THE REINTERPRETATION
OF VICTORIAN LITERATURE

THE
REINTERPRETATION
OF
VICTORIAN
LITERATURE

EDITED BY JOSEPH E. BAKER

FOR THE
VICTORIAN LITERATURE GROUP
OF THE MODERN LANGUAGE ASSOCIATION
OF AMERICA

PRINCETON, NEW JERSEY
PRINCETON UNIVERSITY PRESS
1950

PREFACE

THE Victorian Literature Group of the Modern Language
Association of America, at the 1939 meeting in New Or-
leans, agreed to put out this volume to further the reinterpretation of a literature of great significance for us today.
The writers of Victorian England first tried to salvage
humane culture for a new world of science, democracy, and
industrialism. We owe to them—and to Pre-Victorians like
the prose Coleridge—a revival of Christian thought, a new
Classical renaissance (this time Greek rather than Latin),
an unprecedented mastery of the facts about nature and
man—and, indeed, the very conception of "culture" that
we take for granted in our education and in our social plan-
ning. In that age, a consciousness that human life is subject
to constant development, a sense of historicity, first spread
throughout the general public, and literature for the first
time showed that intimate integration with its social background which marks our modern culture. In protest against
this came the aesthetic movement, another Victorian phenomenon that still commands and repels so much of our
modern literary mind. These "new" attitudes cannot be
understood without reading the literature that made them
current. The Victorians are indispensable to bridge the gap
that too often yawns between the traditional thought and
art of the great ages of European mankind, and the immediate pursuits of present-day writers and readers.

That there is a place for a volume like this was first suggested by the success and influence of *The Reinterpretation
of American Literature*, but the two books are not exactly
parallel, since this one is not national in its interest. We
have not substituted a British for an American point of
view. Thackeray is our best critic concerning our own van-

ity fair; we laugh at our own quiet struggles for rank and prestige in *Barchester Towers*; our proletarian novel goes back to Dickens, and, further, to the humanitarian approach to industrial problems developed by Carlyle. We have taken Victorian literature as the best expression in our language of certain phases of modern civilization, certain experiences common to Western man.

In most libraries, the Victorians probably take up about half the space devoted to English literature before 1900, and the same is true of the past literature still indulged in for pleasure and enlightenment by the reading public. Yet only a fraction of the valuable scholarship and sound literary criticism by professional men of letters has been devoted to this vast and valuable treasure. It is so unexplored that often only specialists seem to have any real knowledge of the relevant facts and significant movements, even when these come closest home to us. Those who are not specialists in Victorian research have had no adequate guide to Victorian scholarship available at all. Those of us who are professors of Victorian literature have suffered from a lack of general informed discussion and synthesis. But the present series of essays, embodying the latest results of study by scholars who have been working in that field, should do much to supply the needed illumination and to provide a usable map for further explorations.

This book deals with specifically Victorian contributions to our culture. Hence we have not tried to sketch the history of any idea or form merely because it can be found in nineteenth-century England. Still less have we wished to include studies of single authors. It has been our intention rather to offer a frame, or various frames, within which these other kinds of studies could be worked out with fresh perspective. For instance, it was in this period that fiction reached its height in the older manner, and then passed over into new forms—just as the transition was being made from traditional forms of verse to "modern" poetry, and from the "essay" to our modern prose and epigram. Even important biographical facts about many of the Victorians are as yet almost unknown, and facts that have been discovered have not been assimilated in adequate biographies. What could we learn about the literary background of Victorian writers —and their public—by investigating their school curricula? How do current news items in any given year of the Queen's reign help us to interpret the force of a political generalization, a poetic allusion, a dramatic scene, or a fictional caricature? British insularity came to an end—for better or for worse. English literature rediscovered Italy and the Germanic cultures. Meanwhile, the wall of antipathy between Burke and the democratic spirit of Jefferson, Shelley, and Republican France was being broken down as Burke's traditional English wisdom was made accessible to us by his Victorian successors. And to maintain the sanity of our own culture in these trying times, it would be well to recognize that Victorian literature preserves for us a rich treasury of comedy, wit, and humor.

To stimulate the widest possible range of interest in Victorian study, we have encouraged diversity of approach in this book. The unity that has been given it resulted from the work of the committee put in charge of this project: Joseph Warren Beach, Charles Frederick Harrold, Howard F. Lowry, Bradford Booth, Joseph E. Baker. Each contribution was read by at least two members of the committee, often by three, and sometimes by other contributors. Though most of the essays have been given final form after careful discussion, we have not felt that differences should be ironed out. It seemed a more civilized policy to leave each contributor solely responsible for the statements he chose to make and the methods he wished to emphasize. No system has been imposed, no demands made or implied, save that each should offer an invitation to further intellectual adventure whereby we can better appropriate to our use, enjoyment, and understanding the wealth of Victorian literature.   J.E.B.

Iowa City, November, 1948

CONTENTS

THE REINTERPRETATION
OF VICTORIAN LITERATURE

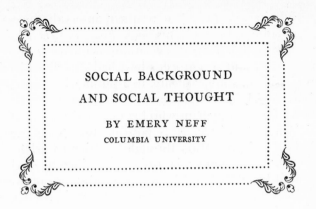

SOCIAL BACKGROUND
AND SOCIAL THOUGHT

BY EMERY NEFF
COLUMBIA UNIVERSITY

THE Victorian poets, even more than the Romantic, felt what Keats called "the burden of society." In the diatribe in *Maud* against mid-Victorian evils, Tennyson charges that "chalk and alum and plaster are sold to the poor for bread." A footnote in Marx's *Kapital* confirms this shameful practice by citing the report of the "Committee of 1855 on the Adulteration of Bread."[1] The Parliamentary Committee heard testimony of chemical experts between July 13 and August 8 of that year; *Maud* was on sale in the last week of July, simultaneously with a *Times* editorial of July 24 supporting the investigation. Nothing could have been more timely than Tennyson's allusion to a national scandal involving a great variety of foods and drugs. His information did not come from the expert testimony, for he had sent *Maud* to press on July 7, six days before the opening of the hearings; but the Parliamentary Blue Book and letters to the *Times* correcting details in its editorial give clues to his anticipatory accuracy. The first witness before the committee, Dr. Arthur Hill Hassall,[2] had published analyses of

[1] More precisely, "the Select Committee on the Adulteration of Food." (Parliamentary Papers, Session of 1854-55, VIII, 221 ff.) Marx's note 51 to page 138 of his first edition (Hamburg, 1867) mentions alum and chalk only, but plaster (of Paris) appears in the committee report.

[2] Dr. Hassall's discovery that the microscope could detect chicory in ground coffee, which started *The Lancet* on its campaign of exposure, ex-

foodstuffs in *The Lancet* at frequent intervals since 1851 and had collected them in his book, *Food and Its Adulterations* (1855). The *Lancet* revelations, confirming his experience with fraud as a grocer's boy, had stirred a Birmingham physician, John Postgate, to a publicity campaign for national legislation, which gained the support of a Radical member for Birmingham who became chairman of the investigating committee. It is possible that Tennyson obtained other information through his friend Carlyle, ever on the alert for commercial dishonesty, since he obviously borrowed from *Past and Present* the substance of another verse in *Maud*: "When a Mammonite mother kills her babe for a burial fee."

Such is the variety of relations in which a line of Victorian poetry may stand to the society in which it was written. Here is a typical instance of *belles lettres* lending aid to a movement for legislation[3] protecting health and morals, and incidentally becoming associated with scientists, a crusading medical journal, a philanthropic citizen and his parliamentary representative, newspaper publicity, an author turned social prophet, and a heterodox economist. Among other "passing interests of the day" touched by Tennyson's verse Mr. G. M. Young has noted apparently prosaic chancery procedure, company promoting, industrial insurance and the provision of coaling stations.

As the earliest machine-age society, Victorian England has special claims to our attention. In it we see the problems of our own time emerging, may trace growing awareness of them and endeavors to find solutions. In this awareness and these endeavors, men of letters bore a distinguished part, for they had a sense of social responsibility to a high degree. Many, including Tennyson, felt the lingering feudal obligation of paternalism, which Disraeli's Young Eng-

---

plains Goldwin Smith's sarcasm in reviewing *Maud*: "To wage 'war with a thousand battles, and shaking a hundred thrones' in order to cure a hypochondriac and to get rid of the chicory in the coffee is a bathos" (*The Saturday Review*, I, 14).

[3] The Adulteration of Food and Drink Act of 1860, England's first general pure food law.

land group tried to make paramount. Others, like John Stuart Mill, derived humanitarian concern from an opposite quarter: from the eighteenth-century *philosophes* and the principles of the French Revolution. In a period of religious revival the duty to be one's brother's keeper and the example of the Hebrew prophets were potent: often both were reinforced by the Romantic conception of the literary genius as the inspired enlightener of his contemporaries. In certain authors, notably Carlyle, all four motives were operative; in many others, such as Ruskin, George Eliot, Matthew Arnold, and Charles Kingsley, two or three.

Men of letters had at their disposal information immensely exceeding their personal observation, for the era, unprecedently self-conscious, was prolific in social statistics. Never had a society examined itself with such conscientious thoroughness. The national census, begun in 1801 and extending with each decade the scope of its inquiries, was supplemented in the thirties and after by more intensive and accurate special investigations, public and private: parliamentary investigations into conditions of labor in factory, shop, and mine, into public health and morals in the new industrial cities; reports of the Board of Trade, of royal commissions, of statistical societies (the Manchester Statistical Society dates from 1834), of philanthropic societies and public-spirited individuals. It was almost impossible for a writer of prose or verse to be unaware of the repercussions of the industrial and commercial revolutions in class conflict, in politics, in morals and religion, in matters of general welfare. For whether to trumpet the amazing increase in production through mechanical invention as evidence of "unexampled prosperity" and "progress," or to express grave concern for "the condition of England," the periodical and newspaper press gave wide publicity to pryings into almost every nook and cranny of the social structure. Since the Victorians used paper more durable than the wood pulp which is dooming much of the twentieth-century record to oblivion, the historian of literature, its sources and background, is thus faced with a task of peculiar difficulty. Practically everything we wish to know about the Victorians must lie somewhere in print or manuscript. Nowhere are a scholar's theories so likely to meet contradiction by stubborn fact.

It is not surprising that literary historians and critics should have hesitated to deal with the social background of literary works and the social theories of writers when confronted by such overwhelming bulk of evidence: evidence, moreover, with which their usual linguistic and belletristic training had not equipped them to deal. The border region between literature and the social studies was earliest entered by economic and political historians, prepared to cope with Blue Books and statistical tables. A pioneer work, *John Ruskin: Social Reformer*, was published by the English economist J. A. Hobson in 1898; and Fabian Society pamphlets ventured ahead of literary critics. But whether from lack of the necessary detachment from the recent past of their nation, whether from reaction against Victorian moral preoccupation or from an illusory belief that the problems of the "hungry forties" could not recur (H. D. Traill, when editing the Century Edition of Carlyle in 1896-1897, remarked that "his boding prophecies . . . are marred for us to-day by an ever-present consciousness of their subsequent falsification"), Englishmen were slower than foreigners to undertake social interpretation of Victorian literature. Schulze-Gaevernitz's Leipzig dissertation, *Carlyle's Stellung zu Christentum und Revolution*, dates from 1891; Louis Cazamian's *Roman social en Angleterre*, which has served as a model for similar studies, from 1904. Vida Scudder's richly suggestive *Social Ideals in English Literature* appeared in 1910. In 1913 Cazamian's essay, *"Histoire littéraire et Histoire social,"* could announce "the transformation of literary history. . . . Just as everywhere the end of the last century saw the necessary adoption of the notion of organic connections and interdependences between the physical, moral and social elements of reality which scientific analysis had naturally separated too greatly, so now it seems no longer possible to study the literature of a people, or a single literary work, without reuniting them to their environment. This requirement has become a veritable intellectual necessity, which no longer needs to be demonstrated or justified. Henceforward the study of languages and literatures seems linked with that of societies, in which institutions and manners are developed, in which are formed economic and political systems, great movements of ideas and feeling: all the forces of which languages on the one hand, literary works on the other, are the expressions."[4] The impact of the First World War upon a generation which read Shaw, Wells, and Galsworthy impressed this view upon British critics and scholars; but no British university has done so much in the social interpretation of Victorian literature as Robert Morss Lovett and his followers at Chicago or Ashley Thorndike and his followers at Columbia;[5] nor has any unacademic British critic rivaled in discernment Edmund Wilson's essays on Dickens. Nevertheless, the social approach has only begun to touch American textbooks and anthologies, which are often deficient or inexact in social information. A school edition of *Past and Present* identifies "the late Manchester Insurrection" as Peterloo, although "late" could scarcely apply to an event so far back as 1819; the reference is obviously to the "Plug-Plot," an early example of organized sabotage, put into effect in August, 1842. In the same text, a note on "Saint-Simonism" runs as follows: "After Carlyle published *Chartism*, he was approached by some of the followers [of Saint-Simon] with the idea that he might become a disciple." For *Chartism* one should read "Signs of the Times," a decade earlier.

The present socially minded generation of Americans is advantageously situated to interpret the Victorians, for because of a cultural lag we are acquainted with religious and ethical taboos substantially Victorian and live in a nation emerging belatedly from "rugged individualism." Many

[4] Taine's *History of English Literature* (1863) had promoted this view of literary history in France.

[5] *The Cambridge Bibliography of English Literature*, although going so far as to include Bentham, fails to list the foremost critical work concerning him, Halévy's *La Formation du Radicalisme philosophique*, and an indispensable biographical study, Charles W. Everett's *Education of Jeremy Bentham*.

literary scholars, furthermore, are now trained in the methods and the materials of social studies, which have put at their disposal authoritative works of reference, such as Elie Halévy's *Growth of Philosophical Radicalism* and *History of the English People in the Nineteenth Century*, J. H. Clapham's *Economic History of Modern Britain* and the Webbs' *History of Trade Unionism*, and key biographies like Graham Wallas's *Francis Place* and G. D. H. Cole's *William Cobbett*. Unfortunately Halévy did not live to execute his project of a social survey of England in 1860 to match his England in 1815, but the lack is somewhat supplied by the unequal cooperative study, *Early Victorian England*, edited by G. M. Young, which endeavors "to create for the reader of the history and the literature of the time the atmosphere which will bring their details into perspective and relief." Through such means we are in a position to understand the Victorian scene more fully and more accurately than the Victorians themselves, and to acquire standards for estimating the social intelligence and instinct of Victorian men and women of letters.

At the opening of Victoria's reign, the experiments of factory inspection and of a "scientific" Poor Law had been begun, and sanitary surveys, the sequel of cholera epidemics, were revealing the horrors of mushroom industrial cities. The forties opened in the midst of the worst industrial depression England had experienced, with the Chartists demanding unrestricted manhood suffrage when the Reform Act was the freshest of memories and the French Revolution loomed bodingly in the background; they met in mid-course an Irish famine that obliged the dubious experiment of Free Trade; and they closed with another depression complicated by repercussions of the continental revolutions of 1848. The reign ended with the Consolidated Factory Act of 1901, following close upon the first Workingmen's Compensation Act and the launching of the Labor Party, signs of steadily constructive domestic policy which were offset by uneasiness as to Britain's relation to the rest of the world stirred by the Boer War then still in progress. The *Times* editorial on the occasion of the

Queen's death confessed: "At the close of the reign we are finding ourselves somewhat less secure of our position than we could desire, and somewhat less abreast of the problems of the age than we ought to be, considering the initial advantages we secured. The 'condition of England question' does not present itself in so formidable a shape as at the beginning of the reign, but it does arouse the attention of those who try to look a little ahead of present business. Others have learned our lessons and bettered our instructions while we have been too easily content to rely upon the methods which were effective a generation or two ago." The sixty-three years of the reign had seldom been free from the stress and strain of a society in often bewilderingly rapid change, trying desperately to preserve in a life increasingly industrial and urban the human values of the past. Into this effort practically every form of literature, even art criticism and superficially "pure" poetry, was drawn.

The historian of literature must discover what drew the individual writer in, and what means for easing the growing pains of society he proposed. Inquiry must go back to the influences shaping his youth. What was his social class, the occupation of his family? Was his early environment agricultural or industrial, village or urban? Was he taught to be his brother's keeper out of religious or feudal duty, or for reasons of social efficiency? What sort of schools formed him, what intellectual, artistic and class values was he taught to cherish? In such matters the historian must try to penetrate behind the author's rationalizations, to perceive his unconscious assumptions. He must give special attention to the form in which the writer first encountered social maladjustment and class conflict. Charles Kingsley, as a schoolboy of twelve, saw the Bristol riots of 1831, when a populace enraged by a rejection of the Reform Bill broke open prisons, set fire to the city hall, and destroyed the bishop's palace. "When the first excitement of horror and wonder were past," he recalled, "what I had seen made me for years the veriest aristocrat, full of hatred and contempt for those dangerous classes, whose existence I had for the first time discovered. It required many years—years, too, of personal

9

intercourse with the poor—to explain to me the true meaning of what I saw." Thomas Cooper, a plebeian from an agricultural community, was shocked by the manufacturing population of Leicester: "The fierce and open opposition in public meeting of working men to employers, manifested in derisive cries, hissing and hooting, and shouts of scorn ... utterly unlike to the earlier old Lincolnshire life I had known, wherein I mingled with the poor and saw a good deal of their suffering, yet witnessed not merely the respect usually subsisting between master and servant, but in many cases the attachment of the peasantry to the farmers, and of the farmers to the landlords."

Regarding the maturing writer, other questions are basic. How did his literary interests lead him to social problems? Familiar illustrations are Ruskin's chapter "On the Nature of the Gothic" and Arnold's essay, "The Function of Criticism at the Present Time." What novel social theories, domestic or foreign, did the writer encounter? Note here J. S. Mill's debates with the Owenites and the efforts of Saint-Simonians to convert Mill and Carlyle. Finally we may ask, what subsequent events, economic or political, modified the writer's opinions? These considerations and their like form a pattern for the study of an author's social views. Such studies have been made, notably for Arnold, Carlyle and Ruskin, but need extension to many others.

Of like interest is the collective response of one or more generations of writers to some social institution, condition, or doctrine. By including newspaper and periodical writing, one may take fair samples of articulate opinion. The veil of anonymity is being lifted by histories of periodicals, already including the *Quarterly, Westminster, Fortnightly,* and *Saturday Reviews, Fraser's Magazine, The Athenaeum* and *The Monthly Repository*, which identify a large proportion of contributors. The transition of *Punch* from its early crusading days, when it published "The Song of the Shirt" to its twentieth-century offering of class distinctions as the staple of humor, needs to be traced. Most of these studies of periodicals, fortunately, have not limited themselves to literature and the arts, but summarize opinion on manners and morals, on economics, politics, and science. Some offer samples of class or group opinion, Marchand's *Athenaeum* that of the substantial middle class, Bevington's *Saturday Review* that of Cambridge and Oxford intellectuals. Periodicals, newspapers, biographies, and creative works may be drawn upon for attitudes toward "classical" economic theory, trade unions, employment of women and children in factories, the decline of British agriculture, etc. The immense stir made by Malthus, from his Principle of Population (parent of the "iron law of wages") through his basing upon the law of diminishing returns his doctrine of differential rent (an illustration of, and an incitement to, class conflict) to his shaping of the thought of Darwin and Spencer, is the subject of a forthcoming book. Other convenient barometers of changing social opinion would be trade unions, slow to live down their Napoleonic era reputation as fomenters of political conspiracy and murderous violence, and the "sacred" right of private property, invoked in Glasgow against municipal carting away of filth accumulated in courts surrounded by tenements, and defended against other encroachments of the state by the Private Enterprise Society. The recent disclosure that Nassau Senior, first professor of political economy at Oxford, while upholding laissez-faire as an inviolable principle in his signed writings, advocated considerable departures from it in anonymous articles, measures the repressive force of respectable opinion and the courage of Carlyle, Ruskin, and Arnold in publicly braving it.

Monographs like J. A. Hobson's *John Ruskin: Social Reformer* have by no means exhausted the subject of positive contributions to economic theory by men of letters. Probably most interesting to the literary historian are the stages, brilliantly sketched in the opening chapter of Margaret R. Grennan's *William Morris: Medievalist and Revolutionary*, whereby the Middle Ages, a source of thrills for the tale of terror and Coleridge, of pageant for Scott and Keats, became a storehouse of lessons for the reshaping of Victorian economic life. Carlyle's contact with the medieval tradition was fortuitous and ironic, by way of the Cambridge Camden

11

Society, propagandists for the ritualism he despised, and of
Scott's novels; but he gave more than he received, especially
by adapting Scott's praise of chivalry to the contemporary
scene in his famous contrast of the ethics of the knight with
the buccaneering of the industrialist (one wonders if the
devisers of New Deal "codes" were aware of their ancestry).
With Ruskin, the economic application of medievalism becomes more varied; Gothic architecture teaches the lesson
of the free craftsman, which points toward guild socialism
and the aesthetic movement, where Morris joins in with
A Dream of John Ball. The germ of aestheticism was already in Southey's *Colloquies* (1828) with Sir Thomas
More, which Macaulay's review triumphantly reduced to
absurdity: "We are told, that our age has invented atroci-
ties beyond the imagination of our fathers; that society has
been brought to a state compared with which extermination
would be a blessing; and all because the dwellings of cot-
ton-spinners are naked and rectangular. Mr. Southey has
found a way, he tells us, in which the effects of manufac-
tures and agriculture may be compared. And what is this
way? To stand on a hill, to look at a cottage and a factory,
and to see which is the prettier." Macaulay was confident of
his 1830 readers; thirty years later many readers would have
turned the laugh against his Philistinism. Utopias imagined
by Victorians reveal various forms assumed by the desire to
escape from the ugliness and cruelty of the contemporary
scene. Ruskin's claim to be the first economic theorist who
understood the fine arts indicates the source of his superior-
ity even over J. S. Mill, the most cultivated and humane of
the contemporary economists, in creating a theory of value.
The recognition by certain Victorians that, in a society of
unrestricted competition, peace is but war under another
name, led toward William James' "Moral Equivalent of
War." Diogenes Teufelsdröckh declared: "There is no
Social Idea extant . . . each, isolated, regardless of his neighbor, clutches at what he can get, and cries 'mine,' and calls
it Peace, because, in the cut-throat scramble, no steel knives,
but only a far cunninger sort, can be employed." The opening stanzas of *Maud* point out the same anomaly. *Past and*

Present and *Latter-Day Pamphlets* propose the diversion of the martial energies and virtues into cooperative struggle to subdue the forces of nature to human advantage; and James could hardly have failed to notice J. S. Mill's hope for a moral revolution that would make "a common man dig or weave for his country as readily as fight for his country." These are far from exhausting the ways in which "classical" economic theory has been corrected and modified by values from literature and the arts, from religion and ethics.[6]

Americans born in and conditioned to an advanced stage of urban industrialism are in danger of being less than just to Victorian inadaptability to its early and crude forms. They should make the effort to comprehend the agricultural mentality of most Victorian writers, more firmly fixed by the recent Romantic feeling for nature. The established morality and culture were founded upon a patriarchal village family living close to the soil. Thence the strong moral protest against the tendency of the factory system to break up the family by drawing women into work outside the home and by offering to young people financial means of hiring lodgings to avoid the restraint of family discipline. Authors were slow to understand the industrial life of women and to see the good that might come from its offering them a degree of independence.[7] Thence, too, the hostility to an industrialism which divorced great masses of the population from nature and divided the nation into two mutually uncomprehending groups. Many less articulate could sympathize with Matthew Arnold's seeking in Kensington Gardens repose from the uproar of London. The extent to which literature clung to, and tended to sentimentalize, village life has been described by Julia Patton's *The English Village: A Literary Study*. Nostalgia for a way of life that was passing should be traced beyond Professor Patton's chronological limit of 1850; for the decline of British agriculture followed the repeal of the Corn Laws with deceptive slowness, and became obvious only after 1870, when

---

[6] Christian Socialism has been studied so fully as to seem to need little further investigation.

[7] See Wanda Fraiken Neff, *Victorian Working Women*.

rapid and comparatively cheap Atlantic transport brought in underselling American grain. The fullest and most sympathetic annalist of this tragic decline, and of the conservative resistance to the mechanization of agriculture, was Thomas Hardy, whose readers had been prepared for him by the fresh rural scenes of George Eliot and many lesser novelists. Professor Clapham's economic history presents means to confirm and to illustrate Hardy's accuracy. The converse study of the emergence in literature of the industrial city, and of the psychology of its workers, would be welcome.

Adaptation or creation of educational institutions for the needs of a society in such rapid change was a major Victorian concern. Literary studies have been made of the resistance of Oxford, "the home of lost causes," to a narrow utilitarianism,[8] and of the concessions of the public schools to the moral and practical complexion of the era;[9] others might be prepared concerning Cambridge, Edinburgh, and London Universities, in various degrees more hospitable to science, to social studies, and to modern languages, and concerning the campaign, led by Matthew Arnold, for better schools for the middle classes. Literature is rich in illustration of the need for nationalized elementary education, long delayed by laissez-faire dogmatists and by the incompatible demands of rival religious sects and groups. One thinks of the extremes of the dame school kept by Mr. Wopsle's great aunt, of Dotheboys Hall, and of the up-to-the-minute forcing school of Mr. and Mrs. M'Choakumchild, which had a painfully real parallel in James Mill's tutoring of his precocious son. Sissy's mistakes in statistics are brilliant ridicule of the preposterous teaching of political economy to children. Education of women is a scarcely explored theme. I do not think it has been observed that Richard Feverel was given substantially the training of the Victorian girl, an implied parallel with satiric significance.

A social tension chart has correlated political unrest in nineteenth-century England with unemployment and high

8 William S. Knickerbocker, *Creative Oxford.*
9 Edward C. Mack, *Public Schools and British Opinion*, 2 vols.

food prices. A similar chart would throw light on literary production. It was the boom culminating in 1825 that tempted Carlyle into professional authorship; the subsequent crash, which ruined Scott, forced Carlyle to leave Edinburgh for cheaper living in Craigenputtock. His isolation there, putting him out of touch with the reading public, and the political and economic uncertainty in the years between the French Revolution of 1830 and the Reform Act, made *Sartor Resartus* unsalable in book form. The often remarked literary interregnum between the Romanticists and the Victorians in the late twenties and early thirties is partly explicable by these impediments to the book trade, which drove much of the best literary work, like *Sartor*, into periodicals. Attempts by enterprising publishers, notably Colburn and Bentley, to force sales against this unfavorable market by imitating and improving upon the advertising techniques of manufacturers and shopkeepers account for Carlyle's shrinking from publicity in the thirties. Subsequent economic and political crises account for his other works of exhortation and prophecy. The long depression of 1836-1842 called forth *Chartism* and *Past and Present*; the revolution of 1848, *Latter-Day Pamphlets*; the Reform Act of 1867, *Shooting Niagara*.

A chapter on the publishing career of Colburn incidental to Matthew W. Rosa's study of a fictional type, *The Silver-Fork School*, and Leslie Marchand's account of the *Athenaeum's* campaign against puffery indicate probable rewards from further investigations of the business relations of literature. Unfortunately A. S. Collins' *The Profession of Letters* does not go beyond 1832 and is sketchy and amateurish beside Beljame's *Le Public et les Hommes de Lettres au 18ᵉ Siècle*. Authorship as a profession for women, an essentially Victorian phenomenon, deserves attention. A study of the activities of a typical literary agent, John Forster, is now in progress. The activity of publishers' readers, such as George Meredith and Leslie Stephen, should be explored, in spite of the frequent unwillingness of publishing houses to supply information as to sales of books or contracts with authors.

Of the literary genres created by social change, the most conspicuous are the novel of industrial and political life, examined by Cazamian, and "silver-fork" fiction, described by Rosa. The former is largely concerned with the condition of the poor; the latter specializes in the manners of the rich. Novels of the first sort we have with us abundantly, but there is no exact twentieth-century counterpart of the novel of fashionable life which flourished from 1825 to 1840 in response to the curiosity of post-war new rich concerning the manners of the aristocracy, which they aspired to acquire; although in a similar post-war atmosphere books of etiquette were prominently advertised in American newspapers and periodicals of the nineteen twenties. Fashionable novels made the fortune of Colburn, their chief purveyor. They are not pictures of the life of the aristocracy in its eighteenth-century prime, but follow the dandy in his descent from Beau Brummell to the Count d'Orsay, Disraeli, and Bulwer, the two latter the best authors in the genre. Their chief significance in literary history is the ridicule they provoked, from Carlyle's savage chapter, "The Dandiacal Body," to Thackeray's subtler impaling of snobs. *Vanity Fair*, which Mr. Rosa styles "a fashionable novel to end fashionable novels," is the flowering of what began as catering to the aspiring curiosity of profiteers.

Jos Sedley represents an earlier type of *nouveau riche*, the "nabob" returned with the spoils of India, whose literary career from the time of Warren Hastings to Kipling is being studied. Opposition to the class system developed into a formula of castigation of the faults of each class, conspicuous in Carlyle, reaching subtler form in Arnold's "Barbarians, Philistines and Populace," and continuing beyond Bernard Shaw's novel, *An Unsocial Socialist*, which proposes a classless society. Victorian literature, especially fiction, should be explored for evidence of the increasing fluidity of classes, of the shifting evaluation of the country gentleman and of the relative social standing of the professions, of trade, finance, and manufacture. O. F. Christie's *The Transition from Aristocracy* is a disappointingly amateurish book on a theme demanding a highly skilled hand.

The anomaly of British provincialism in a time of greatly improved communication, a provincialism largely the result of the national isolationist policy and the rise of the middle class, was a staple of Arnold's satire and was developed by George Eliot into a fictional type. *A Study of Provincial Life,* the subtitle of *Middlemarch,* which portrays a community inimical to influences from outside, whether railroads, political liberalism, medical science, or German historical scholarship, would also have served to describe *The Mill on the Floss,* whose chapter entitled "A Variation of Protestantism Unknown to Bossuet" is an extraordinarily acute essay in social analysis. A study in comparative literature could connect these novels with similar works springing up on the continent in the latter half of the nineteenth century: *Madame Bovary, An Enemy of the People, Fathers and Sons, The Three Sisters,* and with twentieth-century studies by Arnold Bennett, Sinclair Lewis, and Mauriac. The time-worn device of an imaginary foreign commentator on the narrowness of British horizons appears from Teufelsdröckh and Arminius to *Letters from John Chinaman.*

The passing of a Victorian fetish, the patriarchal family, confirmed statistically by the fall of the birth rate among the comfortable classes after 1875, is reflected in a group of novels of which the best is *The Way of All Flesh.* Butler's dual interest in the revolt of the individual against family dominance and in hereditary resemblances had already appeared in *The Ordeal of Richard Feverel.* Other types of family novel follow the rise of a family in the social scale (as in Thackeray's significantly named *Newcomes*) or the decline of an aristocratic family, the latter a frequent theme of minor fiction in which technicalities concerning entail display the author's virtuosity. A study now under way will link such novels with continental counterparts, such as *Buddenbrooks.*

Social influence upon literary style can be identified most surely in the didactic works so much a sign of the times: not only in the writing down to a barely literate populace begun by Hannah More and Cobbett, and carried into the

Victorian era by the Societies for the Diffusion of Useful
and of Christian Knowledge, but also in the more artistic
reaches of books addressed to the middle class and the self-
educated workingman, such as the popular essays of Carlyle, Ruskin, and Arnold. The chronic repetitiousness and
verbosity of these writings by authors capable of the greatest concision betrays conscious effort to reach slow minds,
minds moreover accustomed to a diet of sermons. In the
novel, a similar condescension gives us Thackeray's asides.
Carlyle, though despising sensational journalism and advertising, could not resist the temptation to enlist their methods in a good cause. His pictures of social types, Bobus
Higgins, Plugson of Undershot, Sir Jabesh Windbag, have
the effectiveness of cartoons and signboards. Like advertising slogans and newspaper headlines are his catch phrases:
"Morrison's Pill," "Captains of Industry," "Devil take the
hindmost," "paralytic Radicalism," "the dismal science,"
which exploit the means whereby the man in the street is
swayed. In this technique Ruskin and Arnold followed and
probably imitated Carlyle.

Investigation of the social implications and relations of
Victorian literature has scarcely begun. Yet not every
scholar should be called to labor in the vineyard. The investigator must be no bondsman to the printed word, such
as he who in seeking the sources of Carlyle's hero theory
spread so wide a net as to include Confucius and Plato, yet
failed to consider the laissez-faire anarchy which Carlyle
had before his eyes. He must have definite social opinions,
tested by observation of the contemporary scene, else he
will not know what to look for; yet he must not be so attached to these opinions as unconsciously to maim literature to fit the Procrustean bed of Marxian or of "classical"
economic theory. He should be equipped not only with the
methods of the social sciences, but also with those of the
psychologist and the anthropologist. He should be willing
to immerse himself in social documents until he can distinguish the original opinions of an author from the assumptions of his generation or his social class. Finally, he
should be sufficiently an artist to present background mate-

rials in organic relation with literary productions, instead of contenting himself with the makeshift of putting background in one compartment, literature in another, on the supposition that the reader will observe their interconnection. To such a flexible mind, the rewards of research will be rich, not only in understanding of the past, but also in insight into analogous situations and problems in the present troubled scene.

19

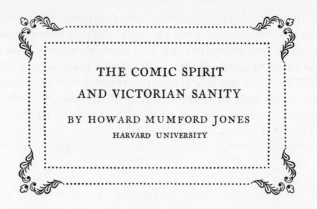

THE COMIC SPIRIT AND VICTORIAN SANITY

BY HOWARD MUMFORD JONES
HARVARD UNIVERSITY

WE ARE all too familiar with the attacks on the Victorians. They conjure up the hair-cloth sofa, the Sunday-school tract, the antimacassar, the what-not, the bustle, and the unhygienic skirt. Victorianism is the elder generation. Victorianism is the pretense that if you do not name a thing, it isn't there. Those who dislike to discuss sex merely in terms of biology are apt to be classified with the lady who noted sadly the difference between the home life of Cleopatra and that of our dear Queen. Those who admire Gladstone (if anybody does) are Victorians, albeit those who admire Disraeli (and the Victorians admired him enough to make him premier) are not. To talk of duty, honor, the obligations of being a gentleman, the responsibilities of matrimony, or the sacredness of religious belief is to be Victorian. The Victorians were so bent on being moral that they ignored the unpleasant aspects of life. They had no use for art which was not ethical; they displayed, it is alleged, an embarrassing familiarity with the purposes of the Almighty. Did not one of them proclaim that God's in his heaven and all's right with the world, though the world was palpably maladjusted? Did not another sing aloud that he was going

NOTE: The substance of this chapter was originally published in *Scribner's Magazine*, February, 1933, under the title: "Those Eminent Victorians."

to be Queen of the May? Victorian stuffiness, Victorian decorum, Victorian prudery, Victorian solemnity!

Well, in one sense they had a right to be solemn. The first half of the century, like our own, was a period of recurrent crises, but whereas we have confined our discussions principally to "serious weeklies" and long-faced conferences and ineffectual newspaper editorials, the Victorians were of the opinion that the national conscience was concerned, and sought in their writings to arouse thinking on the subject. Our own fiction has been monotonously compounded of sex, horror, and psychology. The Victorians thought otherwise. From the day when Bulwer Lytton in his first novel converted Pelham to utilitarian thought, to the day when George Gissing laid down his pen, a consciousness of the importance of man to society and of society to man is a constant theme in nineteenth-century fiction. Mrs. Gaskell and Charles Kingsley cry out against social injustice. Thackeray studies the adjustment of the parvenus and the upper classes. Disraeli outlines a political philosophy in the Young England novels, and Trollope, in the Parliamentary novels, uttered more than parliamentary wisdom. George Eliot bases her books on a social philosophy; to George Meredith a reading of life is a reading of earth. Similarly the poets— Tennyson, Mrs. Browning, Swinburne, Kipling—are aware of political issues and turn them into beautiful and enduring verse.

I am far from thinking that literature is any better for being sociological, but most of us will agree that literature tends to be better when it is written with a large discourse, and I confess that the relative thinness of American fiction after our own Victorian age had ended seems to me to arise from the fact that it was based on a very narrow reading of life—a reading which sees the be-all and the end-all of the novelist's business as sex and psychology. And I wonder, in view of the relative brittleness of that fiction, whether we are quite entitled to patronize the Victorian novelist? Have we mastered the art of the novel so completely that we can afford to dismiss as naïve a Dickens who, more than any other single figure, in the opinion of his contemporaries, made readers aware of social chaos in England? Our solitary exhibit in the way of broad canvases and social satire was for a long time Sinclair Lewis (perhaps some would add Dreiser), a humorist of great power, but is it not odd that whereas we produced only one of this kind, the Victorians produced a score?

I have said that the problems of that period and our own were similar. On the one hand, there was, for example, the inherited system of the universe. There was God, whose wondrous hand the nightly stars hymned as of old. There was an intricate and reasonably formed universe which He had invented, and everywhere traces of His handiwork could be found. There was the Anglican Church as by law established. There was man, who certainly had a body, and who was presumed, as even Shelley admitted, to have a spirit and probably a soul. There were the Queen, God bless her, and England's wooden walls, and the Duke of Wellington. In fact, there was a noble world inhabited by noble beings. And then there came crashing down on the Victorians a bewildering variety of changes, discoveries, and revolutions.

Startling theories of geology ruined the comfortable chronology of the King James Bible and reduced the life of man to an inconsiderable second in infinite time. Astronomical investigations extended the regions of heaven until earth was lost in infinite space. More and more it appeared that man was a great deal lower than the angels, and about the middle of the century he appeared to be a good deal closer to the animals. A succession of brilliant investigations in science smashed the good old comfortable mathematical universe of the eighteenth century into bits. In the heavens there was only anarchy, and on earth nature was red in tooth and claw. The Anglican faith was split by a schism which sent some of its most brilliant minds into the Roman Catholic fold, and Arnold later pleaded in vain with the Puritans to return to the established church. Could it be that the old system was wrong? The system that seemed as certain as the Duke of Wellington and as invincible as the Life Guards at Waterloo? Amidst the wreck of matter and the crash of worlds the Victorians clung to one essential belief—they were not under any circumstances going to admit that human life was any less interesting or important or dignified or noble, even though the heavens fell and hell blew up—in fact, one of them, Frederick Denison Maurice, helped in the explosion. They did their best to reconcile the smashing impact of the new science, which threatened to reduce everything to anarchic materialism, with their inherited belief in the dignity of human life. If we are today anything more than certain worms writhing in midnight, we owe our sanity to the Victorians. They conserved the human tradition, and without the human tradition, we should be stark, raving mad.

While the physical universe was crashing around them, the political and social world, too, seemed to be going to pieces, as Carlyle and others gloomily observed. The fixed and immutable laws of political economy, traced logically to their tragic conclusion by Ricardo, McCulloch, and the Manchester School, seemed to indicate that modern life would have to be one of increasing misery. They saw poverty in the streets and heard revolutions across the water. From 1820 to 1870 the Victorians struggled with depressions at home and counted a succession of crashes abroad; yet the streets of London, unlike the streets of Paris, Berlin, Vienna, or Richmond, never ran red with blood, nor echoed to the tread of a conquering army. The Victorians went into the nineteenth century with an England that was in many ways the little old England of Walpole's time, and they emerged with an empire that, with all its defects, was the most remarkable the world had seen since Rome. Theirs is one of the most extraordinary examples of national continuity and astonishing readjustments in the history of mankind.

How did they manage it? I suspect we have overstressed Victorian prejudice; for they managed it by a tolerance for unexpected developments which far surpasses ours. They were capable of absorbing strange food. They made a Jewish novelist prime minister of England, despite his curls and his waistcoats; and I need not comment on the chances of either a Jew or a novelist, much less both, being elected

President of this enlightened republic. They elected an atheist to Parliament, and when Parliament threw him out, they continued to elect him until not atheism, but Parliament gave way; and I hardly need mention the possibility of electing a Charles Bradlaugh to the Senate of the United States. They suffered a group of aliens to tie up the business of the House of Commons night after night under the leadership of Parnell and his followers; and I cannot imagine delegates from the Hawaiian Islands and Puerto Rico enjoying the same liberty in the House of Representatives. Huxley told a bishop to his face in a public meeting that he was a liar; yet Huxley served on more public commissions (so his biographer states) than any other British scientist. Would an American professor in a state university be similarly honored? I think we have talked too much about Victorian moral conformity.

I I

You cannot, said Burke, indict a whole people; and it is difficult to indict a whole century. That the Victorians (to confine ourselves to them) had their characteristic weaknesses is evident; but one grows weary by and by of so monotonous and one-sided an argument and longs for a little more attention to a few obvious facts.

For example, one is confronted by the charge of moral prudery. It is evident one can retort that the Victorians were often refreshingly immoral, and if this form of argument is hilariously absurd, it will at least awake the jaded attention of modern critics. Against the charge that the Victorians insisted upon the standards of middle-class respectability for all forms of conduct, let us set some bits of biography. The period opens in 1837, with the arrest of Thomas Griffiths Wainewright, artist and designer (the friend of Charles Lamb), who poisoned various harmless persons, partly for cash and partly for pleasure, and closes with Oscar Wilde, who wrote charmingly of Wainewright, and whose particular form of vice even our advanced generation has not quite brought itself to condone. The philosophical thought of the age was largely shaped by John

Stuart Mill, who ran off with another man's wife, and its most characteristic novelist is George Eliot, who lived for over twenty years quite openly with a man she was not married to, for the sufficient reason that he was another woman's husband. The most amusing essay of Thomas De Quincey, who did not die until 1859, is a whimsical defense of murder considered as one of the fine arts, and his best-known work is an aesthetic description of the dreams of an opium-eater. Rossetti took chloral; James Thompson drank himself to death; and from Ford Madox Hueffer's absorbing *Memories and Impressions* I cull the following pleasing anecdote concerning a visit paid by William Sharp to the house of Philip Marston, the blind poet: "He found the poor blind man in the clutches of the poet I have just omitted to name, crushed beneath him and, I think, severely bitten. The poet had had an attack of delirium tremens and imagined himself a Bengal tiger. Leaving Marston, he sprang on all fours toward Sharp, but he burst a blood-vessel and collapsed on the floor. Sharp lifted him onto the sofa, took Marston into another room, and then rushed hatless through the streets to the hospital that was around the corner. The surgeon in charge, himself drunk, seeing Sharp covered with blood, insisted on giving him in charge for murder; Sharp, always a delicate man, fainted. The poet was dead of hemorrhage before assistance reached him."

And in the same book I am reminded that Madox Brown, "whose laudable desire it was at many stages of his career to redeem poets and others from dipsomania, was in the habit of providing several of them with labels upon which were inscribed his own name and address." The poets, when too drunk to get about, were then brought by cabmen or others to Fitzroy Square, where the maid and the cabman promptly put them into a bath and made them drink strong coffee, the bath being selected because the poet would "not be able to roll out and injure himself." But let us continue.

Charles Dickens, in the minds of many the chief purveyor of Victorian sentimentality, separated from his wife and quarreled incessantly with his publishers. George Meredith left his first wife, the daughter of Thomas Love Peacock, and celebrated in *Modern Love*, published in 1862, not a triangle situation, but a quadrilateral one. M. Lafourcade, the French student of Swinburne, points out that Richard Monckton Milnes owned a library of erotica, introduced the poet to the works of the Marquis de Sade, and encouraged him to write poems celebrating various sexual perversities, that are unpublished and unpublishable. Among Swinburne's friends was Sir Richard Burton, whose chief masterpiece cannot for obvious reasons go through the mails. Swinburne himself got drunk ("and how drunk he used to get!" writes Julian Field, an Oxford student who knew him); indulged in the most outrageous language; and was frequently referred to by the erudite Furnivall, the Shakespeare editor, as "Pigsbrook." As for the literary groups with which the Victorian period closes, their "morality," as any reader of Holbrook Jackson's *The Eighteen Nineties* knows, was a little to seek—Francis Thompson took opium, John Davidson killed himself, Aubrey Beardsley is remembered for decadent drawings, and Ernest Dowson's brief career was scarcely memorable for ethical balance.

Now of course these tergiversations do not prove anything except as they raise doubts about careless judgments on the Victorians. As it is sometimes argued, however, that facts like these are exceptional and that the true tone of Victorianism is to be sought in the work of Tennyson, Browning, Thackeray, and Dickens, let us look at some of it. There is no doubt that Dickens invented Little Nell and Paul Dombey; that George Eliot wrote a Sunday-school story in *Silas Marner*; that Tennyson was often sentimental; and that Browning was an irritating optimist. But is this all the story? Is there anywhere a more vigorous denunciation of cant and hypocrisy than in the novels of Dickens, the creator of Mr. Pecksniff and Mr. Chadband and Mr. Podsnap? Thackeray certainly complained that he could not write with the openness of Fielding, but if the author of Becky Sharp and Major Pendennis was really hampered in depicting them, the fact is not patent; if there is a more appalling picture in brief compass of human greed and depravity than in the story (too little read) of

the Honorable Mr. Deuceace as set forth by Mr. Yellow-
plush, his footman—if there is anywhere a more succinct
statement of the lack of connection between worldly success and the official principles of that success than *Pendennis*, I do not know where it is. George Eliot undoubtedly
wrote *Silas Marner*; but exactly what moral lesson is to be
drawn from the loss of Mr. Tulliver's fortune, and what is
the precise application of the seventh commandment to the
life of Dorothea Brooke? Has anybody surpassed the sharp-
ness with which Trollope pictured worldly clergymen in
the Barchester series, or worldly aristocrats and parvenus
in the parliamentary novels? Does nobody read *The Way
We Live Now*? Is any reader of Disraeli still of the opinion
that cynicism was unknown in the nineteenth century? Did
or did not the Victorians produce those great eccentrics,
George Borrow and Edward Fitzgerald, the author of *Hajji
Babba*, and the author of *The Way of All Flesh*? The Victorian novel begins, if you please, with Peacock the satirist
and closes with Meredith volleying arrows of silvery laughter; it includes the great apology for the natural man to be
found in *Lavengro* and *The Romany Rye*; and it numbers
among its principal exhibits (a fact frequently forgotten)
the serried titles of one Thomas Hardy, who was emphatically of the opinion that God is not in His heaven and that
all is not right with the world.

As for poetry, let us look at Tennyson, that arch example
of all the Victorian qualities. Arthur, it must be admitted,
is not much of a man, but what about Ulysses? *Enoch Arden*
is rather bad, but what about the poem which reads:

> Raving politics, never at rest—as this poor
>   earth's pale history runs—
> What is it all but a trouble of ants in the
>   gleam of a million million suns?

I cheerfully surrender Galahad to anybody who wants him,
but this same Tennyson wrote "The Revenge"; and if the
true test of poetical worth is pessimism (for so our modern
argument seems to run) I submit in evidence this product
of Tennyson's last years:

Act first, this Earth, a stage so gloom'd with woe
    You all but sicken at the shifting scenes.
And yet be patient. Our Playwright may show
    In some fifth Act what this wild Drama means.

And then there is Browning. On the literary exchange
Browning stock has at present sunk to its lowest level since
the organization of Browning clubs, and there are almost
no takers. I do not count myself among the Browning enthusiasts, but even the author of *Pippa Passes* is entitled to
fair play; and I would merely observe that the famous
phrase about the exact whereabouts of God with respect to
the rightness of earth is not spoken by Browning *in propria
persona*, but sung by Pippa herself as part of the dramatic
action of the story, which has for its end to show the unconscious effect that the words of one human being may
have in the lives of others—a theme not unknown to our
stream-of-consciousness novelists. And this same Browning, so cheery, so irritatingly glad, had a fine eye for a
scoundrel, as witness "Mr. Sludge the Medium" and
"Prince Hohenstiel-Schwangau" and "The Bishop Orders
His Tomb at St. Praxed's Church"; argued on occasion
that it was better to be vitally immoral than passively
moral; stole an invalid woman from her father; and (unless I am much mistaken) set a fashion for writing dramatic
monologues which the admirable E. A. Robinson and other
modern poets are still following without surpassing.

III

The truth is that, instead of inventing "Victorianism,"
the Victorians engaged in incessant warfare against the
cant and hypocrisy they inherited from the maudlin sentimentality of the eighteenth century. At the opening of that
epoch Shaftesbury taught that there was inherent in the
human heart a something which his disciple, Hutcheson,
was to label the "moral Sense." In the innumerable volumes of Daniel Defoe England read that nothing succeeds
like success; that when you have money you ought to in-
vest it prudently; that a bad woman can be made good by

putting her funds out at six per cent; and that a wicked pirate becomes respectable when he retires to trade and to overreaching his fellow man in a bargain. The fashionable pens of Steele and Addison were presently at work refining female manners in the direction of modesty, good sense, and prudery; admonishing noblemen not to duel, drink, or gamble, but to follow the example of Sir Roger de Coverley and look after their tenants benevolently and morally. On the stage you learned that female delicacy is always to be protected—read the *Conscious Lovers* for an example; and if you attended the *London Merchant*, which moved the acid Mr. Pope to tears, you learned a good sound moral lesson as to the fate of the idle boys—for the apprentice takes up with a prostitute, embezzles money, shoots his good old uncle, is caught, repents, and is hanged, to the accompaniment of such a salvo of moral platitudes as no Victorian novelist ever dreamed of.

And the doctrine was continually preached throughout the eighteenth century. What are the novels of Richardson but involved Sunday-school lessons in a low and prudential order of morality? What is Fielding's *Amelia* but an object lesson in the domestic virtues? What are the *Night Thoughts* of Edward Young except lessons in religiosity? What is *The Vicar of Wakefield* (in this connection at least) but a lesson in impossible goodness, and what is Samuel Johnson, among other things, but a dispenser of ethical commonplaces? No, it is not in the Victorian age that heroines begin to faint on the slightest provocation; it is in the novels and plays that preceded the nineteenth century. Nineteenth-century writers, with all their faults, never preached so ostentatious a morality as did Richardson, nor taught, like Defoe, that money is the test of virtue. No religious poetry of the Victorian era is as lugubrious as Young's *Night Thoughts* or Hervey's prose *Meditations among the Tombs*. The moral story for the young was really founded by the heavily virtuous female writers of the eighteenth century, and the moral tale flowed from the pens of Samuel Johnson, Mrs. Barbauld, Hannah More, and John Gay long before Little Nell died and Colonel

Newcome was called away and Tito ruined Romola's life.

Of course this is not the whole truth about the eighteenth century, but it is a truth critics of Victorianism ignore when they declare that the Victorians, forgetting the glorious freedom of Byron and Shelley, invented a pall of morality and snuffily turned from art to the sermon. Their leaders did nothing of the kind. They took what had been given them and made the best of it. They were a race of rebels. They had little use for ethical codes which had cramped average human conduct for a hundred years and which, reinforced by the eighteenth-century reasoning of the utilitarians and the laissez-faire economists, threatened to cramp human conduct still. Indeed, we read them ill if we continue to forget that they were struggling with the great burden of "morality" which they inherited from the century before them.

IV

There still remain, however, the undeniable Victorian Sunday, the black clothing, and the sober faces in the faded daguerreotypes; the solemn discourses of John Ruskin and Matthew Arnold; Herbert Spencer and Bishop Wilberforce, Mrs. Hemans and Mrs. Humphry Ward. But even granting them, there is yet another aspect of the Victorians which we all too often neglect. We fail to remember that this gloomy age is likewise the age of British humor and that the nineteenth century has actually given more first-rate humorists to English literature than any other century in the long roll of English letters.

The wit of the century which invented *Punch* is perhaps its most enviable possession. The Victorians did not take themselves half so seriously as we take them now. Anecdote after anecdote exists to prove that the period was a time of exuberance and gaiety. William Morris, for example, stepped to the head of the stairs in that amazing household which contained the pre-Raphaelites (when they were not joyously quarreling) and called down to the cook: "Mary, those six eggs you served me for breakfast were bad. I ate them, but don't let it happen again." There is Edmund

Yates's biting comment on Thackeray's first lecture when, asked his opinion of the performance, he meditated solemnly and remarked with becoming laconicism: "Very good. Wants a piano." Swinburne on one celebrated occasion met Tennyson at the house of a friend and said, "We understand, of course, that Arthur is Prince Albert and Guinevere is Queen Victoria, but Tennyson, who is Launcelot?" There is W. S. Gilbert's famous comment on Beerbohm Tree in *Hamlet*: "Funny, without being vulgar." There is, in short, an endless stream of anecdote and persiflage which makes Victorian letters and memoirs an infinite delight.

In fact, when drollery is almost a major theme in the Victorian period, it is wonderful to see how critics forget to account for it. The age begins with Sydney Smith, who once dryly remarked: "Benevolence is a natural instinct of the human mind; when A sees B in grievous distress, his conscience always urges him to entreat C to help him"— and from that witty punster goes its scintillating way to Oscar Wilde, the epigrammatist. Was there ever such a feast of humor as Victorian fiction alone presents—the brilliant pages of Disraeli, the inimitable Dickens; Thackeray, over whose "Victorian" novels there plays a constant stream of satire and fun; George Eliot with her great comic peasant creations; George Borrow with his joy in life and humor; Trollope and the vagaries of cathedral life; the wit and wisdom of George Meredith? And as if this were not enough, there are the great eccentric novelists from Peacock, the irresistible, to Mallock's *The New Republic*, Oliphant's *Piccadilly*, and John Davidson's half-mad concoctions. There is Browning, a master of grotesque satire; Tom Hood—and when next it is argued that the Victorians could not call a woman's "limb" by its right name, let the cynic read *Miss Kilmansegg and Her Precious Leg*; there is the long succession of verse humorists from Father Prout to Charles Stuart Calverley. How in the name of common sense can a period be writ down as unmitigatedly solemn which produced Edward Lear and the *Ingoldsby Legends*, Lewis Carroll, and W. S. Gilbert? Has anyone

31

arisen in this earnest age to create another Pooh-Bah or a new *Pirates of Penzance*? Had anybody until *Of Thee I Sing* was written laughed at the Senate as Gilbert laughed at the House of Lords, and do we dare treat our bishops as airily as that great man depicted the Bishop of Rum-Ti-Foo? It would appear from all this that the Victorians were not all such grave deacons as the world imagines. In fact, I believe that the absurd seriousness with which we read novels based on the fairy-tales of Freud, and ponderous works of fiction based upon the insubstantial fabric of dis-ordered syntax and stream-of-consciousness anarchy must awaken mirth among the departed Victorians. And I think we might profit from the Gargantuan gales of laughter which come to us across the what-nots and set the patent rocking-chairs a-rocking, and which, blowing more softly, sigh through the woods where Alice and the White Knight walk forever to the delectation of mankind.

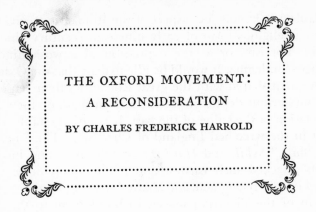

THE OXFORD MOVEMENT:
A RECONSIDERATION

BY CHARLES FREDERICK HARROLD

IN OUR present years of crisis it is appropriate to reconsider a movement which in itself was the product of a crisis, and which looked backward and forward to a series of culminating forces which give the word "modern" a meaning at once hopeful and ominous. For the Oxford Movement was not merely the work of what someone has called "a band of Oxford parsons," but an event—a continuing event—which has especial significance for anyone contemplating the fateful years of 1789, 1830, 1848, 1870, 1914, and 1939.

In the framework of this historical perspective, it is no longer possible to follow the traditional accounts of Trac-

NOTE: Professor Harrold was engaged in revising his essay at the time of his death. His friends associated with him on this project take the occasion to express their sense of personal loss, and their recognition that America has lost one of the leading Victorian scholars of the twentieth century. At a time when the Victorian age was often considered too modern or too difficult for professional study, his own wide learning and his interest in vital issues produced a model of profound scholarship, *Carlyle and German Thought*. He then turned to John Henry Newman, who became to him more than a subject for study. Charles Frederick Harrold reached certain personal convictions that we found challenging indeed in our "age of crisis." Even those who did not share his sentiments were impressed by the soundness of his scholarship, and grateful for his serious handling of significant ideas. It seems to us appropriate that his power to stimulate intellectual effort in others should be carried on by the publication of his essay under the auspices of the Modern Language Association, to which he had contributed so much.

tarianism as largely an "aspect of the Romantic Revival,"[1] or as a religious form of early nineteenth-century obscurantist Toryism, or as the expression of a weak-minded hunger for dogma. It would be idle to deny that the Oxford Movement shared with the great Romantics their sense of the mysterious depths in nature and in man, or their appreciation of the value of the past. It is unforgettable, too, that in the wretched England of Chartism, "The Song of the Shirt," *Sybil*, and *Hard Times*, Newman and his cohorts attacked such earnest and admirable reformers as Mackintosh, Brougham, and Shaftesbury for permitting the plight of the Victorian masses to blind them to the importance of the "Apostolical Succession" and "the prophetical office of the Church." It is true, again, that the Newmanites frankly preached the necessity of dogma, though in a far different spirit from that attributed to them by readers ignorant alike of dogma and of the true nature of religion.

We shall find it profitable to consider the Oxford Movement in terms less temporal and controversial, regarding it, rather, as a part of a vast European effort to retrieve and to warn. Unfortunately, most of the literature resulting from the movement has suffered from the difficulty and the remoteness of its language. The "educated" man of today no longer understands the highly specialized theological traditions of his own culture. Now that religious education has gone the way of theological education—becoming the possession of the expert—the average person is simply a religious illiterate. Newman and Keble and Pusey

[1] The true relation between Tractarianism and Romanticism has been ably stated by Yngve Brilioth, in *The Anglican Revival* (London, 1925, 1933), pp. 57-58, 71: "The Oxford Movement . . . can only to a small extent be explained by the literary currents of the age. It was prepared for by these, and appropriated some of their thoughts; but it was not evoked by them, nor can it . . . be classified only as part of the Romantic Movement." A more recent, and very cogent, account concludes that in the light of history, and by any accurate use of words, "the core of the Revival is a faith which stands in eternal opposition to the Romantic spirit"—Hoxie N. Fairchild, "Romanticism and the Religious Revival in England," *Journal of the History of Ideas*, II (1941), 330-338.

speak to him in a dead language, about ideas of which he has never heard, on premises which seem to him preposterous, and for purposes which strike him as fantastic and superstitious. Yet at the core of the Tractarian teaching, there lay a set of intelligible convictions which have relevance not only to "the stupid nineteenth century" but also to the "highly informed" twentieth century.

Originally, of course, the Oxford leaders were concerned with problems which demanded an immediate solution: the assertion of the spiritual independence of the church from the state; opposition to the rationalism of the "Noetic" group (Whately, Arnold, Hampden) in Oriel College;[2] a search for a firmer foundation than current theology for the Catholic tradition latent in Anglicanism; and a recovery of the tradition of piety, spirituality, and authority, as found in the English divines of the seventeenth century (Hooker, Andrewes, Vaughan, Ken) and in the great Church Fathers of the fourth and fifth centuries. The determination of the Tractarians, in the fourth decade of the nineteenth century, was boldly to realize the primitive "apostolic" conception of Christianity, and to apply it uncompromisingly to modern conditions. This was at once the great strength of the movement and the great obstacle to its acceptance. Yet in the degree that it brought itself into collision with the main spirit of its own time, it remains today a continuing power against the forces which have largely produced the world crisis of the twentieth century. Its very radicalism—a religious radicalism more explosive in its potentialities than any conceivable secular radicalism—throws into sharp relief some of the basic ills of modern society.

[2] Mark Pattison has maintained that the Oxford Movement, far from reacting against the Noetics, was in fact an outgrowth of their teachings; the Oriel school "implanted the germ" (see Pattison's review of T. Mozley's *Reminiscences* in *The Academy*, July 1, 1882, quoted by S. L. Ollard in *A Short History of the Oxford Movement*, London, 1915, p. 15). However, we have Newman's word that, in 1828-29, he came sharply to resist his own Noetic tendency "to prefer intellectual excellence to moral"—*Apologia*, ed. Wilfrid Ward (London, 1913), p. 116.

One is therefore justified in asking precisely in what respects a movement so theological can throw light on our own time, on the problems of economic injustice, social dissolution, competing political ideologies, and atomic warfare. The light will often be indirect, as we shall see. But a close study of the Tractarian point of view may convince some of us that, as Nicholas Berdyaev pointed out,[3] we have reached the bitter end of Renaissance secularism, in the increasing dehumanization of man, in the loss of spiritually organic social unity, in the vast and barbarous conflict which comes from the exploitation of nature rather than in a sacramental use of it in the service of the human spirit. A kind of "liberalism" had "burst out in infidel fury at the French Revolution," and so naturalized itself in England that even Greville regarded it in 1830 as "the spirit of the times . . . a movement no longer to be arrested,"[4] and which "believed that rational intelligence, education, and civilization would cure all the evils and sorrows of mankind."[5] This is not to say, of course, that the splendid gains of nineteenth-century liberal culture are to be denied reality. We shall see that it was not liberalism in the deepest sense that the Tractarians opposed, but a secular liberalism which looked to a millennium based on the spirit-denying, Philistine proposition that to make men perfect is no part of mankind's objective, but to make imperfect men comfortable.[6] We shall see that the Tractarians attacked liberalism, and its bourgeois world, because for them it meant the

[3] *The End of Our Time* (London, 1933), Chapter 1; also the same author's *The Fate of Man in the Modern World* (London, 1935), pp. 9, 26-27, 113, etc.

[4] See *sub ann.* 1830 (August 31), *Leaves from the Greville Diary*, ed. Philip Morrell (London, 1929), pp. 109-110.

[5] Ollard, *op. cit.*, p. 9. See also, for a satire on the superficial progressivism of the time, Thomas Love Peacock, *Crotchet Castle*, Chapter II, "The March of Mind."

[6] Utilitarian secularism found its great prophet, for many early Victorians, in Lord Bacon, rather than in Bentham or James Mill. Macaulay represents this more theoretical "liberalism," and founds his own middle-class philosophy upon the "two words which form the key to the Baconian doctrine, Utility and Progress. . . . To make men perfect was no part of Bacon's plan. His humble aim was to make imperfect men comfortable." See Macaulay's essay on *Lord Bacon*.

ultimate victory of secularism. They had a dim premonition, based on a profound knowledge of religion and human nature, that secularism would destroy the last remnants of organic social order. They could not foresee the specific shape of things to come, but from the general nature of their teachings, we may draw the conclusion that the *total* secularization of life leads to the depersonalization of man in the triumphant despotic state.

II

The Oxford Movement was not of course an isolated phenomenon. As is well known, it was a part of the general European reaction against the spirit of the *Aufklärung* and of the French Revolution. It was indeed a part of the English effort in the early nineteenth century to re-enter the circle of European life. At bottom, it was, as Guido De Ruggiero has pointed out, "an expression of the same universalistic attitude which inspired . . . the Radicals, economists, and Liberals."[7] This effort to break down the isolation imposed by the pride of past generations of Englishmen, this tendency to Europeanize itself, forms one of the most striking characteristics of Victorianism. In the field of religion, the Oxford leaders, in thus reaching out for contact with what they regarded as the central tradition of continental Christianity, shared the general recoil of the conservative spirit against revolutionary liberalism. This reaction was far from being as simple as is sometimes believed: it was at once religious, intellectual, and political. Everywhere, whether in France, in the work of Chateaubriand, De Maistre, De Bonald, and Lammenais, or in Germany, in the labors of Görres, Friedrich von Schlegel, or Novalis, the spiritually conservative mind—sensing the mystery of loyalty, imagination, the soul—looked with distrust upon the dangerously facile intellectual statements of eighteenth-century revolutionism—the "rights" of man, and of reason; the contractual nature of society; the ideals

[7] *The History of European Liberalism,* translated by R. G. Collingwood (London, 1927), pp. 121-122.

of liberty, equality, and fraternity.[8] It sought, on the contrary, to resuscitate the sense of corporate and organic order, with authority (the rights of God and of governors) as the only true basis of such order, and with a concrete and total conception of man's nature to oppose the abstract, fragmented view of man as a rational animal. To such a mind, valuable as is liberty, advantageous as is equality, Christian as is fraternity, there was one fatal flaw in the revolutionary program: it was conceived in terms of human self-sufficiency, in terms of rebellion to divine authority. To such a mind, European Christendom for the past three hundred years had been progressively apostate to authority. No genuine reform could be effected without the humbling of human pride before an authority transcending the instabilities of human nature. This seemed to have been proved by three centuries of change. "The literary revolt of the fifteenth century, the religious revolt of the sixteenth, the philosophical systems of the seventeenth, the political revolution of the eighteenth, were all parts of a whole, successive steps in the dread argument that had been fulfilling itself in history."[9]

In England, where the revolution had been won gradually, and was at last legally and peacefully accomplished, there was less need of the swift and politically militant counter-reformation which occurred in France; it could afford to be more personal and religious in character. The

---

[8] The revival of French Catholicism, in theocratic Ultramontanism, was of course heralded by Chateaubriand's *Génie du Christianisme* (1802), which was so successful as to lead De Maistre to formulate his hierocratic doctrine of papal authority as the guarantee of royal power (*Du Pape*, 1819). De Bonald had already ascribed sole sovereignty to God, who transmits it to the pope and thence to the king (*Théorie du pouvoir politique et religieux dans la société civile*, 1796). Lammenais, hoping to "ensoul" the liberal gains in France, gathered about him such ardent disciples as Lacordaire, Montalembert, and Maurice de Guérin, and molded a whole generation with his famous *Essai sur l'indifférence en matière de religion* (1817-21), which argued for authoritarian religion as the basis of social order. The German reaction may be observed in Joseph von Görres' *Christliche Mystik* (1836-42), in Novalis' *Die Christenheit oder Europa* (1799), and in F. von Schlegel's *Geschichte der alten und neuen Literatur* (1815).

[9] A. M. Fairbairn, *Catholicism: Roman and Anglican* (London, 1899), p. 101.

Oxford Movement was not concerned with rehabilitating the old hierocratic doctrine of political authority as resting upon the spiritual authority of a divine institution. It was, however, concerned with discovering an authority capable of resisting that mild, persuasive, "reasonable" "Liberalism" which, in England, was the equivalent for the violent but less insidious Gallican "Revolution."[10] It was not merely interested in defeating the Whigs' intentions of disestablishing the church (of which there was really little danger in 1833), or in asserting the essence of the church to lie in the doctrine of Apostolical Succession or of the three-fold ministry of bishops, priests, and deacons. There were other and less ecclesiastical objectives, and it is these which have especial relevance for us today.

The Oxford leaders were as acutely aware as were Coleridge and Carlyle (and Burke before them) that the new secularism, founded in eighteenth-century empirical skepticism, and developed in modern materialistic industrialism, was to be the supreme enemy of man's spiritual identity. Once the revolutionary democracy of 1789 came into functional service with the machine and the laissez-faire market, the time was ripe for social dissolution and the progressive emptying of man's meaning for himself as an individual. All truly final authority—transcending the never-ending contingent authorities of nature and man—would yield to competing secularisms, and men would find themselves isolated in the mechanical meshes of an atomic social "order." This was the nightmare of Coleridge, Carlyle, Maurice, Ruskin, Arnold, and all those Victorians who failed to be quickened or comforted by the gospel according to Lord Bacon and Jeremy Bentham, or by their evangelists Macaulay, Brougham, Peel, and John Stuart Mill. Many took heart at Carlyle's oft-reiterated affirmation, "There is a Godlike in human affairs. . . . Man is still Man,"[11] and not a "Patent Digester" or "Motive-grinder"[12]

[10] *Ibid.*, p. 112.

[11] "Characteristics," *Collected Works*, Centenary Ed. (London, 1896-99), XXVIII, 42.

[12] *Sartor Resartus*, ed. C. F. Harrold (New York, 1937), pp. 210, 160, 162, etc.

and social order is a "mystic, miraculous, unfathomable Union"[13] of men in the bonds of spirit, not a contractual "partnership-agreement in a trade of pepper and coffee, calico or tobacco . . . to be taken up for a little temporary interest."[14] The seat of authority for man and society must be sought in a sphere transcending the mechanisms of logic, on a plane where man's spiritual wholeness will be inviolable. By 1870, many could feel, with Ruskin, that when confronted by the "dry-featured dwarfish caricatures" of men,[15] one's own contemporaries, one had the eerie sensation of talking to specters: "in our modern life . . . you not only cannot tell what a man is, but sometimes you cannot tell whether he *is*, at all!—whether you have indeed to do with a spirit, or only with an echo."[16] Most popular "advanced" religious thought of the day followed Coleridge, or Carlyle, or Thomas Erskine of Linlathen, or Maurice. These sought to rehabilitate man's spirit by pointing to the universality of genuine spiritual *experience*, hoping somehow, by means of it, to divinize history and nature. Whether in the transcendental idealism of Coleridge, in the "natural supernaturalism" of Carlyle, or in the Christian-Platonic doctrine of the *logos* in Julius Charles Hare, Erskine, or Maurice, there was persistent hope in seeing in "God's universe a symbol of the Godlike . . . [in] Immensity a Temple . . . [and in] Man's History, and Men's History [biography] a perpetual Evangel."[17] This was the cen-

13 "Characteristics," p. 11.

14 Burke's words, quoted here, are a satirical statement of the secular-utilitarian concept of society as held by eighteenth-century left-wing Whigs and French Jacobins (*Reflections on the Revolution in France*, London, 1790, p. 143).

15 On the despiritualizing of man in the Victorian epoch, much stimulating thought will be found in H. V. Routh's *Money, Morals, and Manners as Revealed in Modern Literature* (London, 1935); see also his better known *Towards the Twentieth Century* (London, 1937).

16 *Lectures on Art*, in *Works* (London, 1904), p. 94.

17 *Sartor Resartus*, pp. 253-254. The appeal to "experience," as the basis of religious evidence, in the thought of Coleridge, Carlyle, Erskine, and Maurice, had already been made in Germany by Kant and Schleiermacher. However, in men like Hare, Maurice, and Erskine, man and nature are redeemed from finitude by "a continual inflowing of the Logos"; thus the spiritual unity and authority which they sought really comes from the neo-

tury-long hope, the creation of what amounted to little more than a new "nature myth." It was eventually to vanish in the rose-colored mist of Victorian pantheism, leaving behind it the iron god of Mammonism, worshiped by those who had divinized nature just enough to sanctify labor, money, and property.

The Tractarians, on the other hand, protected by the Pauline and Augustinian emphasis on "the transcendence of the supernatural order and the incommensurability of Nature and Grace,"[18] felt none of the seductions of nature, but instead saw in the Church, as divinely established, an instrument which alone could provide a principle of order beyond the reach of "the all-corroding, all-dissolving skepticism" of the intellect where it is permitted unrestricted freedom in dealing with man's nature or with the character of the world. For the Tractarians, nothing but a divinely authoritative religion could cope with the unique predicament of man, that of being fated to live in two different orders: in his own "existence," which is always personal although full of super-personal values, and in the objective world, which is always non-personal and quite indifferent to human values. If man defined himself solely in terms of the second order, he would end by denying his own essence. All the religious sanctions for the power which had held society in an organic unity would collapse, and with the fall of religious authority, a new and remorseless authority would take its place: the Caesarism of the all-embracing secularist state.

One of the first stages in the triumph of the secularist spirit was the enthronement of the middle class. Thus, long before there rose the threat of "the Man versus the State,"[19]

Platonic element in Christianity, as expressed in the Fourth Gospel. See Vernon F. Storr, *The Development of English Theology in the Nineteenth Century: 1800-1860* (London, 1913), pp. 337-356; and L. E. Elliott-Binns, *Religion in the Victorian Era* (London, 1936), pp. 131-152.

[18] Christopher Dawson, *The Spirit of the Oxford Movement* (New York, 1933), p. x.

[19] See Herbert Spencer, *Man versus the State* (London, 1884) for a late-Victorian secularist realization of the dilemma produced by the conflicting authorities of the individual and society when neither has any longer a spiritual significance.

the Tractarians could easily see—what was celebrated by Macaulay, denounced by Carlyle, and satirized by Matthew Arnold—the "bourgeoization" of standards and values. On religious grounds alone this was highly repugnant to men like Newman. The still popular theological utilitarianism of William Paley—"doing good to mankind . . . for the sake of everlasting happiness"[20]—was but the counterpart of that cruder utilitarianism of the reformers which organized society for the making of money and disorganized it for anything else. It smiled upon the principle that the secular rules of the market justified the merchant in using for his own benefit whatever gifts had been bestowed upon him. As one critic has already noted, it might well have taken for its motto those words from Tyndale's translation of the Bible which R. H. Tawney has placed at the head of his account of the Puritan-Capitalist movement: "And the Lorde was with Joseph, and he was a luckie felowe."[21] This spirit of adjustment of religion to worldly success—one of the least admirable aspects of the "Victorian compromise" —was especially hateful to the Tractarians, for whom, as we shall see, all things have properly a sacramental value. They could easily foresee that condition in England which later, in the 1860's, Bishop Creighton saw in Oxford, after the defeat of Newman and the advent of Mill's *Logic* as the dominating influence there: "At the close of the 'sixties it seemed to us at Oxford almost incredible that a young don of any intellectual reputation for modernity should be on the Christian side."[22] The triumph of "modernity"— liberalism, secularism, mechanical civilization—inevitably nourished the conception of religion as at best merely an investment, and at least as a moral and emotional stimulant. Under the influence of the middle-class spirit, the English Church had drunk deeply of the temper, ideas, and laws of an ambitious and advancing civilization; it had become

[20] *Moral and Political Philosophy* (London, 1785), Book I, Chapter 7.

[21] See William George Peck, *The Social Implications of the Oxford Movement* (New York, 1933), p. 102; and Tawney, *Religion and the Rise of Capitalism* (London, 1926), Chapter 4.

[22] *Life and Letters of Mandell Creighton*, I, 75, quoted in Elliott-Binns, *op. cit.*, p. 323.

respectable, comfortable, sensible, temperate, liberal; it had laid its blessing on what Dean Church designated as "triumphant Macaulayism."[23] And to the Tractarians, as to Carlyle, the outlook was inexpressibly dreary as the "Gospel of Mammonism" surrendered humanity to the tender mercies of industrialism.

It was precisely in the social dissolution resulting from an advancing industrialism that the Oxford men saw one of the greatest threats to that high organic idea of society which Burke had held, and which Coleridge, Southey, and Carlyle were keeping alive in the mind of many an enlightened conservative. In fact, as we shall see, the Toryism of the Tractarians was not that of the "two-bottle orthodox . . . the thoroughgoing Toryism and traditionary Church-of-England-ism" which Newman found in the colleges and convocation of Oxford;[24] it was, instead, a spiritual Toryism which opposed endorsing remedies for reform derived solely from a philosophy fundamentally individualist and secular. Its aim was, in fact, twofold: "Tractarianism not only brought Industrialism under the condemnation of the Church. It set itself also to recover a right doctrine of 'the World,' in opposition to the Evangelical identification of it with 'some particular set of persons, or pleasures, or occupations,' "[25] and in opposition to the economic liberals' conception of it as a mere quarry for exploitation. It hoped to retrieve the seventeenth-century conception of the church and state as organically one, when, in Coleridgean terms, "the National Church was no mere State-institute" but rather the "State itself in its intensest federal union, . . . the guardian and representative

[23] *Life of R. W. Church*, p. 27, quoted by Ruth Kenyon in "The Social Aspect of the Catholic Revival," *Northern Catholicism: Centenary Studies in the Oxford and Parallel Movements*, ed. N. P. Williams and Charles Harris (London, 1933), p. 377.

[24] *Apologia*, ed. Wilfrid Ward, pp. 117, 494.

[25] Ruth Kenyon, in *Northern Catholicism*, p. 379, quoting from Newman's "The World Our Enemy," in *Parochial Sermons*, VII, iii. See also Newman's sermon on "Doing Glory to God in Pursuits of the World," in *Parochial Sermons*, VIII, xi.

of all personal individuality."[26] In the 1840's, it was this lost organic unity and humanity which was disturbing all classes. It was by no means an accident that the authors of the *Communist Manifesto*, in 1848, deplored in the language of *Past and Present* the modern "nexus between men" as being nothing but "callous 'cash payment.' " Marx and Engels lamented in almost Romantic terms the fact that the bourgeoisie had "put an end to all feudal, patriarchal, idyllic relations" among men, "those feudal ties that bound man to his natural superiors." The rapacious mercantile class had "drowned the most heavenly ecstasies of religious fervor, of chivalrous enthusiasm, of philistine sentimentalism, in the icy waters of egoistical calculation."[27] This is the language not only of nineteenth-century Marxians but also of Burke and Cobbett. Something incommensurable with money was vanishing from the world.

It was partly to redeem men from such despair of the supersensible that Newman emphasized the sacramental character of the world. Though Newman himself seldom speaks of nature in definitely sacramental terms—the Calvinist in him never died, and "the whole world lieth in wickedness"[28]—nevertheless there are innumerable passages in his works where the notion is clearly present:[29] the Christian will of course "see God in all things," but he will more specifically "see Christ revealed to his soul amid the ordinary actions of the day, as by a sort of sacrament."[30] All objects and events are at once profane and sacred, finite instrumentalities for the realization of divine ends, ends which alone can give meaning to the groping significance

26 *Aids to Reflection* (London, 1859), p. 238: "For the Church is the shrine of morality: and in morality alone the citizen asserts and reclaims his personal independence, his integrity."

27 Karl Marx and Friedrich Engels, *Manifesto of the Communist Party* (Chicago: Charles H. Kerr and Co., n.d.), p. 15.

28 *Parochial Sermons*, VII, 31.

29 On the sacramentalism of Newman's general philosophy, see C. F. Harrold, "Newman and the Alexandrian Platonists," *Modern Philology*, XXXVII, 283-288.

30 *Parochial Sermons*, VIII, 158, 165. See also *The Idea of a University*, Discourse V, final paragraph.

of nature's symbols. To seek a meaning solely among the symbols, to seek a humane ideology among economic or political secularisms, is to follow false gods, to cut man from man, and frustrate tragically the fierce longing of man to solve his social and individual problem. For by some strange fact of his constitution, man continually discovers that "so long as the economic [or political] operation is conceived as the human end, no truly humane ideology can be evolved. The strange but characterizing feature of humanity is that the principle of its true socialization cannot be discovered within earthly horizons, and must be sought in a transcendent sphere. It is only when work is governed by the sacramental idea of realization of spiritual ends through visible means, that a distinctly *human* co-operation emerges."[31] The lost sense of the spiritually organic unity of society, which Carlyle sought to revive through transcendentalism, the Tractarians sought to revive through "sacramentalizing" the world and restoring man to his dual citizenship in the two orders of nature and spirit.

It was Tractarian sacramentalism which, when applied to social order, gave rise to the superficial belief that the Oxford Movement was, after all, merely the religious aspect of the hidebound Toryism of Eldon and Wellington. But the official Toryism dominant in Newman's early career was just as secular at heart as was the Liberalism which the Newmanites opposed, and had not even the humanitarianism and the moralism which were at least two undeniably redeeming characteristics of the best Liberals. If we are to call Newman a Tory, then his Toryism was of a singularly revolutionary kind, with its emphasis upon the divine issues of social order, the supernatural value of every man, and the sacramental relation of the world to the spirit of man. "In so far as the Oxford Movement was Tory, its Toryism was not that of the defenders of vested interests, the 'Conservatives' who aroused Hurrell Froude's scorn, but that of Southey and Coleridge and the young Disraeli who were among the first to denounce the injustices of the Industrial

[31] W. G. Peck, *op. cit.*, p. 197.

Revolution."[32] Indeed, for a time in 1833, Newman seems to have moved astonishingly close to Radicalism, noting how, at least historically, "the people were the fulcrum of the Church's power."[33] And in more specifically social terms, not only Newman but also Pusey and Keble were able to rise above the barriers of cultural and intellectual inequality in their personal attitudes toward poor and humble folk.[34] While the Tractarians never cast their thought in the mold of social science, and never familiarized themselves with contemporary economic problems, the fact remains that they boldly criticized existing social conditions, condemned injustice and oppression, and clearly asserted the radical conflict between the aims of industrial capitalism and the aims of the Christian religion. Thus we find Pusey denouncing the prevailing idolatries: "Covetousness . . . is the very end and aim of what men do, the ground of their undertakings, to keep and enlarge their wealth. . . . In our eager haste to heap more comfort to ourselves, we beat down the wages of the poor, in order to cheapen or multiply our own indulgence."[35] And it is Newman who lashes out at the money-hungry middle class in his famous sermons at St. Mary's, in which he flagellates the early Victorians for their "avarice, fortune-getting, amassing of capital."[36] In the sermons of the Tractarians there are unmistakable hints that they heard the ominous rumblings of world-wide disaster. "The kingdoms of this world," said

[32] Christopher Dawson, *The Spirit of the Oxford Movement*, p. xi. See also Southey's dialogues on society, *Sir Thomas More*, and Macaulay's brilliant but superficial reply in his review-essay on Southey's volume.

[33] "If we look into history, whether in the age of the Apostles, St. Ambrose's, or St. Becket's, still the people were the fulcrum of the Church's power," wrote Newman in 1833, on returning from the Mediterranean full of hatred for the reforming Whigs and the inert Tories. "Expect on your return to England to see us all cautious, long-headed, unfeeling, unflinching Radicals." *Letters and Correspondence*, ed. Anne Mozley (London, 1891), L, 454; also p. 450.

[34] See Peck, *op. cit.*, pp. 62-63, for Isaac Williams' astonishment at John Keble's affection and reverence for the humble folk of his parish.

[35] Quoted from the sermons on "The Danger of Riches" and "The Sin of Judas," in Peck, pp. 66-67.

[36] Quoted by R. W. Church, *The Oxford Movement* (London, 1892), p. 140.

Pusey in his *Christianity without a Cross,* are "retaining an outward civilization, [but] they are fast decaying and becoming uncivilized."[37]

The Tractarian opposition to Liberalism as a method of regulating the economic process rested, one should add, on what in their own day, as in ours, provoked the opposition of innumerable intelligent readers: namely, on the very limited value which they placed upon the historical spirit. It is because the Oxford Movement has long been dealt with through an overworked historical sense that it has so often been seen in a false light. To account for the movement solely in terms of historical cause and effect is to fall into the very secular fallacy which they saw overtaking their contemporaries. It is to judge an absolute standpoint from a relativist point of view: valid only to a certain degree, but fatally missing the essence of the thing judged. For it must always be remembered that when we are dealing with a movement based upon theological propositions, the essence of the movement will transcend the limits of historical definition. Like the fundamentals of metaphysical truth, the basic dogmas of theology do not change. And it is on this vantage ground that the Tractarians were able to overcome that "historicism" which Etienne Gilson has shown to have vexed the minds of later nineteenth-century historians,[38] that imprisonment in historical relativity which prevented any genuine solution of real problems, because the only leverage for dealing with nature and history must be found outside the circle of cause and effect. Put into social terms, this means that Tractarianism naturally finds no help for man's deepest needs in the state. The state is not concerned with life, but only with the ordering of life, with organization and control. The real friend of life, the only true source of spiritual power, is to be found ultimately in religion. Men like Keble, Newman, and Pusey had no need to be reminded, as most of us do, that all genuine forms of religion—contemplation, sacrifice, unselfish action—are a

37 Peck, p. 69.
38 *The Unity of Philosophical Experience* (New York, 1937), p. 319.

turning away from the external, centrifugal, non-vital activity to the heart of life, to sources of power inaccessible by the crude hand of secular or civil authority. The Oxford leaders were relatively indifferent to the claims of the new "historical spirit" because they felt that it dealt, after all, with "fallen" human nature, which needs something supra-historical: a new principle of life which would reveal the inadequacy of human knowledge and human civilization, and heal and restore them. The Tractarians were no more indifferent to the Corn Laws than were the early Christians to Roman slavery; they were no more eager to destroy the Victorian secular civilization around them than were the early Christians to destroy the Roman empire. They were not social idealists. On the other hand, they were blessed with a sophistication far more profound and far more profitable than that of the hard-headed social reformer: a religious sophistication, by which they realized man's dilemma more intensely than the most fervid secular idealist, since they saw it as an inner, "inherited" burden of evil which could never be lifted by any political or economic program, but which required, for its eradication, a turning to a frame of reference transcending the flux of history.

We should now be able to understand the grounds on which the Tractarians distrusted "Liberalism." To them the word "Liberalism" referred to a twofold modern movement, at once intellectual and political. In 1833, it was the intellectual aspect of the movement which disturbed them; Newman has defined it clearly in the *Apologia* as "the exercise of thought upon matters, in which, from the constitution of the human mind, thought cannot be brought to any successful issue. . . . Among such matters are first principles of whatever kind; and of these the most sacred and momentous are especially to be reckoned the truths of Revelation."[39] The application of what Newman calls "liberal" reason to philosophy and theology results in positivism, in the scientism of popular thought, in the de-supernaturalism of the "social Christianity" of Protestantism,

[39] *Apologia*, ed. W. Ward, p. 483. For Newman's complete definition and illustration of "Liberalism," see the Note, on pp. 491-502.

and in the general absorption of religion into the secularized culture of the modern world. The political side of
Liberalism laid less claim on Newman's attention, but it
represented the outer or practical manifestation of the
same spirit. It has been conveniently summed up by Matthew Arnold, in *Culture and Anarchy*, as "middle-class liberalism, which had for the cardinal points of its belief the
Reform Bill of 1832, and local self-government, in politics;
in the social sphere, free trade, unrestricted competition,
and the making of large industrial fortunes; in the religious sphere, the Dissidence of Dissent and the Protestantism of the Protestant religion."[40] Liberalism in either sense
represented the effort of man to solve the problem of life
"without the aid of Christianity."[41]

It was the conviction of the Tractarians—as of many
other religious Victorians—that nineteenth-century Liberalism could be but a temporary phenomenon, a transition between a Christian culture and one that is completely
secularized. It was plain to them that European culture had

[40] *Culture and Anarchy*, ed. J. Dover Wilson (Cambridge, 1935), p. 62.
[41] Newman, in his famous *Biglietto* speech, on attaining the cardinalate,
in 1879, summed up the subject as follows: "Liberalism in religion is the
doctrine that there is no positive truth in religion, but that one creed is as
good as another. . . . It is inconsistent with any recognition of any religion,
as *true*. It teaches that all are to be tolerated, for all are matters of opinion.
Revealed religion is not a truth, but a sentiment and a taste; . . . and it is
the right of each individual to make it say just what strikes his fancy. . . .
It is as impertinent to think about a man's religion as about his sources of
income or his management of his family. Religion is in no sense the bond
of society. . . . Hitherto, it has been considered that religion alone, with its
supernatural sanctions, was strong enough to secure submission of the
masses of our population to law and order; now the Philosophers and
Politicians are bent on satisfying this problem without the aid of Christianity. Instead of the Church's authority and teaching, they would substitute first of all a universal and thoroughly secular education, calculated
to bring home to every individual that to be orderly, industrious, and sober
is his personal interest. . . . It would provide the broad fundamental
ethical truths, of justice, benevolence, veracity, and the like; proved experience; . . . natural laws . . . in society, in social matters, whether physical
or psychological . . . in government, trade, finance, sanitary experiments,
and the intercourse of nations. As to Religion, it is a private luxury, which
a man may have if he will; but which of course he must pay for, and
which he must not obtrude upon others, or indulge in to their annoyance."
Wilfrid Ward, *Life of Newman* (London, 1912), II, 460-461.

already ceased to be Christian in the eighteenth century, and that while it retained the inherited moral standards and values of a Christian civilization, it succeeded only in erecting a quasi-religious substitute for faith. For the time being, it was living on the spiritual capital inherited from historic Christianity; as soon as this was exhausted, something else must come to take its place. Once society were really launched on the path of secularization, it could find in Liberalism only a half-way house; it must go on to the bitter end: some form of "state-ism"—what the twentieth century was to know as "totalitarianism." The Tractarians could have no knowledge of the exact forms which secular Liberalism would take, but there is an inner logic in any secularism, a logic which can easily enough be seen in the programs against which the Oxford leaders fought. For if we believe, with the secularists, that the Kingdom of Heaven can be established by political and economic programs, then we have no right to object to the claims of the state to embrace the whole of life in order to produce and distribute its secular goods, even though it demands—as it logically will in time—the absolute submission of the individual will and conscience. The realization of this fact drove the religious conscience of the Victorian age to disapprove of unrestricted liberal doctrine. Not only the Tractarians, but also Maurice, Coleridge, Carlyle, Ruskin, and Arnold were outspoken in their distrust of mass-democracy and economic individualism. The universal expectation of a liberal millennium[42] was scoffed at by Carlyle in his social writings, in which he gave Europe two hundred years in which to learn, painfully, that the worship of Mammon must end in some form of power-leadership.

For Newman the very word "progress" was merely a "slang term."[43] For him "the progress of the species" meant

---

[42] For a picture of the heyday of liberal optimism (1831-32), in which "every clique, every sect, almost every middle-class family believed that . . . every question could be solved instantly and forever by the triumph of right—that is, of themselves," See Thomas Mozley, *Reminiscences: Chiefly of Oriel College and the Oxford Movement* (London, 1882), I, 272-275.

[43] Ward, *Life of Newman*, II, 81.

greater and greater loss of spiritual nourishment for mankind. He was not unaware of the possibility of a proletarian revolution; as the masses were increasingly deluded with the expectation of the fruits of secularism, and at the same time bored and angered by the spiritual vacuity of their lives, a new barbarism would generate from within the very heart of civilization. "Who are to be the Goths and Vandals who are to destroy modern civilization?" asked one of Newman's friends in 1871; and answered, with Newman's approval, "The lowest class, which is the most numerous, and is infidel, will rise up from the depths of the modern cities, and will be the new scourges of God." "This great prophecy," adds Newman, "is first fulfilled in Paris [of the Commune]—our turn may come a century hence."[44]

III

Such words make any reconsideration of the Oxford Movement a study in the implications which it has for our own time. Making allowances for what the Oxford leaders did not say, or did not intend to say, it is possible nevertheless to draw up some very pertinent conclusions based on the general tendency of their thought. Of these, perhaps the most notable at present is the fact that the secularism which they feared and fought has attained precisely the proportions which could have been predicted at the time when Newman wrote his first tracts. It is not too much to say that in the apparently beneficial soil of secular Liberalism, there lay the seeds of totalitarianism, whether in form of Fascism or Communism, or in the form of national mobilization by democratic nations for that "total warfare" which is the natural offspring of nineteenth-century middle-class industrialism.

The debacle of civilization is not merely a failure in

---

[44] The friend was F. M. Capes, editor of *The Rambler.* See Ward, II, 344. For a glimpse of the spread of rationalism and atheism among the Victorian working classes, see Amy Cruse, *The Victorians and Their Reading* (New York, 1935), pp. 122-123: "When the youth comes out of the hall [of the Socialists], he has a printed paper in his hand, a leaflet issued by the Society of Rational Pioneers, Leeds. It is headed, *Twenty-five Reasons for Being an Atheist.*"

leadership, as Carlyle had maintained; it has been a failure of *spiritual* leadership. For generations, religion has steadily retreated into man's inner life; it has left social and economic life to the state and to a civilization becoming secularized. Losing its hold on social life, religion loses its hold on life altogether. By the end of the nineteenth century, it could no longer be said of any nation that "Christianity was the law of the land." Never before in the history of the world had civilization become so completely secularized as was that of the late-Victorian and Edwardian periods. Soon the new secularism was to cease being content to dominate the outer world, leaving man's inner life—his loyalties, his enthusiasms, his imagination, his capacity for sacrifice—to religion. Within a generation it was to begin claiming the whole man. New and bastard religions were to arise, appealing to man's mystical instincts, in the name of "Race," or of "the State," or of "the Proletariat." These show a phenomenon new in history: the "Kingdom of Anti-Christ" fully equipped with political form and substance, standing over against the Christian church as a *counter-church*, with its own dogmas, moral standards, hierarchy, and militant will to world conquest.

All this may seem a far cry from Newman's original grievance against Lord Grey and his Reforming Whigs of 1830, but there is an unbroken continuity underlying the advances and retreats of Liberalism from those early years to the present. Political liberalism, such as Gladstone's, is now dead.[45] But the secularism on which it fed has crowded out that spiritual authority which once was sovereign over all temporalities. Even in the democracies it threatens to erect a new "church," what has been called the "omnicompetent State," which will mold the mind and guide the life of its citizens from the cradle to the grave, developing a kind of democratic *étatisme* which, while being less arbitrary and inhumane than Communism or Fascism, will make just as large a claim on the individual and demand an equally whole-hearted spiritual allegiance. Both in war and in

[45] See George Dangerfield's *The Strange Death of Liberal England* (London, 1935).

peace, it will continue to differ from the "police-state" of the nineteenth-century Liberals, but will become "a nurse, and a schoolmaster and an employer and an officer—in short, an earthly providence, an all-powerful, omnipotent human god—and a very jealous god at that."[46] This will be the logical outcome of setting up the City of Man as an end in itself. Men will have forgotten that even the pagans knew that social order rested on a center not its own, i.e., on a divine center. Men have always felt that civilization did not exist merely for the gratification of needs and desires, but that it ought to be a sacred order resting on what Plato called "the divine Law."[47]

That the Oxford Movement is so frequently seen in only its narrower aspects—in relation to theology, church history, and the problem of belief—is no doubt owing to the scarcity of studies dealing with its larger implications. As we have already noted, it was a part of a wide European movement in search of a true principle of authority or sovereignty. Various writers have touched upon the Tractarians' relation with France, notably in the work of Fairbairn, Knox, and Laski,[48] but we need a full treatment of it as a separate subject. If, as Knox says, "the religious Romantics of France were indirect, but far from insignificant

[46] On the possibilities of the triumph of the god-State, even in the Western democracies, see Christopher Dawson, *Religion and the Modern State* (New York, 1940), Chapter 6, "Religion and Politics," especially pp. 105-110.

[47] "To that Law," says Plato, "he who would be happy holds fast and follows it in all humility and order; but he who is lifted up with pride or money or honor or beauty, who has a soul hot with folly and youth and insolence, and thinks that he has no need of a guide or ruler, but is able of himself to be the guide of others, he, I say, is deserted of God; and being thus deserted, he takes to himself others who are like him, and jumps about, throwing all things into confusion, and many think he is a great man. But in a short time he pays the penalty of justice and is utterly destroyed and his family and state with him" (*Laws*, IV, 716).

[48] A. M. Fairbairn, *op. cit.*, pp. 96-110, 128 n., etc.; E. A. Knox, *The Tractarian Movement: 1833-1845, a Study of the Oxford Movement as a Phase of the Religious Revival in Western Europe in the Second Quarter of the Nineteenth Century* (London, 1933), Chapter 3, "Oxford and France"; Harold J. Laski, *Studies in the Problem of Sovereignty* (New Haven, 1917), Chapter 3, "The Political Theory of the Oxford Movement," and Chapter 4, "The Political Theory of the Catholic Revival."

factors in the development of the Oxford Movement,"[49] then it would be well to know precisely how such works as Lammenais' *Essai sur l'indifférence* and *Des progrès de la révolution* affected Newman and Hurrell Froude. Much remains to be discovered about Newman's correspondence in 1837 with the French Abbé, M. Jager, about the Roman Catholic influence on many Englishmen when England opened her doors to refugee clergy, monks, and nuns in 1789-1790, about the surprising similarities between the early issues of Lacordaire and Montalembert's new journal, *L'Avenir*, and the first *Tracts for the Times*, about the "secret" efforts of Bloxam and Ambrose Philipps de Lisle, even before the publication of Tract xc (1841), to make the Oxford Movement a means of uniting the Church of England with the Church of Rome. Little as has been written on the Oxford Movement and France, still less has been written on the Oxford Movement and Germany. The best study we have is L. A. Willoughby's,[50] which surveys the affinities of two points of view, leaving detailed treatment for other students. Here the relations are indeed tenuous, real German echoes of Newman coming only late in the century, from Ignatius Döllinger, the Modernist.[51]

The relation of the Tractarian Movement to the social and intellectual changes of the nineteenth and twentieth centuries has received considerable attention, but special studies still remain to be done. The general work in this field has been carried on, for the most part, by clergymen;[52] but students of Victorian literature have an equal interest in the subject inasmuch as the Oxford Movement was both

[49] Knox, pp. 45-46.

[50] "On Some German Affinities with the Oxford Movement," *MLR*, xxix (1934), 52 ff.

[51] See Ward, *Life of Newman*, I, 438-446, 479, etc.; also II, 375, 379-380, 466. See also C. Broicher, "Anglikanische Kirche und deutsche Philosophie," *Preussischer Jahrbücher*, cxlii (1910), 205-233, 457-498.

[52] The best work of this kind is by William George Peck, *The Social Implications of the Oxford Movement*, the Hale Lectures, 1933 (New York, 1933). He makes profitable use of the labors of C. C. J. Webb, G. C. Binyon, V. A. Demant, Ruth Kenyon, M. B. Reckitt, and P. E. T. Widdrington, listed in his bibliography, pp. 333-337. See also Christopher Dawson, *The Spirit of the Oxford Movement* (New York, 1933).

the background and the material for much Victorian prose and poetry. It remains to be proved "how little [the Movement] touched [the] characteristic and creative minds" of the period.[53] It is true, as Storr has said, that "none of the greater poets of the nineteenth century yielded themselves to its spell. Tennyson and Browning show no sympathy with Anglo-Catholicism."[54] Yet just what impact it made on such men, as well as on Clough, William Morris, Swinburne, and various minor poets, makes an interesting speculation. The often-noted parallels between elements in Coleridge's thought and that of the Tractarians still remain to be systematically examined. If Carlyle's acerb observation be true, that from Coleridge's "Cloud-Juno" came "spectral Puseyisms, monstrous illusory Hybrids,"[55] then there is room for a definite statement of just how that "seminal mind" affected, not Newman himself, but the atmosphere in which the Oxford Movement generated its power. The degree in which the movement found expression and opposition in Victorian fiction has already been well indicated by Joseph E. Baker;[56] but there still remain the wider fictional backgrounds which throw the movement into sharper focus. According to T. S. Eliot, three distinct stages can be traced in the attitude of Victorian novelists toward Christianity. In the first "the Faith is taken for granted, but omitted from their picture of life; in the second it is contested or worried about; in the third (which was reached with the present generation) it is treated as an anachronism."[57] Scott, Thackeray, and Dickens show considerable interest in religion, but are somewhat unfair to nonconformity and evangelicalism. Later in the century, Kingsley's *Alton Locke* conveys, perhaps unintentionally,

[53] Fairbairn, *op. cit.*, p. 312, also pp. 313-315.

[54] V. F. Storr, *op. cit.*, p. 272.

[55] *Life of Sterling*, Centenary Ed. of *Works*, pp. 61-62. Broicher, *op. cit.*, is a good example of how one may overstate the similarities between the ideas of Newman and those of Coleridge (pp. 469-471, 473-484).

[56] *The Novel and the Oxford Movement* (Princeton, 1932).

[57] See L. E. Elliott-Binns, *Religion in the Victorian Era*, p. 343, paraphrasing from T. S. Eliot's chapter on "Religion and Literature," in *Faith that Illuminates*, p. 39.

a rather vulgar and materialistic account of nonconformity. It is the women novelists, George Eliot and Mrs. Gaskell, who give a juster picture of the religious life of Victorian England. By the end of the century, Hardy, Meredith, and Butler reflect the moral and spiritual conflict around them; religion has become a problem. How accurate such generalizations as these may prove to be, can be shown only by special studies. The varieties of Victorian religion, as seen through Victorian fiction, are still to receive adequate treatment.

In any reconsideration of the Oxford Movement, whether on its theological, intellectual, or literary side, it is no longer sufficient to think of it as a backwater in the onward rush of nineteenth-century enlightenment. It had its own center, its own motive-power, and its significant place among those articulations of modern uneasiness which now may be seen as more prophetic than even the Victorians could have believed. Perhaps its greatest significance for a time of crisis, such as ours, is to remind us that man is so constituted that even in his idealism, if such idealism is turned to his own glorification, he gravitates toward materialism and boredom and destruction. The great idealisms of the nineteenth-century Liberals resulted, strangely enough, in the crass acquisitiveness of capitalism, and led onward to the vast and anonymous savagery of mechanized wars. Thus, with all their intellectual limitations, and in spite of the technical objectives at which they aimed, the great Tractarians remain, in the general grounds of their thought, singularly prophetic of much that astounds us in the wreck of our modern world.

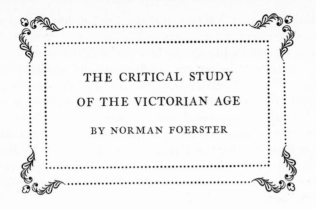

THE CRITICAL STUDY

OF THE VICTORIAN AGE

BY NORMAN FOERSTER

WITH the growth of perspective, some remarks now seem to be in order concerning the excellent and indispensable nineteenth century, especially that portion of it which we conventionally term Victorian. The fact that we use the term Victorian is, I suspect, indicative of a certain insularity in our point of view. We tend to restrict our vision to England, just as scholars in American literature tend to restrict their vision to America. We are too prone to think of the era called Victorian as an isolated and very British Arcadia of "cupolas, mansard roofs and fretwork, of hair furniture, antimacassars, dried flowers and Venus de Milos with clocks in their stomachs, of hoop skirts, frills, and bustles, of tight lacing and much fainting, of lap dogs, and lovers wooing on their knees, a period which prided itself on its 'diligence in business,' its large families, its correct thinking, and its smug piety,"[1] a period, in the words of Amy Lowell quoted in Webster's dictionary, of "that long set of sentimental hypocrisies known in England as Victorian."

It is true that this middle-class fairyland once existed, and it is true that it colored the stream of English literature, especially the novel, during the period; but it is not true that it marks the course of that stream. The course of the

[1] Harry M. Ayres, Will D. Howe, and F. M. Padelford, *The Modern Student's Book of English Literature* (New York, 1924), p. 538.

stream, we too often forget, was not English but European.
As the excellent and indispensable Matthew Arnold saw
clearly, we need a literary history and a criticism which regard "Europe as being, for intellectual and spiritual purposes, one great confederation, bound to a joint action and
working to a common result." There was a time when the
intellectual and spiritual life of Europe as a whole was
dominated by neo-classicism; it was dominated in the next
era by Romanticism; and then it was dominated by Realism, which developed into Naturalism. This is obvious, of
course, but as often happens to the obvious, its implications
are slighted.

In France the realistic dispensation arrived in the 1830's.
In logical France, where literary movements are usually
sharp and decisive, it announced itself in the work of Stendhal, Mérimée, and Balzac, and soon became the naturalism
of Flaubert and Zola. So vigorous was the movement that
by 1885 Realism and Naturalism had pretty well accomplished their task.

Very different was the situation in Germany, incurably
romantic Germany, which was not invaded by the French
movement till the 1880's, beginning with Fontane, continuing with Sudermann and Hauptmann. German aversion
to Realism and Naturalism is symbolized by the fact that
Wagner's *Parsifal* came as late as 1882, and that Hauptmann was not long in relapsing from his realistic austerity
into a *Märchendrama* like *Die versunkene Glocke*.

In England, on the contrary, Realism had strong native,
eighteenth-century roots. In the decade in which Scott and
Coleridge died came the first significant work of Dickens,
followed in the next decade by Thackeray, both of whom
built upon the prose fiction of the eighteenth century. By
the 1850's and early sixties a mild and modest Realism had
reached full flower, in a literature which Joseph E. Baker
has well characterized as one of "humorous, romantic realism; kindly but penetrating criticism of social and individual faults; common sense; pleasant domesticity; a love
of balance and permanence that to our own hectic age is

as strange and restful as the incredible insularity, or even parochialism, of the circles in which life moved."[2] That is the mood in which nineteenth-century English Realism responded to the same forces which produced a very different Realism in France. The mood lingered on, yielding slowly to a growing asperity, until about 1880.

To think of the new dispensation in England as realistic is to focus attention at once upon its fundamental relationship with the continental literary movement, upon its fundamental basis in the scientific spirit of the century so eloquently described by Taine, and upon the genesis of the Naturalism that accompanied and succeeded Realism. To think of it as Victorian, on the other hand, is to isolate it from the continental movement, to emphasize its social harmony rather than its mordant and innovating scientific spirit, and to leave the movement of Naturalism unexplained.

Furthermore, to think in terms of Victorianism is to become involved in sundry awkwardnesses and artificialities. For example: The Victorian era, it is generally agreed, ends about 1880, that is, a full two decades before the end of the Queen's reign.

· Again, one of the foremost Victorians, Thomas Carlyle, had the ill grace to be born the same year as one of the foremost Romantics, John Keats, and it seems to be necessary to keep the first half of him with the Romantics, as Professor Bernbaum has done in his *Guide through the Romantic Movement*, or else to regard him as a Victorian misfit. Wordsworth, an even earlier Romantic than Keats and Carlyle, lived till 1850 and died a respectable Victorian. Premature death obviated the problem of what to do with the three great later Romantics, Byron, Shelley, and Keats, who had no chance to affront or conform to the new era, but who, if they had lived as many years as Wordsworth, would have died between 1868 and 1875, near the close of the Victorian era. Had they lived, it is possible that our textbooks would have had no Victorian era but

[2] *The Novel and the Oxford Movement* (Princeton, 1932), p. 144.

59

would simply have described the conflict between Romanticism and Realism, as they describe the previous conflict between neo-classicism and Romanticism.

I am well aware that the terms Romantic and Realistic are vague, but so is the term Victorian, and it has the additional objection, from a literary point of view, of being political and social. It may or may not suit well what was happening in politics and society; it certainly does not suit well what was happening in literature. It suggests nothing of that civil war between Romanticism and Realism which was the central literary feature of the period. The earlier conflict between neo-classicism and Romanticism had been a war between two visions of life in basic conflict with each other, a war between aliens. But the ensuing conflict between a triumphant Romanticism and a challenging Realism was of a different order, a conflict between two forms of naturism, the one imaginatively emotional, the other endeavoring to be rational in the spirit of modern science— both, however, inwardly at one in their conception of man as a part of nature rather than separate from nature as in the Christian and classical dispensations. That is why, throughout the period of triumphant Realism and Naturalism, from 1870 or 1880 down to the present year, it has been possible to stage romantic revolts against the grimness of the new movement, without leaving the domain of naturism. From "Nature's holy plan," as described by Wordsworth, to Nature's unholy plan, as described by Thomas Hardy, is no great distance: either way, it is Nature's plan, and the distance is merely that between the two sides of the same coin.

There was Victorianism in America also. I can testify to the fact myself, having been brought up in a social environment that had the aspect and the tone of late Victorianism, a modified form of that earlier Victorianism of whatnots and antimacassars, vicious corsets and smelling salts, diligence in business and in procreation. English visitors like Dickens, Thackeray, and Arnold were sufficiently at home in our American paradise of the middle class. But did we have an American Victorian literature? I think not.

After an early brood of mild Romantics including Irving, Bryant, and Cooper, came a distinguished group of writers, all born between 1803 and 1819, which included Emerson, Hawthorne, Longfellow, Poe, Thoreau, Lowell, and Whitman, the writers of our Romantic movement. Had these writers died at age 31—the average life range of Byron, Shelley, and Keats—Emerson would actually have died two years before his first book was published and the entire group would have been gone by the mid-century. Had they died at age 40, as Poe did, all of them would have been gone by the time of John Brown's raid. But they were good actuarial risks and, like Joaquin Miller's Columbus, they sailed on and on, two of them into the 1890's. If some of them took on the color of Victorianism, the central fact remains that they were our Romantics, responsive above all to the currents of European Romanticism, especially British and German.

٠Since the phenomena of literary history in America usually follow after an interval those of literary history in England, we should naturally look to a later generation for our distinguished American Victorians. Actually, however, no prominent writers were born in the United States for sixteen years after the birth of Lowell and Whitman in 1819, so that we must move on to 1835, where we come upon the birth of the un-Victorian Mark Twain, followed by the tolerably Victorian William Dean Howells, and the very definitely modern Henry James. Nor are such lesser contemporaries as Harte, Miller, Lanier, and Cable to be thought of as good Victorians. Our public read the English Victorians, and it read magazines and annuals redolent of Victorianism, but the important American literature of the period was not Victorian. Even more than in England, the term is appropriate to third-rate writers, inappropriate to the first-rate writers.

And in America, even more plainly than in England, the significant change is from Romanticism to Realism. If we let Romanticism begin in 1819 with Irving's *Sketch-Book* recounting the worshipful musings of an American dreamer

61

in Europe, we may well bring it to a close in 1869 with Mark Twain's *Innocents Abroad*, recounting the irreverent observations of a fact-facing American in Europe. From that year till about 1910 the United States had a literature of Realism, the racy, boisterous Realism of Mark Twain ending in the Naturalism of *The Mysterious Stranger*, the genial Realism of Howells, imitator of Jane Austen and admirer of Tolstoy, the cosmopolitan and sophisticated Realism of James, the careful, picturesque Realism of the local colorists, all of them preparing the way for the increasingly naturalistic Realism of the period after 1910, when we come to a writer like Theodore Dreiser and America has at length caught up with Zola. Such, I think, is plainly the story of our nineteenth-century literature, and it should not be obscured by placing in the foreground such concepts as New England Transcendentalism, or Knickerbocker writers, or writers of the early or later national periods, any more than the story of English literature should be obscured by a narrowly conceived Victorian era.

I cannot but think that it is time for us to be attempting a more penetrating, more significant, literary history of the nineteenth century. Our entire scheme needs fresh study and fresh thought. The same may be said of many specialized subjects of investigation, subjects calling for the steady endeavor of a scholar's lifetime or the efforts of groups of scholars.

We need studies, for example, of the influence of various continental cultures upon England, such as the subjects already suggested by the Victorian Group of the MLA, ranging from French Positivism and the Higher Criticism to the modern revival of classical scholarship. Especially valuable would be a more penetrating view of what Goethe meant in England, of the relations between the *romantische Schule* and the Romantic tradition in the Victorian age, of the influence of the post-Kantian philosophy, of the relation between German scholarship and English criticism.

We need studies of the relation between what was going on in literature and what was going on in the fine arts, especially the way in which literature came to be divorced from morality. The tradition of aestheticism running from Keats to Wilde needs fresh exploration, fresh evidence, and, above all, a fresh critical insight from a point of view neither aestheticist nor moralistic but classical at its best.

We need many studies of the relations between literature and science—not merely the new knowledge, but also the method, the criteria, the temper and attitude, and the effect of these upon idea, form, and style in the various literary *genres* of the period; and particularly the interplay of science with other motivations of Realism.

We need further studies in the relations of literature with the latter-day fortunes of Christianity; studies dealing with the continuance of the theory of natural goodness; studies of all the ways of sentimentalism, and of its presence in writers professing disdain for it; studies of emotional and practical humanitarianism; studies of primitivism and the idea of progress; studies of various concepts of individualism: the ethical and spiritual individual of the classical and Christian traditions, the romantic ego, the rugged individual of laissez-faire. And all of these things and many others, if they are to be done well, will demand wide interests, trained powers of reflection, and critical standards capable of organizing material to serious ends.

Instead of which we are in the main studying literature *in vacuo*, isolating it from its sister arts, quarantining it from the other value-judgment subjects such as philosophy and religion, in a sense not studying literature at all but only literary history, and commonly reducing literary history to discrete (and discreet) facts. With joy or without, we go on adding fact to fact, facts about authors' lives, facts about books and periodicals, facts about reputations of authors and books, facts—and purported facts—about sources and influences. Well do we merit the charge that we are lost in a chaos of information and materials. Even the nineteenth-century type of scholarship in which we were schooled risked a certain breadth wanting in our piecemeal and aimless Positivism. When we speak of the use of literature in education, we try to speak nobly of intangibles, but when we write as scholars we employ another language, a dull medium that betrays our limitation to the tangible or matter-of-fact. One becomes respectable, it seems, by avoiding sensitive perception and intellectual vigor.

What is the remedy? First, I should say, an interest in the history of ideas. From an interest in the phenomena of literary history to an interest in the history of ideas is not a difficult step. We need not be frightened at ideas so long as they march in a dignified parade instead of lurking behind a bush. It is fascinating to watch them as they go by in ever changing uniforms to the music of ever changing bands. In time the ideas become familiar and friendly figures, and we begin to take an interest in them *per se*, not merely in their historical progression. We perceive that if, as Lytton Strachey once said, "Human beings are too important to be treated as mere symptoms of the past," ideas also are too important to be so treated. We perceive that ideas must be viewed, not only as early or late, but also as sound or unsound. Then we are on the way to achieving a whole framework of ideas, a working philosophy capable of giving our efforts order and meaning. We have now advanced from a merely phenomenal literary history, through the history of ideas, through ideas themselves, to critical standards.

It is safe to predict that some such development from historical analysis toward critical synthesis will presently be accelerated. Back in the middle 1930's the MLA committee on Trends of Scholarship raised the question whether "a reorientation of research is now due in this country, and overdue." Naturally the committee could not expect any sudden or widespread change, recognizing as it did that many scholars "lack the ability or the courage to relate their discoveries to general ideas," and that "the last thing the mature teacher wants to do in most cases is to reexamine painfully and conscientiously the objectives of his work." A decade and a half later, the limited conventions of the old nineteenth-century type of scholarship still prevail in the United States, though they were widely departed from in Europe between the two wars. Our experience of depression, of a second world war, of the recent blend of prosperity and anxiety, has not yet markedly affected our inertia and complacency. It is true that the need of change is now granted by a consensus of the profession, at least in lip-service, and change itself has gradually occurred: modifications of doctoral training in a few institutions, the appointment or promotion of types of scholars who would have been neglected in the pre-depression period, the publication of types of articles and books more critical and humane. Yet it must be said that the reorientation is still "overdue," and can hardly arrive till the younger professors of letters have extended their record of teaching and publication and a few of them have attained key positions of power and influence in academic departments.

If the younger scholars are to lead us away from aimless discoveries and unorganized compilations, they will have to destroy the curious notion built up in the Victorian period (largely in Germany) that sound scholarship is simply scientific method applied to literature. This notion is understandable only in the light of the fact that the nineteenth century as a whole was "an orgy of scientific triumph"—a phrase given to the middle period of the century by the philosopher Whitehead. Philosophy itself, the traditional queen of the sciences, was finally overcome by the sciences of nature. Today, scientific triumph continues unabated, but is no longer an orgy; most intellectuals are aware that science cannot settle everything in a hurry, if at all. Besides, the basic concepts of science have changed, and in a manner favorable to more humanistic philosophical and literary undertakings. Literary scholars schooled in the science of our time should feel freer than scholars felt in the nineteenth century to affirm that the method of study in any subject should be relative to the subject, that the method in literature and the other value-judgment subjects must be different from that in science, even though

65

the method of science should be used wherever it is applicable. They should be ready to say, plainly, that literature is an art and hence occupies a region, the region of human values, where the neutrality of science is inappropriate. The center of the art of letters is forever value, aesthetic-ethical value, and consequently the end of scholarship is criticism. And the end (as Aristotle said) is the chief thing of all: it determines the beginning and guides the process by which literary study attains its end.

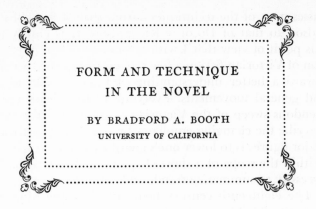

FORM AND TECHNIQUE IN THE NOVEL

BY BRADFORD A. BOOTH
UNIVERSITY OF CALIFORNIA

It is both curious and significant that while we are accustomed to speak of the "history" of poetry and the "history" of the drama, we so often speak of the "advance" of the novel. Restricted to the pre-Richardsonian novel, such terms as "growth," "evolution," and "development" would be properly descriptive of the history of English fiction; but surely the question of improvement during the last two hundred years is at the very least highly debatable. Yet even critics who have not thought of the novel as a succession of ever greater achievements have inadvertently laid traps for the unwary with easy generalizations about "advance." The implication is that later writers, in building new structures, have avoided all the bad architecture of the past and have committed no new errors—that *The Ambassadors* and *Grapes of Wrath* are necessarily better novels than *Tom Jones*. They may be. But if so, it is because Henry James and John Steinbeck are men of greater vision and understanding than Henry Fielding, not because they inherited a more highly developed literary form. We have witnessed a subtilization of technique and form with no marked intensification of over-all merit. For this reason I think it best that we drop the old descriptive phrases and speak merely of changing emphasis in the technique of the novel. Actually, the Victorian novel encom-

67

passes most of the techniques—from that of Samuel Richardson to that of Dorothy Richardson. It is chiefly from this point of view that I wish to offer for the reinterpretation of Victorian fiction a few suggestions for further study toward a better understanding of both specific novelists and general movements. Everyone familiar with the tremendous sweep of the Victorian novel will realize that to describe the changing emphases by reference to only a few major figures is to lower one's guard against the superficial. Within the scope of a short chapter one is forced by hard necessity to summarize trends and influences.

The eighteenth century bequeathed to the nineteenth century a flexible novel of loose structure, richly suggestive in its possibilities, though susceptible of the novel's highest reaches by only first-rate minds. The inferior writers of the last quarter of the eighteenth century were unable to perpetuate Richardson's psychological character study, Fielding's comic epic in prose, Smollett's picaresque virility, or Sterne's mischievous eccentricity. With an unimaginative persistency that threatened for a time to absorb fiction's hard-won gains virtually all but Godwin refused to grapple with reality, retreating to the absurdity of the Gothic tale of terror, the inanity of the novel of fashion, or the sentimentality of the love story of far-away lands. Then appeared two novelists of genius. Jane Austen swept away the extravagances of Mrs. Radcliffe as she laughed at the romantic sensibilities and domestic manners of the English, and Sir Walter Scott cleared the ground of pinchbeck sensation and crude melodrama.

For the prosperity which the novel came to enjoy in the Victorian era Scott is responsible. Though Defoe had addressed common citizens, the novel had formerly been, with poetry, in general the possession of the intellectual few. But after *Waverley* there was a tremendous middle-class public ever alert for a rattling good story. When Scott exhibited a gallery of hard-hitting characters amid the gorgeous panoply of romance, he did more than widen the field of the novel. He assured its triumph in the Victorian period and perhaps its permanent leadership in the family of literature.

But though Scott succeeded in making the novel the most democratic literary form, he did not succeed in convincing all men that he was a great novelist. Zola complained that Scott wrote for boarding-school girls, that he offered nothing to serious and mature readers. That is also the view of most contemporary critics. Scott was a story-teller; a mere story-teller, if you choose. His expansive genius bubbled gaily in extemporized romance; and if thousands closed each chapter with a breathless, "What next?" he was satisfied. It is charged that he had no artistic conscience. That is true. The novel in his day was not an art with a formal canon of "musts" and "don'ts." It was so amorphous that the writer could make of it pretty much what he chose. Scott chose to interest, to amuse, and to edify a variety of readers with a variety of spirited characters and scenes. He knew nothing of restricting the point of view, of dramatizing discursive philosophy, of presenting character from the inside. The principles of the well-made novel had not yet been set down. So his facile pen raced haphazardly over the pages in the deep of the Abbotsford night.

Technically, Scott added two important legacies to the Victorian inheritance. First, he made description an integral part of the novel. Even with Fielding description had been rudimentary. With the Gothic romancers it became a highly stylized atmospheric property. But Scott with the poet's and the painter's eye set his scenes and sketched his characters so tellingly that he may be said to have established description for its own sake as a basic novel technique. Second, Scott frequently broke with the tradition of the novel of fashion, popular when he began to write fiction, that the principal characters must be high-born. When he succumbed to current tastes, as he frequently did, he failed. When he permitted his colorful peasants and rugged townsmen to shoulder the narrative, he was at his best. Jeanie Deans almost makes us believe that he had learned from Jane Austen the novelist's most important lesson—that the essence of dramatic conflict lies not in the violence of the action but in its emotional significance for the characters. It is at this point, however, that Scott is most vulnerable to criticism, for he was uncertain how best to answer the rival claims of character and action, and lapsed at times into an unsatisfactory compromise.

Disraeli and the silver-fork novel of high life perpetuated the older fashion after Scott's heyday, until the Newgate rogues of Bulwer and Ainsworth, and the sporting hot-bloods of Egan and Surtees, stormed the bastions of refinement and blew the trumpets for Dickens's proletarian comedy. Such, very briefly, was the state of the novel in 1837—at the accession of Queen Victoria and the publication of *Pickwick Papers*.

Dickens spoke *to* and even *for* a new public. In the story of the Victorian novel no fact is so important, and none has been so consistently disregarded. Virtually every feature of the novel of this period can be accounted for in terms of public taste, of which, as yet, no satisfactory study exists. The implications for fiction of general cultural levels are such that a literary history written from that point of view might well supplement those which regard a writer's subject and style as matters of personal idiosyncrasy only. After Scott, the novelists become increasingly valuable as social historians.

The poet, though he may be heartened by an approving public, will not be disheartened by neglect; but the novelist, like the dramatist, *requires* the cordial of an approving public. To procure that approbation in the Victorian age he had to fall in with current standards, address a "family" audience, and set his seal on conventional morality. This the Victorian novelist was willing to do. So a new public, a middle-class public nurtured on the literary pap of annuals and the Minerva Press, set up the novelist as puppet king and became itself the tyrant of nineteenth-century literature.

Over fiction the tyrant of public opinion ruled with vicious despotism. Particularly harmful was the prudery of the age, which, of course, none of the arts escaped. Thackeray's protest is well known.[1] Even Dickens admitted privately that the rich wine of real life had to be watered for

[1] See the preface to *Pendennis*.

public consumption.[2] The normal conservatism of English morality had been reinforced by the abnormal asceticism of the Methodist revival, and few writers cared to brave the wrath of Mrs. Grundy, especially since the Queen was of the same persuasion.[3] Harriet Martineau's remark that she could not read *Vanity Fair* because of the moral disgust it occasioned shows how far rational criticism was warped by irrational ethics.[4]

Nothing is more commonplace—or more futile—than to attack the conventions of Victorian society. That they were absurd is patent; the limitations and affectations of another age are always absurd. But the Victorians proved such easy game that the word itself has come to carry a pejorative connotation of prissiness, hypocrisy, and meretricious piety; and the warm humanitarianism and eager intellectuality of the age are lost in a foolish scorn of its foibles. Nevertheless, there is often an air of unreality about even the best of Victorian fiction. This is not occasioned by the absence of profanity and obscenity from the dialogue, but rather by the passionless quality of the love scenes, against which even Charlotte Brontë protested. To treat the carnal appetite as though it were a matter of scented handkerchiefs and waltzes is to perpetrate a travesty on human nature. But when such an organization as Mudie's, which circulated 10,000 books daily, refused to stock a novel which treated love frankly,[5] honesty was not the best policy.

[2] See George Gissing, *Charles Dickens* (London: Duckworth, 1898), p. 68.

[3] She wrote to Gladstone in 1870, protesting against men and women medical students studying the human body together. See *The Queen and Mr. Gladstone*, ed. Philip Guedalla (London: Hodder & Stoughton, 1933), I, 227.

[4] *Autobiography*, ed. Maria Weston Chapman (Boston, 1878), II, 60. She praises *Pendennis* and *Esmond*, however, speaking of the latter as "*the* book of the century."

[5] See George Moore's *Literature at Nurse* (1885) and "Books from Mudie's" in Amy Cruse, *The Victorians and Their Reading* (Boston: Houghton Mifflin, 1935), pp. 310-336. George Meredith wrote to Augustus Jessopp: "Does she [Pallas] know that my literary reputation is tabooed as worse than libertine in certain virtuous Societies? . . . that there have been meetings to banish me from book-clubs? And that Pater familias has given Mr. Mudie a very large bit of his petticoated mind concerning me?" *Letters of George Meredith*, ed. W. M. Meredith (London: Constable, 1912), I, 59. See also Hardy's "Candour in English Fiction."

The reading habits of the new public substantiated Thomas Moore's worst fears. In 1834 he had written in his journal: "Broached to him [Wordsworth] my notions (long entertained by me) respecting the ruinous effects to literature likely to arise from the boasted diffusion of education; the lowering of the standard that must necessarily arise from the extending of the circle of judges; from letting the mob in to vote, particularly at a period when the *market* is such an object to authors."[6]

To serious fiction the dissemination of popular culture was a body-blow, for though the buying public was enormously enlarged, taste was debased. The desire to improve one's self mentally is, of course, wholly laudable, but the world has long known the dangers of a little knowledge. It led Queen Victoria, among others, to think Martin Tupper a fine poet, though one is tempted to discard as untypical the judgment of a reader whose favorite book had once been the Bishop of Chester's sermons! More important, it encouraged novelists to cater to starved emotions, hungry for excitement. It assured the success of Dickens, Reade, and Collins, "sensation novelists." On a lower level it meant fortune, and even a kind of evanescent fame, for an indefatigable crowd of scribbling women: Dinah Mulock, Mrs. Henry Wood, Mary Elizabeth Braddon, Rhoda Broughton, and Ouida.

In 1863 *The Quarterly Review*, attempting to fix responsibility for the alarming growth of sensation novels, pointed to cheap newspapers and magazines, circulating libraries, and railway bookstalls.[7] It seems obvious now, though the few studies of the subject deal only in generalities, that the novelists were answering, not creating, a demand. During the eighteenth century, newspapers and periodicals were able to maintain a relatively high standard, for they were addressed to persons of some education; in the Victorian period fierce circulation wars to capture

---

[6] *Memoirs, Journals and Correspondence*, ed. Lord John Russell (London, 1853-56), VII, 46. Moore adds, "Those 'who live to please must please to live,' and most will write down to the lowered standard. All the great things in literature have been achieved when the readers were few."

[7] "Sensation Novels," CXIII (April, 1863), 483.

the new reading public forced standards ever lower. Such a publication as *Reynolds' Miscellany* must have brightened the dull lives of oppressed laborers, but it established a level of taste that strangled art. The circulating libraries peddled a brand of culture several cuts higher. If there was a single literary dictator, it was Charles Edward Mudie. He ran with benevolent righteousness an organization which in 1861 stocked 800,000 volumes.[8] A whisper that he was buying heavily pre-publication would make an unknown novel a best-seller, sight unseen. A whisper that he would not handle it—and it fell stillborn from the press. In 1846 W. H. Smith began buying up old copyrights. He issued a series of cheaply printed volumes which when sold from stalls in railroad stations proved enormously popular. These were the famous "Yellow Backs." Designed for persons who wished to relieve the tedium of an uncomfortable journey in the carriages, they came to play a part in shaping the reading habits of the English people. A fuller understanding of the impact of all these forces should precede further study in most aspects of Victorian fiction.

The concessions which the novelists made to the culture and morality of the new public give their work significance as social history.[9] Perhaps a growing consciousness of the responsibilities of their position as leaders of public opinion led many of them to balance their drollery with the solid substance of contemporary thought. I do not wish to discuss here the social novel *per se*, but before turning to the changes in technique it might be well to recall the leading features in the social and intellectual life of the age. In his valuable little book *English Thought in the Nineteenth Century*, D. C. Somervell lists six trends: industrial and commercial enterprise, the growth of democracy, Benthamite legislation, Evangelical piety and philanthropy, the Anglo-Catholicism of the Oxford Movement, and the popularizing of scientific theories of evolution. All of these topics found expression in fiction, yet only one—the Ox-

[8] Cruse, *op. cit.*, p. 321.
[9] Dickens "describes London like a special correspondent for posterity"— Walter Bagehot, *Literary Studies* (London, 1879), II, 197.

ford Movement—has been adequately studied from this point of view. Our critical approach has always been too belletristic for a form which has never wholly abandoned characteristics of the essay. It is true that for a time in the nineteenth century the novel was considered by neither reader nor writer as a serious literary genre equipped to comment on social problems. But that is no reason why contemporary studies should continue to take the form of mere appreciations. Pleasant essays on the individual writers are about as thick as rubbish in Tophet—and about as valuable. The history of Victorian fiction would be made much clearer by such studies as those with which Professor Parrington illuminated American literature. I should urge, then, a more vigorous study of the Victorian novel, not simply as the development of the conscious artistry of isolated genius, but also as a product and as an expression of the changing culture of the period. This could be done without the sacrifice of aesthetic values.

Wilkie Collins had a simple recipe for successful novels: "make 'em laugh, make 'em cry, make 'em wait." The master of humor, pathos, and suspense was not Collins, however, but his mentor Dickens. When Dickens began to write he had to compete with such popular entertainers as Pierce Egan, Thomas Hood, Theodore Hook, Douglas Jerrold, Lever, Lover, and Marryat. It is said that illiterate charwomen gathered monthly for a reading of the latest installment of the new Dickens novel. The reading experience of this new public, which no reputable novelist had ever before reached, had been principally in comic annuals and almanacs. It is a mistake to think that Dickens consciously wrote down to this group,[10] but it is just as great a mistake to think that he was not aware of public taste. At any rate, humor and pathos of a rather obvious sort were the staples of his appeal.

Dickens's humor arises principally out of character and dialogue. For the purposes of amusement his method was to extemporize characters, then scurry around for plot sit-

[10] It is recorded, however, that he deleted from one of his manuscripts the word "trousseau," as probably not in the vocabulary of his readers.

uations in which they might exhibit their amiable eccentricities. Smollett had on occasion done the same. But then Smollett had been content to introduce only a comparative handful of characters and to tell a story which, though rambling, was less episodic than that of Dickens. Scott, too, had successfully managed a troupe of humorous minor characters, but whereas he had tickled his readers with a sideshow of whimsical personalities, Sam Weller, Sarah Gamp, and Mr. Micawber perform under the big tent. The humor of Dickens's "originals" was not, as it was with Scott, an act strategically reserved to capture flagging attention, but rather the central performance of a well-planned program. At times his humor is marred by boisterous grotesquerie. Certainly the quiet modulations of Jane Austen's playful vein were beyond him. But for originality, quick inventiveness, appropriateness of dialogue, and sheer richness of humor, he has never had his peer in the English novel.

It is on the score of his handling of pathos that most modern readers quarrel with Dickens. We no longer weep for little Nell or Paul Dombey.[11] Since our age finds nothing quite so venal as the insincerity of the false pathetic, Dickens's bones have been picked clean by the critical vultures. Every literary historian has repeated the statement that Dickens was the child of his age, but to distinguish between the temper of the age and the personality of the man is a task too delicate for most observers. In order to satisfy oneself on that point it is necessary to read widely in the minor Victorian novelists. Few critics have done so. The whole immense terrain of the minor novel is a strategic no-man's-land which nobody has had the courage to attack. It is the gateway to the easy command of major points beyond, yet we continue to butt our heads futilely against the familiar citadels.[12] Much of Dickens's unimpeachable senti-

[11] In his big set pieces Dickens is often melodramatic; in briefer episodes (such as in *Dombey* Cap't. Cuttle's reception of Floy, and Walter's return) he controls the emotional impact with consummate skill.

[12] Heartening signs of developing interest in the minor fiction are the republication of several novels of Emily Eden, the notable exhibition of 1947 by the Book League of London, the appearance in 1948 of the first

ment is drowned in maudlin sentimentality, but only those familiar with the excesses of the popular novel of the day can judge of Dickens's relative restraint.

Of all the novelists before Henry James, Dickens, as author and editor, was most interested in the technique of telling a story. Paradoxically, however, few writers have been so vigorously assailed for faulty structure by students of the art of fiction. No doubt by nature Dickens would have succumbed to the English novel's most common complaint: plot trouble; but virtually all his defects can be traced to the vicious influence of serial publication. In the first place, the structure of the old comic novel had to be abandoned before the exigencies of concluding each part on an interesting point of unresolved action. The demands of this technique resulted in overplotting—Dickens's besetting sin—and in the substitution of a series of minor effects for one major cumulative effect. Second, little inconsistencies of plot and character inevitably crept in when the author began publication without fully working out the design. Since among the reputable novelists Trollope alone seems to have withstood the temptation to publish before completing a manuscript, a full investigation of this aspect of serial publication would be valuable. Third, men of no will submitted meekly to the tyranny of a public which interested itself in a character and demanded for that character in the name of poetic justice a fate wholly inconsistent with life and logic. Dickens was bombarded with letters calling on him to spare the life of little Nell, and he was persuaded to tack a happy ending on *Great Expectations*. Trollope fortunately refused insistent demands that he marry Lily Dale and Johnny Eames. Hardy ruined *The Return of the Native* by knuckling under to clubwomen who clamored for the sentimental gratification of a marriage, artistically incongruous, between Thomasin and Diggory Venn.

In the technique of characterization Dickens was superior

---

titles in the English Novelists Series, and the imminent publication of Mr. Michael Sadleir's catalogue of his library, the finest of its kind in the world.

to any novelist of his age. Rejecting analysis, he substituted dialogue as the revealing medium and allowed his characters to depict themselves in dramatic situations. The method is presentative and (to use José Ortega y Gasset's word) autoptic. In his capacity as editor Dickens criticized a tyro for relying too heavily on exposition: "The people do not sufficiently work out their own purposes in dialogue and dramatic action. You are too much their exponent; what you do for them, they ought to do for themselves."[13] And again, "My notion is that when I have made the people play out the play, it is, as it were, their business to do it and not mine."[14] Even Jane Austen, subtle as she was, had developed character directly, not dramatically, from the point of view of the omniscient author. In characterization Dickens is sometimes as modern as Hemingway. His knowledge of the theater, though it often led him into cheap melodrama, served him well in this particular. Critical disapproval of Dickens arises not from his methods but from an impression of shallowness given by all authors who deal largely in "flat" characters and in eccentrics.[15] The study of "original" characters, by the way, was given the blessing of science, the trend of which was to regard even trivial eccentricities as a manifestation of serious abnormality and a proper subject for either amusement or satire.[16] But the writer whose characters are particular without being general, who stand only for themselves, may be popular but not great. The finest of the Russian novelists have succeeded in giving life to characters of cosmic significance. Everyman steps out of the morality play into life. To do that is to hoist one's flag atop Parnassus.

Dickens's penchant for the dramatic technique established a new school of fiction. His own comment on method

13 *Letters of Charles Dickens*, ed. Georgina Hogarth and Mamie Dickens (London, 1880-82), III, 162.

14 *Ibid.*, II, 249-250.

15 "The very excellence and diversity of Mr. Dickens's powers makes one long that they should exercise their full force under the broad open sky of nature, instead of in the most brilliant palace of art." Harriet Martineau, *Autobiography*, II, 62.

16 See Walter L. Myers, *The Later Realism* (Univ. of Chicago Press, 1927), pp. 9-10.

is, unfortunately, not so full as that of Collins and Reade, for he modestly refused to set himself up as critic; nevertheless, his principles may be deduced from his practice and from the critical statements of his followers. Like Reade, who titled one of his novels *Christie Johnstone: A Dramatic Story*, Dickens adapted stage techniques to narrative art. Like Collins, he believed "that the novel and the play are twin sisters in the family of fiction; and that one is drama narrated, as the other is drama acted."[17] All three worked with the materials of romance, searching for the extraordinary in the commonplace. If the extraordinary could be found only with the aid of coincidence and accident, Dickens, anticipating Hardy, shrugged his shoulders and called it fate. "Where the accident [Mme. Defarge's death] in such cases is inseparable from the passion and emotion of the character, where it is strictly consistent with the whole design, and arises out of some culminating proceeding on the part of the character which the whole story has led up to, it seems to me to become, as it were, an act of divine justice."[18]

The artistic error of the sensation novelists is that in attempting to draw romance from the familiar they were driven to creating incident for its own sake. The domestic novelists, particularly George Eliot, attempted to draw from the familiar, incident and character of ethical significance.

Dickens's weaknesses are the *défauts de ses qualités*. His fertile imagination could not always be stopped on the safe side of caricature, and his high spirits and facile emotions could not always be brought within the bounds of good taste. But though his reputation has been frequently challenged by the newer criticism, his position among the greatest of English novelists seems not yet to have been seriously endangered. He is himself the sublimation of Victorianism, and all who cherish the foibles of the age will take him to their hearts. The world has chosen to admire Thackeray but to love Dickens.

If Dickens for his sins has been given short shrift by

[17] Collins's preface to *Basil*.   [18] *Letters*, II, 117.

critics interested in technique, Thackeray for different reasons has fared even worse. It has been said that the most significant change in the fiction of our time is the disappearance of the author. Conversely, the trade mark of the Victorian novel is the presence of the author, ever poised to intrude a comment on the action, to interpret the characters, or to write an essay on cabbages and kings. If this is to offend against the "rules," Thackeray is guilty without hope of reprieve. Of course, Fielding, George Eliot, and many another have not allowed the narrative to fend for itself; but Fielding frequently had the good sense to put his extraneous remarks into vestibule essays and intercalary chapters that one can skip, and George Eliot, though often wearisomely didactic, is usually impersonal.

Thackeray was the critic of his age. He detested its snobbishness, its hypocrisy, its insipid sentimentality; and he wittily rebuked it with acute studies of human nature. His satirical temper found a more congenial atmosphere in the rationalism of the eighteenth century, and it was from that vantage point of history that he peppered his contemporaries with stinging shot. Fielding and Smollett were his guides in fiction (he and Trollope both hated the sensation novel), but he was attracted principally by the cool urbanity of the essayists. He played the sedulous ape to Addison and Steele almost as thoroughly as had Benjamin Franklin, and he carried into the novel the intellectual and philosophic attitudes of the essayist. *Vanity Fair* was conceived of simply as "sketches of society." Since Thackeray's interests were not primarily those of the story-teller, he gave little heed to conventional narrative technique. He had virtually no sense of the dramatic, dragging fidgety readers through interminable pages of summary narrative. He lacked the perspective to organize his material on any unified plan. Of the full-length plots only that of *Esmond* was carefully charted before composition. All the others, like Topsy, just grew.[19] Indeed, Thackeray broke with tra-

[19] In *Barry Lyndon*, it might be added, Thackeray is a fine craftsman, but then a picaresque novel has fewer complications.

ditional plot to the point of relying on the interplay of social relationships to carry the interest.

When we are tempted to score Thackeray for faulty technique, we should do well to remember his purpose and his accomplishment. Since he did not attempt popular novels, it is idle to measure him by conventional standards. If his technique was inspired by eighteenth-century models, it was nevertheless his own; and since it has pleased several generations of discriminating readers, it is futile to say he should have employed some other. There are many types of novels: character, dramatic, chronicle, period, well-made; it should be possible for a man of less than catholic tastes to enjoy more than one.

Thackeray's was a vigorous and intelligent personality, and his pages glow with trenchant observations on men and manners. It is quite possible that he will wear longer than Dickens. First of all, he was a master stylist, one of the great prose writers among English novelists. Second, he was less given to "humour" characters and theatricality. Third, he was a pessimist—as Galsworthy used the term when he said: "The optimist appears to be he who cannot bear the world as it is and is forced by his nature to picture it as it ought to be, and the pessimist one who cannot only bear the world as it is, but loves it well enough to draw it faithfully."[20] Only occasionally was Thackeray derelict in his duties to truth. The early novel had been full of such easy solutions to tough problems as the revelation of the peasant hero's high birth or the discovery of somebody's lost will. Scott specialized in this device, a stratagem which probably never convinced the veriest schoolboy. Arthur Pendennis's sudden wealth is as bathetic as such evasions of true art must ever be, for it arises out of chance, not character. Male or female Cinderellas indicate the novelist's unwillingness to come to grips with reality. Trollope never did a wiser thing than to refuse Johnny Eames his heart's desire, though

[20] "Some Platitudes Concerning Drama," *The Inn of Tranquillity* (New York: Scribner's, 1913), p. 192.

because of the sudden acquisition of an unearned fortune he otherwise had the world at his feet.[21]

Trollope was a great admirer and an avowed disciple of Thackeray. Artistically, however, he did not have much in common either with Thackeray or with any other of his contemporaries. He was not a satirist like Thackeray, a moralist like George Eliot, a caricaturist like Dickens. He did not have the passion of the Brontës, nor the ethereal humor of Meredith. He was essentially a portraitist of society. Historians will never find a substitute for his pictures of Victorian life. It is said by his biographers that Anthony Trollope was somewhat irascible, but the novels reveal only a man of the broadest sympathies who observed life shrewdly and was mildly amused by the idiosyncrasies of good people. He was too tolerant to be a satirist, too humble to be a moralist, too realistic to be a caricaturist. He had no passion, and only the quietest kind of humor. Nothing could be less intellectualistic than a Trollope novel— and nothing more solidly satisfying.

Just why Anthony Trollope is so satisfying it is difficult to say, for he had many technical faults. His long, wheezing introductions are both tiresome and inept. His casual, detached way of speaking of his characters is maddening. He shared with Dickens and George Eliot the mistake of trying to carry forward too many sub-plots. *The Last Chronicle of Barset*, for example, is a magnificent novel, but as poorly plotted as *Our Mutual Friend*. One of the narratives is not only extraneous but dull; another, though interesting, nevertheless distracts attention from the central situation. His love stories are conventional and without variety. He was not wholly at ease with such material. But within the cathedral close or the rector's study he stood on firm ground.

In the rector's study and in the squire's drawing room Trollope is master. Both these places would be in Barchester, of course, a bit of England as well known and perhaps better loved than Wessex. Very little of moment happens here, but Trollope had learned that good character is

---

[21] Trollope's Harry Clavering, however, is another Arthur Pendennis.

action. We may forget what caused certain misunderstandings, and how certain differences were finally resolved; but we do not forget Mr. Harding, the Proudies, Josiah Crawley, Archbishop Grantly, and Mr. Slope. Though all else may fade, the clerical characters survive. For this group portrait Trollope had no models, no conventions; so he was able to avoid the steryotyped formulas which date his other novels. He listened to his people talk, and laugh, and quarrel; and he came to love them. Out of such imaginative experience comes great art. Trollope created something new in English fiction, and its freshness has the permanence of universal truth. In general, Anthony Trollope out of Barchester is just another second-rate novelist, but such fine stories as *The Belton Estate* and *Dr. Wortle's School* teach one not to make sweeping statements.

In one other respect Trollope was unique among Victorian novelists: he was not a reformer. I have glanced at the social novel above, and the whole subject of the re-awakening of the social conscience is discussed elsewhere in this book; but since the new subject matter had its effect upon the technique of fiction, a further word might not be superfluous.

The casements out of which Victorians looked were not magic, and they saw not the foam of perilous seas, but the filth of grimy factories. Those who had once looked hopefully down the ringing grooves of change came to see the unspeakable poverty and wretchedness on the one hand, the hollow optimism and self-satisfied futility on the other. Some expressed their horror in speeches, some in tracts, some in novels. For a time, then, in the Victorian period the novel became the artistic expression of the age's intellectual ferment. Disraeli's *Sybil*, Mrs. Gaskell's *Mary Barton*, Charlotte Brontë's *Shirley*, Kingsley's *Alton Locke*, and dozens of other novels protested eloquently against the gaping incongruities between "the two nations." The novelist's conception of his function was rapidly changing. Once a purveyor of sweetmeats to jaded palates, he now assumed the sober duties of historian, philosopher, and teacher. Rousseauistic individualism had run its course in the novel.

The influence of Dickens in reviving the spirit of social responsibility is too familiar for repetition. Virtually every form of civil abuse came under his heavy ferule. Charles Reade, another militant foe of all oppressions, soon picked up Dickens's cudgel and flailed about bravely, if a trifle wildly. Where Dickens had attempted nothing more than truth of impression,[22] Reade worked from documentary materials, compiling huge notebooks of newspaper clippings. The study of his "sources" ought to keep graduate students happy for some time. Collins, too, was a partner in the "indignation" novel, probing boldly into hush-hush subjects. His neglected masterpiece *The New Magdalen* is a fierce indictment of society's stupid treatment of prostitutes.

The humanitarian novel provides a criticism of life by offering a commentary on life. Those who suffer from what Saintsbury calls "the disease of contemporary partisanship" find the humanitarian novel wearisomely obvious and tediously didactic. A thesis is a treacherous nag, to be sure, and the novelist who rides it too hard may find himself unable to halt the beast this side catastrophe. Empty rhetoric and moralistic fulmination are the stuff of impotent pamphlets, not imaginative art. But the Victorian novelists were not only constructive critics of the social order; they were master story-tellers as well. Nevertheless, the intensity of their purpose drove them into type characters rather than personalities. Everyone can recall instances where Dickens overplayed his hand, and won through only at the expense of reality. We view his characters with a telescopic lens, and know their intimate movements, but it is from the outside only that we see them. Then and now, the

[22] Harriet Martineau wrote: "Another vexation is his [Dickens's] vigorous erroneousness about matters of science, as shown in 'Oliver Twist' about the new poor-law (which he confounds with the abrogated old one) and in 'Hard Times,' about the controversies of employers. Nobody wants to make Mr. Dickens a Political Economist; but there are many who wish that he would abstain from a set of difficult subjects on which all true sentiment must be underlain by a sort of knowledge which he has not." *Autobiography*, II, 62. It is interesting to remember that Bagehot spoke of Dickens's "Sentimental Radicalism."

propaganda novel at its worst loses all sight of character in emphasizing the effects of environmental forces. The realism of the great Russian novelists is all the more striking for the revelation *from within* of the human heart and soul. Turgenev never forgot that the novelist's characters must be something more than abstract symbols of economic maladjustment and social disorder.

Mid-Victorian realism, though it hit hard at many abuses, took an essentially optimistic view of society. That is, it had faith in the doctrine of perfectibility, if not the doctrine of progress. This heartening view of life was followed by one of bleak pessimism. The squalid realism of Gissing is sometimes dour, sometimes anemic, but always drab and hopeless. The same is frequently true of George Moore. These writers escaped the unhealthy conventions of Victorian art, and in this respect their influence was salutary. But they were extremists. Their characters never have a chance—they are beaten down under the triple-hammers of inexorable circumstance. It is a question whether a philosophy of futility is more desirable than a philosophy of complacency.

George Eliot must also be included among the thesis novelists, though her interests were not those of the Realists. For her the adjustments of man to society were of far less importance than the adjustments of man to the welter of conflicting forces within himself. These forces she heated in the alembic of subjective analysis, and the distillate was the substance of her own philosophy. From the first George Eliot had assailed the spinelessness of popular fiction. One of her first writings—"Silly Novels by Lady Novelists"—not only ridiculed the literature of escape but advanced her contention that fiction could and should be bent to the purposes of philosophy. From *Scenes in Clerical Life* to *Silas Marner* her own novels carried the weight of sober reflection, but with *Romola* she led the novel out of the amusement park into the academic quadrangle. Among the mid-Victorian novelists George Eliot was undoubtedly most sensitive to the flux of speculative ideas. It was this cultural awareness, coupled with a strong personal philosophy and an unusual facility in rendering the abstract concretely, that produced such a profound influence on both the subject matter and the technique of English fiction. After George Eliot the story elements became less important in the novel, as writers applied themselves to the illustration of philosophic theory and the interpretation of man's relations to the universe.

As one reads the animated pages of Fielding or the placid pages of Trollope, one has the impression of listening to shrewd common sense—the practical though unsystematized philosophy of right-thinking men who have made the most of living in the world. As one reads the worried pages of George Eliot, one has the impression of listening to a unified and systematized philosophy which, though the product of scholasticism rather than experience, has nevertheless a parental and almost proverbial wisdom. There are two roots to the spreading tree of George Eliot's philosophy: the idea of moral responsibility and the idea of moral retribution. Virtually everything she wrote is an illustration in fiction of the working of one or both of these conceptions. The idea of moral responsibility proposes that an anti-social isolation is not possible—that the most reclusive as well as the most gregarious of men will have his effect upon society. English fiction had not before been built of such material, though the thought was current in poetry, and is familiar to readers of Emerson and Browning, among others. Even more important in George Eliot's fiction, as it was in her life, was the idea of moral retribution. For her, fate is simply the inevitable consequences of our actions. We are not sinners in the hands of an angry God, nor are we, as Hardy would have it, the pawns of purblind Doomsters. We are the masters of our fate—"our deeds determine us, as much as we determine our deeds." An enlightened sense of social responsibility makes for the happiness and well-being which an alertness to the forces of moral retribution enables us to preserve. It is in the ring of such a challenging philosophy that one hears the fulfillment of her wish to join "the choir invisible."

Obviously, the technique of fiction which served well the

purposes of Scott and Dickens would not suffice for George Eliot. Her preoccupation with moral problems and consequent mental states necessitated a new kind of psychological character analysis. Richardson and Fielding had both busied themselves with pinning down and studying the psychology of their characters; but the novelists did all the work, the characters remaining passive or entering the action apparently only to corroborate previous testimony. With George Eliot the characters sometimes have an opportunity to speak up for themselves, though in sententious passages, of which there are too many, the author turns ventriloquist. There is no denying that she runs moral issues into the ground as she consistently interferes with the story on behalf of an ethical system. Once in a while she seems to feel that the reader may miss the point; so, as Professor Beach puts it, she "stacks the cards" against "poor Hetty Sorrel." Nevertheless, George Eliot came nearer than had any of her predecessors to establishing for psychological fiction a dramatic technique. Enthusiasts who hailed her as the new Shakespeare were not absurd on every count.

One finds himself qualifying everything he says about George Eliot, for her inconsistencies in method make generalization more dangerous than usual. Her very uncertainty, however, gives her historical significance. One sees her writhing in the death agonies of an old system and in the birth pangs of a new. She is among the last of the old discursive novelists, but she is also the first of the psychological dramatists in narrative.

Speaking of George Eliot, Leslie Stephen many years ago suggested a profitable course of study in the thesis novel: "The future historians of literature . . . will no doubt analyze the spirit of the age and explain how the novelists, more or less unconsciously, reflected the dominant ideas which were agitating the social organism. . . . The novelists were occupied in constructing a most elaborate panorama of the manners and customs of their times with a minuteness and psychological analysis not known to their predecessors. Their work is, of course, an implicit criticism of life."[23] But such a history, describing the effect on the novel of specific social and personal philosophies and of the impact of Victorian ideas in general, remains to be written.

If we knew better the critical opinions of the Victorian novelists, if we knew more of their subjective literary experiences, we might better understand their methods. What were their reading habits? How did they regard their art? Why was their fiction so low-pitched? What was their conception of the special functions of poetry and drama? Trollope, who alone of the great novelists left an autobiography, tells us that he chose fiction only because he failed as a dramatist and realized that poetry, the loftiest of the literary arts, was beyond him. Everyone knows from internal evidence in the novels, as well as from other titles, that the Brontës were poets and that the sensation novelists were dramatists. Yet one must dig out the critical theory for himself. R. Brimley Johnson's *Novelists on Novels* is not more than a suggestion of what might be done to facilitate our understanding of the literary conceptions out of which the different techniques emerged. There is every reason why the novelists, as well as the poets, should be subjected to serious "als Kritiker" analysis. One step toward providing the materials for such studies is the collecting and editing of personal letters. Fortunately, this is at the moment an active field of research,[24] but much remains to be done.

Chronologically the Brontë sisters flourished a decade before Trollope and George Eliot, but historically they have more in common with the later Victorians, Meredith and Hardy. That they were out of place in their own day is obvious. Poets did not write novels in 1847—that *annus mirabilis* in which two country spinsters published *Wuthering Heights* and *Jane Eyre*. And poetry—poetry and passion—were the qualities which they brought for the first time to the English novel. The comic epic in prose had

[23] *George Eliot* (London, 1900), pp. 67-68.
[24] Professor Gordon N. Ray's recent edition of Thackeray letters may well be a model for future collections. In progress at the moment are Professor Gordon S. Haight's edition of George Eliot letters and the present writer's similar edition of Trollope. The Dickens letters, unhappily, are incomplete in the Nonesuch Edition, and some day this task must be repeated.

rightly repudiated the artificial poetics of the old romances, but the complete rejection of poetic intensity that followed is another instance of throwing the baby out the window with the bath water. For a century the English novelist had played Mr. Spectator, ranging the streets to capture impressions of his fellows, but never following them into their homes to watch passion spin the plot and know the tragedy that lies too deep for tears. Then came two women who had scarcely ventured beyond the steps of Haworth parsonage. They are an ever-living rebuke to the sterile novelists who pursue a phantom inspiration from the sands of Tahiti to the bull-ring of Spain—who ignore the poet's dictum: "Look in thy heart and write."

Poetry plus passion is a simple sum that has always equaled tragedy, and with the Brontës, particularly Emily, English fiction began to reach the deeper emotions. What had previously passed for tragedy had been only an awkward series of catastrophes, mightily affecting the volatile sensibilities of Mackenziean men of feeling but ludicrous to all others. The Brontës had the artist's power to re-create one's own experience and to project oneself imaginatively into the lives of others. And though emotion runs high in their work, it is normally under control, for what was false to experience and to human nature they did their best to exclude. Death casts its shadow over the Brontë novel, as it does over the Elizabethan drama, but with this difference: that with the Elizabethans it is the fact of death that is the ultimate in tragedy, but in *Wuthering Heights* it is the necessity of living. Perhaps Charlotte compromised with life and truth more than Emily, solving her theoretical problems by facile expedients in which happiness grows out of circumstance rather than character. Nevertheless, they both brought a new honesty to the novel, particularly in the candid analysis of a woman's instincts that drew down upon them the wrath of the Philistines. Before George Eliot they had subordinated story interest to character study, and through their independence of current fashion they were able to adapt fiction to aspects of tragedy formerly treated by the drama only.

When George Meredith began to write, the artistry of the loquacious eighteenth-century novel was being questioned, and new forces were active, working for simplicity and dramatic condensation. Between the old and the new, Meredith is a transition figure. He can act the part of commentator with all the humor and irony of Fielding, dissecting character and interpreting motive with the confidence of the omniscient. He can be the self-effacing dramatist too, as, smiling obscurely, he sits behind the curtain and creates sound effects for his characters. He can play the philosopher, interfering with the story as he summarizes life in the oracular manner of George Eliot. And he can suggest Browning in the detached objectivity of his dramatic presentation. Meredith's ambidextrous facility in this double technique is not, however, always successful, for some fastidious critics find a shifting point of view annoying.

The rapprochement between fiction and poetry begun by the Brontës was carried forward and intensified by Meredith. From that weird rhapsody *The Shaving of Shagpat*, which George Eliot hailed as a work "of poetical genius," to *The Amazing Marriage*, his pages are incandescent with evocations of pure imagination more poetic than his poetry. For him all is fancy, if not phantasy. "Little writers should be realistic," he once said.[25] Son-in-law of Peacock, fellow-lodger with Swinburne and Rossetti, intimate of all the pre-Raphaelites, Meredith came to regard fiction as one of the fine arts. The novel, he felt, can be more than an *exemplum*, can be more than the illustration of the philosophy of one's poems. As all prose must be, the novel's appeal is primarily intellectual; nevertheless, it can be made to satisfy aesthetic principles of form and style. One does not find in Meredith's prose, then, the flow of Scott's journalistic ease or the headlong tumble of Ruskin's lush prodigality. Instead there is a studied rarity of language that reminds one of Pater and the prose poets.[26]

[25] *Letters*, I, 56.
[26] Professor Joseph E. Baker has called my attention to the anticipation of twentieth-century subjectivity in *Marius the Epicurean*. Influenced by the pre-Raphaelites, Pater rejected eighteenth-century rationalism and

It has been said of all the Victorians that no generalization about them is true. This applies particularly to Meredith. Like a butterfly on its jagged circuit of the garden he wheels and dips out of reach just when one thinks to grasp him. He follows no plan, no rules. He is consistent with no one, least of all himself. Consider, for example, his treatment of character. In attention to detail, *The Egoist* might easily be mistaken for late Henry James. In a long novel very little happens: the author attempts no more than the analysis of a situation. He hovers over his characters with busy hands, knitting up the raveled sleeve of motive with meticulous caution lest a stitch be dropped. Every thought is examined, every flickering eyelid explained. Thackeray is not less dramatic. Yet such shorter novels as *The Tale of Chloe* and *The Tragic Comedians*, and even the longer *Vittoria* are tight, compact, dramatic. Here the characters forge ahead without authorial pulling and tugging.[27] The difficulty arises when Meredith combines his methods, as he does in *Harry Richmond*. Then readers who cannot distinguish between literal and poetic characters are perplexed and charge him with obscurity.

It would be an exaggeration to say that a Meredith novel is usually a group of characters in search of a plot, but something of the sort is very nearly true. The nature of the high comedy which he practiced so successfully demands brilliant talk, and of necessity the more talk, the less action. Still, if the talk is good, nobody in his senses will ask for action. *The Egoist*—"a comedy in narrative"—simply coruscates with good talk. Here is Meredith's idea of the civilization in which alone true comedy can exist. The dull, the

---

nineteenth-century materialism, fashioning a philosophy of subjective aesthetics that recalls Poe and the French Symbolists. Edmund Wilson in *Axel's Castle* traces the somber expressionism of Poe through Baudelaire and Mallarmé to Proust, Joyce, and other modern writers who have abandoned Victorian objectivity.

[27] Meredith knew what the public wanted. Of *Vittoria* he wrote to Jessopp: "All story, tell Mrs. Jessopp; no philosopher present; action, excitement, holding of your breath, chilling horror, classic sensation." *Letters*, I, 143. He knew, too, that *Sandra Belloni* was not what they wanted. See *Letters*, I, 140.

barren, the commonplace of conversation is winnowed out; what remains is so impassioned, so epigrammatic, so aphoristic that in a surfeit of nimble word-play the heartiest of us will cry "Hold, enough!" Of course, versimilitude is sacrificed, for characters to fit such dialogue appear several sizes larger than life.[28] Meredith's humor, however, was not confined to high comedy. There is jest and broad farce, as well as ironic wit and Thackerayan comedy of vanity and snobbery. Nor is Meredith's style always extravagant. True, he was often as euphuistic as Lyly, but when his story demanded simplicity in the telling, as did *Evan Harrington*, he could be almost as plain as Trollope.

To Meredith's suggestions in technique, as well as to his aesthetics, the public was apathetic, if not actually combative. He was too eccentric, too talky, too difficult. But it should have been obvious to all persons of taste that since nothing more could be done with the formless novel of the early Victorians, any progress toward unity and simplicity through control along dramatic lines was sound technically. Meredith, who was not particularly interested in form, made some happy suggestions. It remained for Henry James, who was obsessed by form, to write a technically perfect novel.

Since Thomas Hardy died only twenty years ago, it is sometimes difficult to think of him as a Victorian. Yet *Under the Greenwood Tree* appeared in 1872, the same year as *Middlemarch*; and *Jude the Obscure*, his last novel, in 1896. Chronologically he is well within the period. Furthermore, the way Hardy was tarred-and-feathered for what scarcely amounts to a little mild realism indicates that he was still writing for "Victorians," that there was yet no break in the solid front of moral bias. It is interesting, in addition, to remember that Hardy's first novels were spon-

[28] Where such comedy came from there is no doubt. Molière stood first among Meredith's creditors, and he received his due in the famous lecture on comedy. Studies in Meredith's knowledge of other European writers would be quite helpful. There have been several stimulating essays, but full-length investigations, such as W. D. Ferguson's *The Influence of Flaubert on George Moore*, are essential for fuller comprehension. Meredith's reading in comparative literature, as his letters show, was extensive.

sored by Meredith. The two had much in common, though
the optimism of the one and the pessimism of the other
might seem to place them in quite different categories.
They were both poets, and they both knew something of
dramatic technique, Meredith adapting poetic comedy to
narrative and Hardy following the form and general themes
of Greek tragedy.

Hardy's poetry and his novels are cut from the same
cloth. He reversed the usual procedure, however, after-
wards summarizing in poetic form the philosophical ideas
upon which the novels were based. The pitiless, indiscrim-
inate fate of *Tess* and *The Return of the Native* is the fate
of "Hap" and "The Convergence of the Twain." Everywhere men and women are whipped to their knees, not by
the harsh but remediable agencies of society, nor yet by the
violence of their own passions, but by a blind, irrational
force that strikes the good as well as the evil. Hardy an-
chored his philosophy in his contemplation of "life's little
ironies." He voiced his impatience with the old novel's precise distribution of poetic justice in the aphorism: "The
good end happily, and the bad unhappily; that's fiction!"
In abandoning an artificial system of rewards, Hardy gave
the novel new strength and conviction; but there can be no
doubt that he has lost the hold he had on readers not so long
ago. It is not that we have renounced his conception of
destiny, but that we are no longer moved by a story so de-
pendent on freakish coincidence.

The trouble lies in Hardy's idea of the function of the
novel. "The real, if unavowed, purpose of fiction," he said,
"is to give pleasure by gratifying the love of the uncommon
in human experience, mental or corporeal . . . and the
writer's art lies in shaping that uncommonness while dis-
guising its unlikelihood, if it be unlikely."[29] Now, even
mystery and romance owe some allegiance to likelihood;
certainly a serious attempt to question teleology cannot
afford to have its reality dissipated in a whirlwind of im-
plausibility. So the effect of *The Woodlanders* is lost in a

[29] Florence Emily Hardy, *The Early Life of Thomas Hardy* (New York:
Macmillan, 1928), p. 193.

series of incredible catastrophes, and *The Return of the Native* creaks and groans under the weight of misunderstood motive, undelivered letters, and the ubiquitous reddleman. Such criticism as this Hardy brushed aside with the declaration, "It is not improbabilities of incident but improbabilities of character that matter."[30] Perhaps so. But the greatest writers are those in whose work incident and character are equally representative of life. In a realistic work, as Maupassant understood, the reader should not be called on to suspend disbelief.

Hardy is said to have been chagrined that criticism tended to concern itself with the philosophy rather than the poetry of his novels. If that was an error, it has been rectified. Today many discriminating critics prefer Hardy the poet to Hardy the novelist and find his exquisite descriptive effects the chief virtue of his novels. The novel as a form had been slow to reflect the Romantic love of external nature, but with Scott description began to assume at least a decorative function. Later the social novel, stressing the importance of environment, *demanded* painstaking description beyond the purely pictorial. With Hardy, setting came for the first time to have philosophical significance. Egdon Heath is not an inanimate stage on which the characters are herded to their doom, but is itself the sentient agent of destiny. Not even Conrad gave the technique of description a more functional place in his art.

Before we are to know the whole story of late Victorian fiction two ambitious studies must be undertaken. The first of these is the immensely important and virtually untouched subject of comparative literature in the field of the novel. Everyone knows in a general way that contact with the French and later with the Russian Realists showed the English the possibilities of the novel as a work of art. But few exact relationships have been traced, and the weight of influences is not yet precisely ascertained. We should like to know, for example, to what extent did belated study of Stendhal's microscopic analysis of character or Balzac's tireless examination of motive contribute to the decline of the

[30] *Ibid.*, p. 231.

great Victorians and beat the drums for the advent of Henry James. We know they were widely read, yet specific information is scarce and scattered. Generalizations are ever easy and numerous, documentation difficult and rare.

The second study is the influence of the short story on the development of new techniques in the novel. The scholar who proposes for himself this subject must be prepared to start from scratch and run his own race. It was not until late in the century that English writers began to regard the short story as more than the awkward stepson of the novel, for the advance (and here the word is really apropos) of the short story is the triumph of first American and later of French literature. The names to be remembered are Hawthorne, Poe, and Maupassant; and their secret is simplification. The old overstuffed plots, with their melodramatic incidents and anemic conclusions, were swept away by the inexorable logic of Poe's position in theory, strengthened by the success of that theory in practice. In codifying the "rules" of the new technique Poe made two important points: first, the writer must bend all his attention toward achieving a single effect; and second, he must maintain unity of impression. The first meant the exclusion of all extraneous narrative, and the second meant the maintenance of a single point of view. Both of these principles were adopted by the new school of Realists, though it is worthy of remark that a Romanticist, Stevenson, followed them most faithfully and thereby won the admiration of Henry James. Lest we forget, James spent ten years mastering the technique of the short story before he began the novels of his later period.

Though Henry James is not, strictly speaking, either an Englishman or a Victorian, it would be inappropriate to close a survey of the Victorian novel without reference to the changes which he wrought. In him we see the culmination of all the forces of the last half of the century—and the triumph of the short, artistic novel. Primarily, James's achievement lies in establishing a restricted and unshifting point of view. Stevenson, who had attacked Scott's "ill-written, ragged" romances and Dickens's omniscient point of view in undramatic moments, attempted to rekindle an old fire by clever handicraft. Henry James picked up Stevenson's technique with the narrative of action and adapted it to the narrative of psychological investigation. Secondarily, James pushed the dramatic method of exposition further toward its practical limits for the novel. Disliking a "seated mass of information," he avoided the ponderous expository openings of Scott and Trollope, revealing antecedent action only through the characters and when relevant to a developing situation. There is no moralizing, no nondramatic philosophizing, and virtually no incident. For the Scott-Stevenson drama of the conflict of physical action, James substitutes the drama of the conflict of mind and personality.

James opened as great a chasm between himself and the great Victorians as he did between himself and the average reader. The novel as he saw it was not a narrative but a representational work serving the same ends as the other arts. It must have form, structure, style. But it did not achieve these qualities without the sacrifice of others. The humor, the irony, the broad tolerance, the hard-headed common sense, the human understanding born of wide experience are not often found in a Henry James novel.[31] His was a little world of international sophisticates—cultured, wealthy, idle, too highly bred—a world of circumscribed emotions and no passion. If the Victorian intrusive author failed, he failed on a grand scale, for he attempted much. In the eyes of many of us, however, he did not fail. It is charged that he does not maintain a consistent point of view. What matter, if his characters live? It is charged that he sees human nature only from the outside. What matter, if his view be not distorted? I wonder if the novels of Scott and Dickens with their delightful supernumeraries are not nearer life than those of James, where in the interests of art all persons who do not directly influence the main characters are stubbornly excluded. Much of the criticism of the Victorian novelists is of a kind with the aesthetes' condem-

---

[31] This is unfortunate, for James was not without these qualities, as is made clear in *The Legend of the Master*, a recent collection of Jamesian anecdotes and *obiter dicta*.

nation of Trollope because he wrote to the ticking of his watch 250 words every quarter hour. The only valid criterion is merit.

Most of the recent books on the technique of the novel, beginning with Percy Lubbock's *The Craft of Fiction*, take the stand that Henry James is the rod by which all novelists are to be measured. Mr. Lubbock, who is a keen and stimulating critic, sifts the dramatic and pictorial elements in a pair of novels—and then judges the more dramatic novel the better, though he hedges somewhat at the moment of award. Exactly why fiction should imitate the drama is not made clear. Each has its function. The novel can do many things the drama cannot, as Mr. Eugene O'Neill would doubtless testify; and it is the worst kind of folly not to take advantage of those special opportunities. Techniques change, and it is well for the continued strength of an art form that they should do so. If the Victorians, vigorous and intelligent, touched with fancy and imagination the society of their age and described men and women honestly within the conventions imposed upon them, it is futile for one to wish that they had followed another technique, and undiscerning to suggest that it would have rendered their society more faithfully. The sensible will survey with sympathetic objectivity the wealth of one of English literature's most creative periods, and say with thanksgiving, "Here is God's plenty."

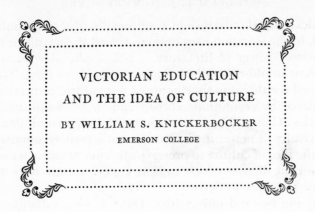

VICTORIAN EDUCATION AND THE IDEA OF CULTURE

BY WILLIAM S. KNICKERBOCKER
EMERSON COLLEGE

"EDUCATE OR GOVERN," wrote John Ruskin, "they are one and the same word."

During the sixty-four years of Victoria's reign, a time of hazardous transition, education in England supplemented parliamentary action as a substitute for revolution, for achieving national change without catastrophic violence. The instruction of the masses, the opening of higher education to women, the establishment of educational institutions for workingmen, and the rebirth of spirit in public schools and universities tended to break down the barriers between classes and to bridge chasms between minds. Educational processes quietly radiated, creating an intellectual climate which vastly favored creative attitudes towards renovating the national social order. Victorian education became England's alternative to successive *coups d'etat* manifested by some other European nations.

Utility or culture—which? New educational institutions tended to abandon the humanistic tradition which had been preserved in England since the revival of the classics, to reject traditional literary bases of education, and to substitute the study of science and of technological machines and processes. Emergence of new educational concepts created a conflict. Aggressive attacks upon the study of the classics aroused resistance by traditionally educated scholars who, in the situation thus evoked, voiced their faith in the formative power of literature, a philosophy of education resident in old established English seats of learning. They resisted the threat to time-honored ways of life, a threat engendered by revolutions abroad and by economic uncertainties at home. They met criticism of their own ideals and the rivalry of newer institutions by militantly recommending the idea of culture to preserve qualities of character and of human dignity which radical experimenters were too prone to ignore or destroy.

Of the two old universities, Oxford more valiantly resisted innovations, and therefore bore the brunt of the struggle. Cambridge was more elastic, more active in developing its inheritance in stressing physical science, less committed than was Oxford in devotion to literary studies as the organizing discipline of higher learning. Defending and extending the idea of culture, the humanization of man in society, were directly undertaken by some Oxford humanists, the most notable of whom were Newman, Arnold, and Ruskin.

I

Unprecedented effects resulted from extending education to hitherto excluded classes. Indispensably a phase of Victorian democracy—both stemming from it in the inchoate and spasmodic efforts to instruct the children of the poor and, inversely, shaping and directing it in the period between the two Reform Bills (1832 and 1867)—popular education enormously increased the numbers of those who could read and write, altered the nature of conditions of authorship and multiplied the phases of national life hitherto untouched in English literature.

Efforts to instruct the lower classes through teaching poor children to read the Scriptures and moral tracts (humanitarian by-products of eighteenth century Methodism) were scattered and unorganized. From 1700 to 1798, twenty "Charity Schools" were founded to provide the rudiments of instruction to the poor, but they too elicited little public interest until they found a champion in Sarah Trimmer whose *Reflections upon Charity Schools* (1792) called attention to their inadequacies while making a plea for their improvement and increase. Maria Edgeworth's *Practical Education* (1798) proceeded further and provided Clapham evangelicals with an educational manual for their humanitarian zeal. For four years (1802 to 1806), Mrs. Trimmer continued her campaign in her magazine *The Guardian of Education*. Some development of the schools resulted from the work of Thomas Stock and Robert Raikes (1780) who succeeded in removing these separated experiments from the wastefulness of amateurism and converting them into the supervised schemes known as "the ragged schools."

Perhaps the intentions of these humanitarians was to rescue children of the lower classes from the blight of gin whose sodden effects were so tellingly depicted by Hogarth. The limited scope of instruction in reading, writing, and a little arithmetic bore fruit in unanticipated results; for once taught to read the poor did not, of course, restrict their reading to the Holy Bible or to pious tracts like Hannah More's *The Shepherd of Salisbury Plain*. They avidly read, in too many instances, whatever came within range of their understanding, including (to the horror of the faithful) infidel and subversive printed matter hawked in the streets —inflaming their sense of discontent with conditions approved by their benefactors. Reaction and suspicion followed as a consequence when Paine's *Rights of Man* and *The Age of Reason* circulated freely among the newly literate poor so that public opinion feared that the mere ability to read was probably more a menace than a blessing—an attitude which became patently evident during the disturbances in England accompanying the progressive violence of the French Revolution. More than one contemporary vigorously questioned, or denounced, all efforts to instruct the poor. Yet extensive popular education as a panacea for the growing problems of ignorance, poverty, and crime lingered in the minds of some who uneasily saw the threatened deterioration of England. Wordsworth, turning to this problem, ventured to descant on its solution in his *Excursion*:

> O for the coming of that glorious time
> When, prizing knowledge as her noblest wealth
> And best protection, this imperial Realm,
> While she exacts obedience, shall admit
> An obligation, on her part, to *teach*
> Them who were born to serve her and obey;
> Binding herself by statute to secure
> For all the children whom her soil maintains
> The rudiments of letters, and inform
> The mind with moral and religious truth,
> Both understood and practiced—so that none
> However destitute be left to droop
> By timely culture unsustained; or run
> Into a wild disorder; or be forced
> To drudge through a weary life without the help
> Of intellectual implements and tools;
> A savage horde among the civilized,
> A servile band among the lordly free.[1]

Wordsworth's lines anticipate Victorian faith in the edifying power of educating the masses. In somewhat cumbersome verse, he phrased in idealistic sentences the vision which inspired Bell and Lancaster in establishing free schools for elementary instruction. Their efforts were consolidated in 1811 by the creation of the National Society for Promoting the Education of the Poor and, three years later (1813), the British and Foreign School Society. Quietly, from 1799 to 1816, Robert Owen was conducting his "New Institute for the Formation of Character" at New Lanark. Wordsworth's lines seem to indicate his sympathy with these movements and with Lord Brougham's agitation to have the government assume the burden of educating the poor: an agitation which, after several years of unremitting energy, triumphed in moving Parliament to appoint a Select Committee to Investigate the Education of the Lower

---

[1] *The Excursion*, Book VIII.

Classes of the Metropolis (1816). In 1818, after publishing his pamphlet "Letter to Sir Samuel Romilly . . . Upon the Abuse of Charities [Schools]" he saw his bill passed for a comprehensive Survey of Educational Charities. Brougham tirelessly worked to supply the unprivileged classes with practical information on a wide variety of topics through the tracts circulated by his Society for the Diffusion of Useful Knowledge, competing with the newly founded Bible Society, which distributed inexpensive editions of Holy Scripture among the literate poor. In 1835 Chambers founded his periodical, *Information for the People*. The establishment of a training school for teachers at Battersea (1833) and the parliamentary grant of £20,000 for People's Schools marked the beginnings of organized, publicly supported, extension of education to the children of the lower classes.

Education of laborers proceeded in a similar hesitating manner. The first of the "Mechanics Institutions," established in 1800, was followed, after almost a quarter century (1823), by The London Mechanics Institute (which later became Birkbeck College). In 1825, Brougham published his pamphlet, "Practical Observations Upon the Education of the People, Addressed to the Working Class and Their Employers." In the same year Thomas Campbell wrote a letter to *The Times* proposing an English university, open to all regardless of creed or social status, modeled on the German university at Bonn. This led, two years later (1827), to the founding of London University. Because this new institution eliminated religious tests for admission, devout Anglicans feared it would spread infidelity and forthwith established King's College, London (1831), to offset its baneful influence. London University did not require residence for its degrees but provided opportunities for examination given in various parts of the kingdom.

Even these provisions did not adequately solve the problem of threatened disaster to the social fabric caused by economic strains and distresses which were dramatically manifested by the anti-Corn Law and Chartist agitations of the thirties and forties and reached their climax in the continental revolutions of 1848. In a passionate speech in the House of Commons on April 19, 1847, Macaulay displayed his anxieties over the severe strains on public security caused by farm hands and artisans in their riots, hay burnings, and ugly threats. "This, then, is my argument," he exhorted his hearers, "it is the duty of government to protect our persons and property from danger. The gross ignorance of the common people is a principal cause of danger to our persons and property. Therefore, it is the duty of government to take care that the common people shall not be grossly ignorant."

In this context, Kingsley's *Alton Locke* is a revealing social document. Perhaps Macaulay's notion of education, narrowly conceived for merely prudential reasons, may have moved Carlyle in his alarming sketch of the condition of England, "Chartism" (1848), to recommend a more humane motive: "Who would suppose," Carlyle wrote, "that Education were a thing which had to be advocated on the ground of local expediency, or indeed on any ground? As if it stood not on the basis of everlasting duty, as a prime necessity of man. It is a thing that should need no advocating; much as it does actually need. To impart the gift of thinking to those who cannot think, and yet who could in that case think; this, one would imagine, was the first function a government had to set about discharging."

From 1848 to 1862 William Ellis founded his Birkbeck Schools and in 1862, Robert Lowe, an Oxford don, gave considerable time to the work of improving elementary education by his Revised Code.

Matthew Arnold's appointment (1851) as one of three inspectors of schools reveals the importance the government placed upon elevating the quality of popular education. Though his biographers cannot dispense with this phase of his life, they have tended to slight it as prosaic and tedious; yet a more realistic view of his experience discloses that, in spite of the drudgery and fatigue the school inspections entailed, they provided opportunities for learning at first hand the conditions of a swiftly changing age, freeing him from the confined outlook resulting from his sheltered upbringing. His duties continued through thirty of the most important years of his life (1851 to 1882) and exacted much from him in the constant travel his duties demanded. But he was compensated by the opportunities offered him, in moving him to write essays which flooded the whole view of contemporary education of the English people with insights which only one with his background and quality of mind could render. The Newcastle Commission, appointed in 1859, delegated him to investigate schools in France, Holland, and Switzerland—an experience which enabled him to see in some perspective the defects and the needs of English publicly supported schools. His report, "The Popular Education of France with Notices of That in Holland and Switzerland" (1861), placed the subject on a plane higher than the solely prudential one which had moved Brougham and Macaulay. It appeared the year that the Taunton Commission was appointed: that commission sent him abroad a few years later to continue his investigations which he presented in another report, "Schools and Universities on the Continent" (1868). By comparing it with Herbert Spencer's *Education, Intellectual, Moral, and Physical* one may see how Arnold's concept of culture infused educational theory with an ideal missing from the great empiricist's proposals. In some measure, it was incorporated in the great Education Act of 1870 constructed by Arnold's brother-in-law, William Forster. Ten years later, in 1880, the Compulsory Education Act definitely legalized the improvements in popular education and made education generally mandatory throughout the realm. The appointment (1894) and the report (1896) of the Bryce Commission, with the enactment of the Education Acts of 1902 and 1903, corrected and adjusted provisions of the 1870 act.

Difficulties which Wordsworth had not foreseen in his *Excursion* passage, quoted above, had arisen through the six decades of Victoria's reign. Should popular education be financed and supervised by voluntary, or by governmental, agencies? Should religion and religious doctrine be an integral part of its program? Should education of the people be confined to the instruction of "skills" or should it primarily seek the development of moral character? "What was proposed in the Acts of 1902 and 1903," wrote Beatrice Webb, "applying to England and Wales only, was that all schools which provided elementary education up to a certain standard should come on the rates, and be controlled by the public authority; but that such of them as had been provided by a religious denomination should be permitted to choose leaders of their own creed, provided that they were efficient in secular subjects, and that, subject to a conscience clause, there should be religious teaching according to the creed of the denominational school."[2]

II

In some sense, not too clearly discernible, professional and higher education of English women in the nineteenth century accompanied the movement for popular education. The "monitorial" system on which Bell and Lancaster relied, using older children to instruct younger, yielded to the need for adult teachers, properly trained in the skill of instruction. This opened new doors for women. Individual women, here and there, like Harriet Martineau and George Eliot, were sufficiently intrepid to venture into fields of higher learning generally then regarded as solely the sphere of men. But teacher training colleges offered an avenue of useful employment for women—apart from the traditional post as governesses in private families—in which they found scope for public service. From this beginning, they broadened their demands for opportunities in higher education and, stimulated by the growing strength of the woman's movement in the Victorian era, slowly succeeded in securing the establishment of women's colleges and the right to enter the universities, including Cambridge and Oxford.

The circumscribed educational field for women was a legacy of the previous century. Dr. Johnson had devised a a triad of educational aims for women: cleverness in learning foreign languages, interest in science, and the general

2 *Our Partnership* (copyright by Longmans, Green & Co., Inc.: New York, 1948), pp. 233-234. Use of quotations taken from this book has been granted through the kind permission of Longmans, Green & Co.

acquisition of quotable facts. These were to make her more attractive as maiden and more convenient and durable as wife and mother. This was a more sensible view than the sentimentalized notion then prevailing, celebrated in *Pamela* and *Clarissa Harlow*, which persisted well into the nineteenth century and was, indeed, illustrated in the good queen herself. It was also reflected in the tender verses of Laetitia Landon, Felicia Hemans, and Jean Ingelow. Mrs. Anne Jameson's *Heroines of Shakespeare*, in its unexcised, original version, frankly stressed the frailties of women who, by various arts of wit and suffering, held up a mirror for Victorian female virtues; it was a moral masterpiece, edifying for women in a world limited to pleasures of the parlor and the martyrdoms of marriage.

Mrs. Ellis's series of conduct-books, *The Women of England*, delineated the whole course of Victorian woman's behavior, from babyhood to the blessedness of the boudoir, gravely exhorting mothers to rear their daughters for careers of patient waiting until won by suitors (or, if not wooed, to endure mutely the long-suffering of inconspicuous spinsterhood); and thereafter as Griseldas in the role of wife and mother. "The first thing of importance," Mrs. Ellis wrote in *Daughters of England*, "is to be inferior to men—inferior in mental power in the same proportion that you are inferior in bodily strength. . . . I confess I do not see the value of languages for a woman," she continued, questioning also the usefulness of the knowledge of science for women beyond making her an "intelligent listener" to men. As for the general acquisition of knowledge, she conceded that a knowledge of facts, however miscellaneous, might be handy "in connection with the proper exercise of a healthy mind," and "necessarily lead to a general illumination." Mrs. Ellis, like the many other women who shared her views, was moved to write in order to preserve and extend the ideal of the "proper female" in a generation whose literary tastes were appeased by the dainty gift books and annuals laden with verse, fiction, and scribblings which satisfied this ideal. It went further, saturating the minds of minor novelists, now forgotten, who conceived their women characters in this atmosphere of "namby-pambyism."

In this milieu and for this public, the young Alfred Tennyson alembicated some of the moods and themes of poets of the preceding romantic generation—of Wordsworth, Keats, Shelley, and even of the sentimental Byron of "Childe Harold"—electing himself the poetic voice of this dominant gynecocracy. Harmoniously in tune with current sentimentalizing of the proper female, he remained faithful to it throughout his life; not even Thackeray's revision of the concept in Becky Sharp, or contemporary women who demonstrated its inadequacy, restrained him in depicting it in *The Princess*. So long as Victoria was Queen, so long was he faithful to her view of woman's status. A glimpse of that view may be seen in the letter written by Mrs. Martin, the Queen's companion, in 1860: "The Queen is most anxious to enlist everyone who can speak or write to join in opposing this mad wicked folly of Women's Rights, with all its attendant horrors, on which her poor, feeble sex is bent, forgetting every sense of womanly feeling and propriety."

Woman's status began to be warmly discussed shortly after Victoria's accession. Critics attacked the notion that women preferred to be sheltered, anemic, deprived of careers. Women struggled for revision of ideas concerning education for their sex despite scepticism, ridicule, and stubborn resistance. By 1848 they succeeded in gaining recognition of their claims: in that year, the year Tennyson published his satiric "medley" *The Princess*, Queen's College, London, opened its doors for the liberal education of women, followed by the Bedford College for Women in the following year. Two graduates of Queen's College, Frances Mary Buss and Dorothy Beale, became notable pioneers in the movement. Others who participated in various ways were Sophia Jex-Blake, Anne Jemima Clough, Emily and Octavia Hill, Emma Cons, Barbara Leigh Smith, and Emily Davis who, in 1864, won a long fight to secure admission of girls to London University Local Examinations, and in 1869 founded the Women's College at Hitchin which, in

1875, moved to Cambridge and became Girton College. The National Union for Improving the Education of Women of all classes was organized in 1871 and was followed, the next year, by the Girls Public School Company. Seven years later, in 1879, London University opened its degree examinations to women; in 1881 women's colleges were founded at Oxford and, in 1884, Oxford permitted women to examinations in some of its Final Schools.

Public opinion grudgingly shifted during the decade of the eighties. Gilbert and Sullivan's *Princess Ida* was a timely parody of Tennyson's *Princess*. John Stuart Mill's *The Subjection of Women* had done its work in persuading many Liberals to adopt more sensible views. George Eliot had eminently demonstrated that a woman was as competent as any of the other sex in fundamental brainwork in philosophy or in fiction. In all fields of intellectual and social action Victorian women were becoming annually more conspicuous in contributing to knowledge and to ways of solving political and economic problems. By 1901, the year of the Queen's death, among the increasing number of notable women—whose achievements were destined not only to expose the inadequacies of Mrs. Ellis's views but were to reveal how a woman, no less "genteel," could attain happiness in marriage while engaged in the severest forms of research—was Beatrice Webb. Her autobiography, *My Apprenticeship* and *Our Partnership*, is a prime sourcebook for Victorian education in some of its later phases. It discloses how an industrious, persevering, intelligent woman continued the efforts, by scientific methods, of Jeremy Bentham, John Stuart Mill, John Ruskin, Robert Owen, and William Morris in assisting the mind of England to confront and solve emerging industrial and economic problems.

III

Education of artisans and mechanics developed concomitantly with that of the children of the poorer classes and of women. Instruction in technological skills undoubtedly made better workmen without necessarily making them better citizens. Its deficiencies moved high-minded Victorians to stress the importance of education as the cultivation of moral attitudes, enlargement of social vision, and the political responsibilities of workingmen as citizens.

Except in individual instances, European consciousness of "a proletariat" found slight acceptance in England, even during the tumults of the forties—partly because of the traditional pride of the Englishman of the lower classes, but more importantly because of the successive series of parliamentary compromises in new legislation, and experimental efforts in creating new colleges and universities to fit the needs of those who either could not afford the expenses of Oxford and Cambridge, or would not consent to the creedal impositions of the two old universities. London University (1827), though not founded specifically for workingmen—it provided university education for dissenters not then admitted to Oxford and Cambridge—made no distinction between the middle and lower classes in qualifications for study. In its first period it was, according to Beatrice Webb, "merely a corporation to confer university degrees. It had no professors; it gave no teaching; it conducted no research; it awarded its degrees to persons coming from all parts, on their passing examinations on papers set by examiners whom they had never seen."[3]

In 1851, Owens College, the experiment which led to the establishment of the University of Manchester, opened in the heart of industrial England. Three years later (1854), the Workingman's College in Red Lion Square, London, was formally dedicated, crowning efforts made by Maurice, Furnival, J. M. Ludlow, Thomas Hughes, Charles Kingsley, and John Ruskin. Ruskin's "The Nature of Gothic," a chapter from his recently published *Stones of Venice*, was distributed to the large audience of workingmen as the rationale of this new venture. In it, Ruskin wrote:

"It is verily this degradation of the operative into a machine which, more than any other evil of the times, is leading the masses of the nations everywhere into vain, inco-

[3] *Our Partnership*, pp. 233-234.

herent, destructive struggling for a freedom of which they cannot explain the nature to themselves. Their universal outcry against wealth, and against nobility, is not forced from them either by the pressure of famine, or the sting of mortified pride. These do much, and have done much in all ages; but the foundations of society were never shaken as they are at this day. It is not that men are ill fed, but that they have no pleasure in the work by which they make their bread, and therefore look to wealth as the only means to pleasure.

". . . The great cry that rises from our manufacturing cities, louder than all their furnace blast, is all in very deed for this—that we manufacture everything there except men; we blanch cotton, and strengthen steel, and refine sugar, and shape pottery; but to brighten, to strengthen, to refine, or to form a single living spirit, never enters into our estimate of advantages. And all the evil to which that cry is urging our myriads can be met in only one way. . . . It can be met only by a right understanding, on the part of all classes, of what kinds of labor are good for men, raising them, and making them happy; by a determined sacrifice of such convenience, or beauty, or cheapness as to be got only by the degradation of the workman; and by equally determined demand for products of healthy and ennobling labour."

Ruskin's exhortation placed the idea of workingmen's education on a high plane, bringing it within a humanistic concept. In spite of strenuous efforts of Ruskin's disciples to make it prevail, it was regarded by practical people as iridescences on floating gossamers. A notable instance is Sir Joshua Mason, a self-made capitalist of Birmingham, who stringently excluded from his projected college (Mason's College, Birmingham, 1881), the study of theology, party politics, and "mere literary instruction." Yet even this college, like some other new institutions, invited men of active affairs—scientists, technologists, lawyers, clergymen, and literary critics—to address its working-class audiences, thus providing opportunities for men with vision to communicate their views.

Freed from inhibitions of statute, custom, and tradition, these colleges explored many avenues of knowledge neglected by Oxford and Cambridge. By adjusting theory and process to newer needs in a world rapidly changing its frames of reference, they enlarged the national mind. The movement was consolidated in the foundation of new urban universities: in Manchester (1880), Birmingham (1900), Liverpool (1903), Leeds (1904), Sheffield (1905), and Bristol (1906).

I V

Influences outside educational institutions also contributed to this extension. The most important were the advancement of natural sciences, the development of trade unions and the political activities of the Independent Labour Party, and the steady propaganda of the Fabian Society.

Annual meetings of the Royal Society constituted, in effect, a "university" of science in which the Baconian method of research, as well as the results of scientific experiments, were publicly announced and discussed. Significant books, like Lyell's *Principles of Geology* (1833) and Darwin's *Origin of Species* (1859), stimulated a shift of thinking which had impressive effects in fundamental thinking and in altering educational concepts in schools and colleges newly founded.

The intricate growth of labor organizations and their effects upon the public mind are recorded in the Webbs' *History of Trade Unionism* (1898). In disputes between labor and capital, and in internal disputes within unions themselves, aggressive personalities found a theater for airing their economic views, analyzing existing conditions, and proposing economic panaceas and policies of tactics. Inadequacies of idealistic proposals made evident the necessity for trustworthy data derived from exhaustive investigation by personal interviews, and by research in musty records of the past. In developing its corporate forms, British labor would have been rigidly materialistic in outlook and purpose had it not been infused by the humanism of Carlyle, Kingsley, Ruskin, and Morris. Indeed, altered by pressures of changing conditions and by shifts of stress, the conflict of humanism and utilitarianism, pointed out by John Stuart Mill in his essays, "Bentham" and "Coleridge," continued in other forms. As the political philosophy of labor evolved, the solution of basic problems (like ignorance, poverty, and crime) veered towards vaguely collectivist proposals; one derived from Robert Owen and his humanitarian experiment at New Lanark, another from John Ruskin's neo-medievalism in the Guild of St. George. Through the conjunction of the influences of John Stuart Mill, of Herbert Spencer, and of the scientific method, the Owen concept of utilitarian socialism and the Ruskin ideal of humanistic socialism fused in the speculative propaganda —buttressed by economic statistics and penetrating social analyses—of the Fabians, on public platforms and through their publications.

Carlyle's *Past and Present*, as well as his later vigorous manifestoes, steadily bombarded the Victorian public, awakening the conscience of the ruling middle class to the perils of the existing conditions which resulted from the less admirable features of capitalism. Superb as a diagnostician, Carlyle contributed a constructive clue to the solution of what he called "the condition-of-England" question: the imperative of retrieving the spiritual and moral dignity of impoverished classes. To achieve this, he urged strong will, emigration to solve overpopulation, and the responsibility of government to educate the masses. His zeal stimulated university idealists. Kingsley's *Yeast* and *Alton Locke*, Hughes' *Tom Brown at Oxford* are fictional footnotes of Carlyle; but the Christian Socialist movement of Frederick Denison Maurice, Charles Kingsley, and Thomas Hughes was industriously engaged in implementing Carlyle's remedies in *Latter-Day Pamphlets*. His chief disciple, however, the eminent Victorian who not only stressed his message but immensely expanded it, was that precocious "graduate of Oxford," John Ruskin, whose pilgrimage, beginning with a search for the central principles of art and beauty, culminated in an apocalyptic vision of a transformed England when labor would be dedicated to the making of beautiful things in a spirit of consecration and of Christian joy.

Carlyle, the Christian Socialists, and Ruskin supplied the vision; but translating the vision into a version was, and still is, a slow, devious, and painful process. Concrete situations, in the cumbersome efforts of laborers to unite in their unions and the subsequent deadlocks in relations of capital and labor, created expediencies in which labor became vocal in stating its concepts, articulate in outlining its demands and programs for their attainment. Discussions in Victorian periodicals (like *The Fortnightly Review, The Athenaeum, The Spectator,* and *The Nineteenth Century*), supplemented by books, brought the problems within the political sphere in the hope that legislation would provide the agency for the correction of economic abuses and distresses. The Second Reform Bill of 1867, by extending the franchise, was a gesture in this direction.

Diverse interests of reformed Parliament impeded action on bills submitted to lessen economic strains. Not content with political action alone, trade unions continued their struggle through their own techniques of economic action. Tradition—thanks to the great advances made by the scientific method in the study of history, which had been appropriated by the schools for the people—became evident in the 1880's, as British labor anticipated the centenary of the French Revolution. The Independent Labour Party, founded during the ugly times of severe economic stress, 1881 to 1885, organized the spirit of discontent by directing its attack on the capitalistic system through a program of revolutionary socialism. Urged by impetuous hot-heads in labor unions, the atmosphere was charged with ominous threats of violence.

More realistic social analysts, acknowledging the imminence of catastrophe, turned towards a method of achieving economic and social advance more truly indigenous, more truly harmonious with the spirit of English tradition of social action: the method of "the inevitability of gradualness" through constitutional socialism. The differences between revolutionary and constitutional socialism were pointed out by Sidney Webb in an address delivered at the tenth anniversary of the foundation of the Fabian Society, "Socialism, True and False":

"In 1884," said Sidney Webb, "the Fabian Society, like the other socialist organizations, had its enthusiastic young members—aye, and old ones, too—who placed all their hopes on a sudden tumultuous uprising of a united proletariat, before whose mighty onrush, Kings, landlords and capitalists would go down like ninepins, leaving society quietly to re-sort itself into a utopia. The date for this social revolution was sometimes fixed for 1889, the centenary of the French Revolution. . . . It was against all thinking and teaching of this catastrophic kind that the [Fabian] Society came to set its face—not, as I believe, because we were any less earnest in our warfare against existing evils, or less extreme in our remedies, but because we were sadly and sorrowfully driven to the conclusion that no sudden or simultaneous transformation of society from an individualist to a collectivist basis was possible or even thinkable. . . . In short, we repudiated the common assumption that socialism was necessarily bound up with insurrectionism, on the one hand, or utopianism, on the other, and we set to work to discover for ourselves and to teach others how practically to transform England into a social democratic commonwealth."[4]

Fabians constituted an educational agency, analyzing economic and social conditions and institutions in England, and disseminating a series of "tracts for the times" which proposed correction of inadequacies in the interests of what they thought was distributive economic justice. The title page of Fabian Tract number 7 explained the name and method of the society: "For the right moment you must wait, as Fabius did most patiently when warring against Hannibal, though many censured his delays; but when the time comes, you must strike hard, as Fabius did, or your waiting will be in vain, and fruitless." According

4 Quoted by Beatrice Webb, *Our Partnership*, pp. 105-106.

to Beatrice Webb, "the Fabian Society studiously avoided any quotations from Karl Marx, preferring indeed Robert Owen: they translated economics and collectivism into the language of prosaic vestrymen and town councillors."[5] "The Fabians," wrote G. M. Trevelyan in *British History in the Nineteenth Century*, "were intelligence officers without an army—there was no Fabian Party in parliament—but they influenced the strategy and even the direction of the great hosts moving under other banners." "The Fabians," wrote Mrs. Webb, "in no way competed with the I. L. P. We were purely an educational body—we did not seek to become a political party. We should continue our policy of inoculation—of giving to each class, to each person, coming under our influence, the exact dose of collectivism that they were prepared to assimilate. . . . Of course, this slow imperceptible change in men's opinions and in the national institutions, is not favorable to the growth of a revolutionary party. There is some truth in Keir Hardie's remark that we were the worst enemies of the social revolution."[6]

Through the legacy of an eccentric Fabian, Henry Hutchinson, the London School of Economics was founded in 1895, modeled on L'Ecole Libre de Science Politique. Sidney Webb collaborated with R. B. Haldane (1856-1928) in drafting a bill for the reorganization of London University: "they were, in their several ways, both entirely free from the subtly pervading influence of the Oxford and Cambridge of those days, with their standards of expensive living and enjoyable leisure, and their assumption of belonging to an aristocracy or governing class." Haldane, graduate of Edinburgh and Göttingen, "among students living sparely in uncomfortable lodgings, undistracted by games, who looked forward to no existence other than strenuous brainwork, . . . believed intensely in the university, not only as a place for 'great teaching' but also as a source of inspiration of 'great minds,' producing in the choicer spirits, a systematic devotion to learning and

[5] *Ibid.*, pp. 106-107.   [6] *Ibid.*, pp. 122-123.

research. . . . He, accordingly, designed a scheme of combining in a single university, of a new type, all three elements: namely, the external students influenced by a system of examinations which could be improved; an organized hierarchy of evening classes which, so far as London was concerned, the Technical Education Board was raising to the highest grade; and the group of autonomous colleges, in which a professoriate in no way inferior to those of Germany and Scotland could be trusted to inspire self-elected groups of earnest students in every subject of study and research."[7]

The government in the summer of 1897 appointed a commission to devise a constitution and statutes for London University, but the London University Act of 1898 resulted merely in continuing the loose external examinations and in recognizing the teaching given in autonomous colleges. "The reorganized University," Mrs. Webb records, "started on what was little more than a formal existence in which the several parts wrangled over and largely counteracted each other's projects and proposals; some fresh convulsion, amounting perhaps to a new birth, was required to give the organism genuine life."

The possibilities for this great metropolitan seat of learning were outlined by Sidney Webb in an essay, "London University: A Policy and a Forecast" in *Nineteenth Century*, 1902. "It may at the outset," he wrote, "be granted that, for any university of the Oxford or Cambridge type, the metropolis is perhaps more unfit than any other spot that could be chosen. By no possible expenditure could we create . . . the tradition, the atmosphere, the charm or grace of collegiate life on the Isis or the Cam. Nor is it possible to secure, amid the heterogeneous crowds of London and its distractions, either the class selection or the careful supervision required by the parents of boys fresh from Eton or Harrow, with two or three hundred a year to spend in pocket money. . . . It may be that we must forego in London University the culture born of classic scholarship

[7] *Ibid.*, p. 403.

and learned leisure. But, if we can show that there is no incompatibility between the widespread instruction of an undergraduate democracy and the most effective provision for the discovery of new truth; between the most practical training and genuine cultivation of the mind; between the plain living of hard-working students of limited means and high intellectual achievements, we shall not . . . appeal in vain. London University must take its own line. They are futile dreamers who seek to fit new circumstances to the old ideals: rather, must we strive, by developing to the utmost the opportunities that the present affords us, to create out of twentieth century conditions new kinds of perfection."

V

Popular education, the development of scientific, technological, and professional training, the creation of new colleges, and the admission of women to university degrees were phases of a noiseless revolution. They filled a need made conspicuous by developments of middle-class and aristocratic education since Elizabethan days.

Seen in the context of the whole Victorian frame, classical grammar schools and the two old universities formed a separate and exclusive system which tended to keep them immune from contemporary concerns. Winchester, Eton, Harrow, Rugby—to name only the best-known public schools—were, though separate corporations, organically connected in their educational policy with Oxford and Cambridge. The corporate independence of each of these institutions, their diversities of administration, in no way affected their consecration to a single inspiring idea, the idea of culture. In large measure, what Oxford and Cambridge thought and taught was reproduced in public schools because teachers of the latter were graduates of the former. Entrenched in custom and protected by tradition, these conservative institutions of learning preserved their standards. In the face of fierce attacks, they framed their "secret" in understandable words, becoming more conscious of the rightness of their procedures and the quality of their discipline. What their critics denounced as their "neglect" and "lethargy" was really their loyal devotion to their own continuities and to their concept of culture derived from a close and continuous study of the classics. They rallied against their opponents and boldly stated their philosophy of education; and, assuming the offensive, ventured to propose it to correct secularizing tendencies then increasingly prevalent.

Though Cambridge accepted Bacon as a supplement to its traditional reliance on Plato, Oxford rested on Aristotle as its guiding mind—the Aristotle of the *Poetics, Ethics, Politics,* and especially the *Logic.* Aristotle stimulated Oxford's tendency to analytical thinking, to the critical scrutiny of Graeco-Latin literature from which it derived and formulated the idea of culture. The play of mind which resulted from the continual criticism by Victorian Liberals caused Oxford humanists to reinterpret the idea of culture in a larger frame of reference. Hence, Matthew Arnold, engaging in the task of permeating middle-class thinking of Victorian England, defined it as "the disinterested endeavor to learn and to propagate the best that has been thought and said in the world," the "love of perfection" which motivates the five powers of life: the powers of manners, of morals, of literature, of science, and of religion.

"The great men of culture," Arnold indicated, "are those who have a passion for diffusing, for making prevail from one end of society to the other, the best knowledge, the best ideas of their time: who have labored to divest knowledge of all that was harsh, uncouth, difficult, abstract, professional, exclusive; to humanize it, to make it efficient outside the clique of the cultivated and learned, yet still remaining the *best* knowledge and thought of the time, and a true source, therefore, of sweetness and light."

From the beginning to the middle of the century, Liberal reformers urged changes which they believed would make these old institutions more truly national, more truly representative. Neither Oxford nor Cambridge considered scientific research its prime obligation and both universities had permitted their professoriate to fall into neglect. Both were loose confederations of colleges in which the tutorial system had developed, over the course of two centuries, at the expense of the university as a single, larger corporation. The successes of German universities—especially of Göttingen, Bonn, and Berlin—in extending the bounds of human knowledge, in Biblical criticism, in philosophy, and in the natural sciences, served reformers as models from which to point out the defects of Oxford and Cambridge. The *Edinburgh Review* maintained a continuous campaign for the reform of the two universities which, in 1808-1810 and 1832-1834, was unusually severe. Its acrimony, and indifference to the peculiar qualities of attitude and scholarly action which had silently developed in the universities, tended to irritate defenders of the *status quo* and, when the issue was taken up by the Liberal Party for parliamentary action, created in both institutions a resolute spirit of resistance.

This agitation for the adjustment of Oxford and Cambridge resulted from a notion that, as *national* universities, they were too exclusive in their conditions for admission, too rigid in insistence on religious conformity for tutors and professors, and too negligent in standards of academic scholarship.[8] Adam Smith in *The Wealth of Nations* (1776) and Edward Gibbon in his *Memoirs* (1795) had caustically criticized eighteenth-century Oxford: Gibbon invented the phrase which became a conventional description of the university: "a place of port and prejudice." Adam Smith had said that it "made no pretence at teaching." But, by 1800, one of the Oxford colleges—Oriel—had begun its own internal reform and, with the aid of influential scholars of other Oxford colleges, succeeded in instituting the "Final Schools," or what might today be called oral comprehensive examinations in the classics, conducted by the university to determine what undergraduates should receive the degree and in what order of merit. These "Final Schools" were the first indication of a willingness by the

[8] *Creative Oxford: Its Influence in Victorian Literature* (Syracuse Univ. Press, 1925) by the present writer sketches specifically the criticisms of Oxford and Cambridge by the *Edinburgh Review* and efforts of Liberals in Parliament to legislate improvement.

independent colleges of Oxford to concede the superior authority of the university, even though, for another half century, they continued as independent corporations, each with its own properties and endowments, its own customs and traditions, submitting to no external jurisdiction.

As a result of this administrative reform, slight though it was, a spirit of competitive scholarly rivalry developed among the colleges as their undergraduates strove for First Class Honors in the Final Schools. By 1837, when Victoria ascended the throne, the chief Oxford college was Oriel. It had, about the beginning of the century, abolished an abuse which prevailed in all Oxford colleges: the custom of electing its tutors for almost any reason except for scholarly merit and achievement. By a daring action, it substituted a scheme to appoint its fellows and tutors from among those students who had won distinction, First Class Honors, in the Final Schools. At the same time, it revised its method of studying Aristotle from memorizing passages of a paraphrase of the *Logic* to mastering its art and applying it in specific issues. Largely by initiating this shift, Oriel became conspicuous as Oxford's "blue-ribbon college." Its dons became gadflies, exercising an agile play of mind on fundamental questions, and were locally described as "The Noetics." One of the most prominent of the group, Edward Copleston, who later became provost of the college, vigorously replied to criticism of Oxford in a tract, *Reply to the Calumnies of the Edinburgh Review* (1810), which Newman had before him a half-century later when he wrote *The Idea of a University* (1852).

From this company of Oriel logicians came Thomas Arnold and John Henry Newman, men whose idea of the church and of the relation of Oxford to the church differed profoundly. Arnold relinquished his Oriel fellowship in 1820 (Newman was appointed to fill the vacancy). He was so successful preparing youth for the universities that he was appointed in 1828 as headmaster of Rugby where, during the following fourteen years (1828-1842), he radically changed the whole conception of education for pre-university students. By laying his stress on the formation of

119

moral character and on the necessity for openmindedness in meeting new ideas, he sent to both old universities a succession of Rugbeians who quickly attained distinction in scholarship and were conspicuous for their liberal attitudes. Thomas Hughes' *Tom Brown at Rugby* and its sequel, *Tom Brown at Oxford*, delineate their moral earnestness, physical vigor, and novel openmindedness: attitudes which in life were displayed by Arthur Hugh Clough. While Arnold was at Rugby, Newman, associating with Oriel Noetics at Oxford, found a new intellectual life which he affectionately records in his *Apologia Pro Vita Sua*. He also records how he came to resist the innovating spirit in Oxford introduced by Arnoldian Liberals. In this struggle he became the "most eloquent" voice of the Tractarians. Employing dialectical instruments which Noetics revived, Tractarians strengthened Oxford as a citadel of the national church. Their agitations alarmed many who disagreed with their propaganda. Liberals intensified their demands for parliamentary reform of the two old universities which culminated in a tactical victory in 1851 when they succeeded in having a commission appointed to investigate Oxford and Cambridge.

By that time Newman was a Roman Catholic priest. While the committee investigated the universities, some of his fellow Catholics in Dublin invited him to deliver a series of lectures in that city to inaugurate a projected university. In those lectures on the nature of university education, Newman found an occasion to counteract the work of the investigating committee by anticipating their proposals for university reform, especially in their tendency to secularize higher education. His *Idea of a University* confessedly developed the idea of Oxford expounded four decades earlier by Copleston. Implicitly it rejected innovations like the lack of collegiate residence and the practice of granting degrees merely by passing examinations, both of which had been introduced by London University: it also resisted proposals to lay inordinate stress on laboratory experiment, a stress which disregarded the harmonious development of all human powers.

The ideal university, Newman asserted, was a place of learning in which a harmony of "sciences" prevailed. To him, "sciences" meant *all* studies, not merely the knowledge of physical phenomena. For the needs of teaching, knowledge was broken into separate subject matters; yet, he insisted, all of these "sciences" have "multiplied bearings one on another, and an internal sympathy, and admit, or rather demand, comparison and adjustment. They complete, correct, balance each other." Theology—the systematic study of God, nature, and man—regulated and organized other "sciences" in a reasonable relevancy, in a qualitative gradation of significant worth. In Newman's opinion, this harmony would be destroyed if theology were eliminated from the scheme of higher learning. Doubtless with London University in mind as something to avoid because it not only eliminated theology but also laid improper stress on examinations taken by students who remained at home in different parts of the kingdom, Newman emphasized the importance of collegiate residence.

"This," he said, "I conceive to be the advantage of a seat of universal learning, considered as a place of education. An assemblage of learned men, zealous for their own sciences, and rivals of each other, are brought by familiar intercourse and for the sake of intellectual peace, to adjust together the claims and relations of their respective subjects of investigation. They learn to respect, to consult, to aid each other. Thus is created a pure and clear atmosphere of thought, which the student also breathes, though in his case he only pursues a few sciences out of the multitude. He profits by an intellectual tradition, which is independent of particular teachers, which guides him in his choice of subjects, and duly interprets for him those which he chooses. He apprehends the great outlines of knowledge, the principles on which it rests, the scale of its parts, its lights and shades, its great points and its little, as he otherwise cannot apprehend them. Hence it is that his education is called 'Liberal.' A habit of mind is formed which lasts through life, of which the attributes are, freedom, equitableness, calmness, moderation, and wisdom. . . .

121

"To open the mind, to correct it, to refine it, to enable it to know, and to digest, master and rule, and use its knowledge, to give it power over its own faculties, application, flexibility, method, critical exactness, sagacity, resource, address, eloquent expression . . . is an object as intelligible as the cultivation of virtue, while, at the same time, it is absolutely distinct from it."[9]

Newman's lectures on the nature and scope of education were probably in the minds of many Parliament members during the debate on the bill for the reform of Oxford and Cambridge. When the 1854 act was passed, only administrative changes were legislated, without radically disturbing educational tradition: it lessened the autonomy of the colleges, it strengthened the professoriate, and abolished religious tests at matriculation.

A noteworthy minor change of the 1854 act permitted the professor of poetry to lecture in English instead of in the customary Latin. Hence, Matthew Arnold, the first incumbent after the reform, found his occasion to continue Newman's effort by employing his powers to preserve Oxford's traditions in a time of uncertain transition. Himself stamped by Rugby and Balliol, and one of those whose spirit had been charmed by Newman, cherishing Oxford's beauty and memories, Matthew Arnold reminded his hearers of the magic of the place when encroaching Philistinism threatened extinction of its alluring traits. His *On Translating Homer, Essays in Criticism, First Series*, and *On Celtic Literature*, first delivered as Oxford lectures, were probably devised as "tracts for the times," illustrating Oxonian moods of urbanity and disinterestedness. His poems, "The Scholar Gypsy" and "Thyrsis," tenderly indicated his attachment to the dreaming spires and the happy leisure of his youth in the surrounding countryside. What he found worthy in literature, ancient and modern, were those qualities which had shaped his own mind and spirit in the Oxford of his youth: high seriousness, love of perfection, detachedness, reflectiveness. "She will forgive me,

[9] *The Idea of a University*, Discourse v, Sect. 1.

I know," he wrote, "if I have unwittingly drawn upon her a shaft aimed at her unworthy son. Queen of romance, there she lies, spreading her gardens in the moonlight, and whispering from her towers the last enchantments of the Middle Age."

His valedictory lecture (1868) became the first chapter of *Culture and Anarchy*, in which he communicated to English readers the saving grace of the Oxford spirit. The book was a penetrating survey of Philistine trends of the times, recommending attitudes and responses to offset too narrow effects of doing good. "There is a view," he wrote, "in which all the good of our neighbor, the impulses toward action, help, and beneficence, the desire for removing human error, clearing human confusion, and diminishing human misery, the noble aspiration to leave the world better and happier than we found it—motives eminently such as are called social—come as part of the grounds of culture, and the main and pre-eminent part. Culture is then properly described not as having its origin in curiosity but as having its origin in the love of perfection: it is a *study of perfection* . . . the aim of culture [is to set] ourselves to ascertain what perfection is and to make it prevail; but also, in determining generally in what perfection consists, religion comes to a conclusion identical with that which culture—culture seeking the determination of this question through *all* the voices of human experience which have been heard upon it, of art, science, poetry, philosophy, history, as well as of religion, in order to give a greater fullness and certainty to its solution—likewise reaches. Religion says: *The Kingdom of God is within you*; and culture, in like manner, places human perfection in an internal condition, in the growth and predominance of our humanity proper, as distinguished from our animality. . . . Not a having and a resting, but a growing and a becoming, is the character of perfection as culture conceives it; and here, too, it coincides with religion. . . . But, finally, perfection—as culture from a thorough, disinterested study of human nature and human experience learns to conceive it—is a harmonious expansion of *all* the powers which make the beauty and worth of human nature, and is not consistent with the over-development of any one power at the expense of the rest."[10]

Neither Newman nor Arnold excluded the study of natural phenomena from their ideal of rounded education, but they did resist attempts to make it central, to substitute it in place of the study of the dignity of man. The development of certain natural sciences—particularly of geology, biology, astronomy, mechanics, and heat—moved earnest educational improvers to demand inclusion of scientific studies in all educational levels from secondary schools to universities. Thomas Henry Huxley (1825-1895), the chief spokesman for scientific education, as principal speaker at the formal opening of Mason's College, Birmingham, overtly challenged Matthew Arnold's concept of culture in the address, "Science and Education." He asserted that "neither the discipline nor the subject matter of classical education is of such direct value to the student of physical science as to justify the expenditure of valuable time upon either"; and that "for the purpose of attaining real culture, an exclusively scientific education is at least as effectual as an exclusively literary education. . . . We cannot know all the best thoughts and sayings of the Greeks unless we know what they thought about natural phenomena. We cannot fully appreciate their criticism of life unless we understand the extent to which that criticism was affected by scientific conceptions. We falsely pretend to be the inheritors of that culture, unless we are penetrated, as the best minds among them were, with an unhesitating faith that the free employment of reason, in accordance with scientific method, is the sole method of reaching truth."

Yet Huxley conceded that scientific education was still "inchoate" and tentative and that he was "the last person to question the importance of genuine literary education or to suppose that intellectual culture can be completed without it. An exclusively scientific training will bring

10 *Culture and Anarchy*, Chapter 1.

about a mental twist as surely as an exclusively literary training." Although apparently he debated the Arnoldian concept, he really was only extending it by a specific application in a particular situation. "Within these walls," he concluded, "the future employer and the future artisan may sojourn for a while, and carry, through all their lives, the stamp of influences then brought to bear on them. Hence, it is not beside the mark to remind you that the prosperity of industry depends not merely upon the improvement of manufacturing processes, not merely upon the ennobling of the individual character, but upon a third condition, namely, a clear understanding of the conditions of social life, on the part of both capitalist and the operative, and their agreement upon common principles of social action." Huxley's slighting reference to Arnold as one of the "Levites of Culture" prompted the latter's retort in one of his *Discourses in America*, "Literature and Science," in which, admitting some of Huxley's contentions, he insisted that Greek and Latin writers "have a fortifying, and elevating, and quickening, and suggestive power, capable of wonderfully helping us to relate the results of science to our need for conduct, our need for beauty. . . . And the more that men's minds are cleared, the more that the results of science are frankly accepted, the more that poetry and eloquence come to be received and studied as what in truth they really are—the criticism of life by gifted men, alive and active with extraordinary power at an unusual number of points—so much the more will the value of humane letters, and of art also, which is an utterance of life . . . be felt and acknowledged, and their place in education be secured."

This famous passage at arms had its background of action in the universities. During the decades of the seventies and eighties, both Oxford and Cambridge were fulfilling Newman's idea that "universities are the natural centers of intellectual movements." Oxford, in particular, continued as a theater of bold speculative discussion. Conflicting winds of doctrine met and modified each other: Rationalism, stimulated by John Stuart Mill's *Logic*,[11] Positivism, Hegelianism, Aestheticism, and Imperialism had each its champions. Fresh ideas freely circulated, creating an atmosphere in which classical authors were reinterpreted. The abolition of religious tests for fellows and tutors at Oxford, Cambridge, and Durham (1871), the beginning of Cambridge extra-mural teaching (1873), were preludes to the Universities Act of 1877. The founding of women's colleges in both old universities during the eighties, and generous scholarships awarded for academic merit, marked other signs of the influences of national thinking on Oxford and Cambridge.

Oxford's devotion to Aristotle as the chief organon of its intellectual discipline yielded to Benjamin Jowett's persistent crusade for the inclusion of Plato. This innovation, with the concomitant introduction of the study of Hegel, had immense effects upon the Oxford mind, tending towards greater pliancy, greater susceptibility to new causes. John Ruskin, brought back to Oxford as the first incumbent of the newly established Slade Professorship of Art (1870), vigorously exhorted his university audiences to their responsibilities in constructing a nobler England. For thirteen years (1871 to 1884) he expounded his ideals of beauty, of duty, and of comprehensive social and economic reconstruction. Scanning perilous horizons, he made his hearers keenly conscious of collisions of capital and labor, the rawness and threats of existing industrial England, and of the social coma of the masses. "Life without dignity is guilt," Ruskin urged, "and industry without art is brutality." During his Slade professorship, he tempered his burning denunciations with the comforting gospel of the holiness of work, when workmen, inspired by piety, loyalty, and noble aspiration, glorified God in their craftsmanship. He addressed himself to two audiences: to university students and (through a series of letters collected in *Fors Clavigera*) to workingmen throughout England. Back of all his books lies the mind of a teacher: as he became aware of imminent

11 Frances W. Knickerbocker, *Free Minds: John Morley and His Friends* (Harvard University Press, 1943).

social disaster after his experience in 1848, his mind played increasingly on the urgency of the need of a right education. His thoughts on the subject were culled by William Jolly, an inspector of schools, who published them in *Ruskin on Education* (1894).

With William Morris, his chief disciple, Ruskin supplied Oxford and England with a new vision of society from which great national art would issue as the expression of inner, moral attitudes: of reverence, of humility, of joy in creative work. Though their social philosophy verged towards collectivism, its power lay in Christian motives. In practical efforts, they attempted to realize their ideas: Ruskin in his Guild of St. George, and Morris in his workshops. Ruskin's permanent memorial in Oxford is the workingman's college there which bears his name: it remains a symbol of the conjunction of two main lines of aspiration in the Victorian era, the instruction of working classes and the inculcation of culture.

VI

Victorian education thus became the arena of three rival forces: of anxiety concerning the unpredictable power of the restless lower classes which middle-class spokesmen believed might be alleviated by nationally diffused instruction; of the demand by workingmen themselves for higher education; and of militant resistance by old established institutions of learning to preserve their inherited concept of culture against encroachments by utilitarians, humanitarians, and economic adventurers. Within the area of controversy and movement, Victorians of all varieties matched their earnestness and energy, agreeing in the faith that education would accomplish a more adequate solution of economic and social tensions than reliance on any form of precipitate violence. In its more admirable forms, this faith expressed ideals of life in a society traditionally committed to the will for good in compulsions of necessity, when necessity was clearly demonstrated by exercise of reason in a condition of freedom. Crises like Chartism and the Reform Bills intensified the discussion, providing occasions for legislative action in solidifying advances in educational vision and practice. Impact of these forces not only raised the intellectual level of the populace but vastly widened the range of literary interest and diversified taste.

Humanists believed that education was incomplete if limited to the accumulation of miscellaneous facts, to appease curiosity, or to master a skill which earned one's daily bread. What gave true worth to education, they thought, was a spiritually directed idea which inspired a search for perfection in all phases of human need: an attitude to which they gave the name "culture." Truly defined, in the light of long experience, education is the process in which culture motivates and shapes the unceasing adjusting of the whole state of individuals and of society. It was aptly summarized by John Morley, statesman son of Oxford, who, addressing an audience of laborers at a mechanics institute, stated: "The great need in modern culture, which is scientific in method, rationalistic in spirit, and utilitarian in purpose, is to find some effective agency for cherishing within us the ideal. Literature alone will not make us good citizens; it will not make us a good man. History affords too many proofs that scholarship and learning by no means purge men of acrimony, of vanity, of arrogance, of a murderous tenacity about trifles. Nor would I pretend for a moment that literature can be any substitute for life and action. . . . It is life that is the great educator. But the parcel of books, if they are well chosen, reconcile us to this discipline, they interpret this virtue and this justice; they awaken within us the diviner mind, and rouse us to a consciousness of what is best in others and ourselves."[12]

In an effort to attain a satisfying mode of action for the democratic process, Victorians found education to be a clue to stabilizing divergent, and frequently conflicting, political and economic claims. It became, indeed, a medium of the era's main effort: to accommodate a conservative national mind to new conditions forced by new tensions in

[12] Morley, *Miscellanies*, Vol. I, "Books."

England, and by catastrophic events abroad, during a period in which she experienced a spectacular rise in international power through her commercial and industrial supremacy. But, by maintaining its lines of communication with its past, by restraining those who veered towards a complete abandonment to materialism, Victorian education developed the humanizing power of man in society through inculcating the idea of culture.

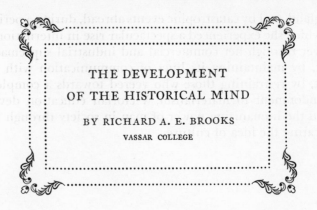

THE DEVELOPMENT
OF THE HISTORICAL MIND

BY RICHARD A. E. BROOKS
VASSAR COLLEGE

A VIVID measure of the popularity of history in Victorian England can be found in the check for £20,000 written by Longmans to Macaulay for royalties on the third and fourth volumes of his *History of England* eleven weeks after their publication.[1] A less vivid but perhaps more significant measure is found in the development of the schools of modern history at Oxford and Cambridge from their humble status in 1800 to being the most popular schools today, for Macaulay was a statesman and man of letters and the present schools are the training grounds for professional historians.

But these schools may perhaps also represent other values accorded to history. A. L. Rowse, Fellow of All Souls College, Oxford, states that "history is of the utmost importance at the universities, as a preparation for the teaching profession, the Civil Service, our political leadership in its highest sense, leaders of the press and public opinion, no less than for politicians. A knowledge of history is indispensable to the higher direction of society; that is why it is especially important in higher education, and the higher

[1] Sir Charles Firth, *A Commentary on Macaulay's History of England* (London, 1933), p. 13. Sir Charles does not make clear that the sum did not wholly represent accrued royalties. I am reliably informed that it was partially advanced royalties.

130

up the more important."[2] He goes on to say that "The truth is that without the sense of human history life as we know it would be unthinkable; history is as fundamental to our lives as that. It is only through a knowledge of history that our own brief lives—such a short span of experience—become one with the record of the human race; it is only through history that we can know anything of the record and can share it. The life of the individual breaks its barriers and becomes coterminous with humanity. Bound as our lives are to the tyranny of time, it is through what we know of history that we are delivered from our bonds and escape—into time."[3]

While it might be remarked that in earlier times literature and the scriptures helped to hand on the story of the past and to make man a trifle less lonely in the present, it is obvious that today history, like many other human activities, has become a specialized study and that it holds an important place in modern consciousness. As M. R. Cohen has said, "the extension of the scope of history throughout the nineteenth century was one of the major events in the intellectual life of Europe."[4]

There had been great historians even before the eighteenth century; and that century itself had its great historians, saw history become interesting to a wider public, and handed on to its successor more skillful methods of historical study than it had inherited. But the more rigorous methods of examining historical documents which the nineteenth century developed and the wider variety of objects and fields of human activity which came within the province of the historian as evidence of man's past, gave a remarkable stimulus to the writing of history and to the public's interest in it. At the same time, too, there were other factors which played—as cause, as effect, and as interacting cause-and-effect—on the study and use of history to produce important results in many phases of European

[2] *The Use of History* (New York, 1948), p. 18.
[3] *Ibid.*, p. 30.
[4] *The Meaning of Human History* (La Salle, Illinois, 1947), p. 14.

life; and not the least interesting are those on English literature, criticism, and scholarship.

Thus, though England did not enjoy that hegemony in historiography in the nineteenth century which she did in industry and politics, one might consider some of the inter-relationships between history and English literature while being mainly concerned with the latter. At the beginning of our century, it would have required temerity for a student of literature to make such an attempt; but contemporary criticism of the theories of history—which, gaining momentum in Germany toward the end of the last century, has recently engaged the attention of English and American philosophers and historians—rather emboldens one to try. Let us briefly narrate part of the sequence of events in the writing of history in the nineteenth century, especially as this relates to the contention between the professional historians and men of letters who wrote histories; stating some of the happenings in the area common to historiography and literature, especially as this area became increasingly accessible to an ever larger public in the middle and lower classes, with no invidious connotation attached to "middle class" and "lower class"; pointing out possible studies which might gain from such a consideration; and evaluating some of the gains and losses in the study of English caused or occasioned by the spread of historical awareness and by the nineteenth century's concept and development of the historical method. If my own ignorances had not limited me to English literature and historiography, the profuse, rich, and complex growth of European historiography and literature would have done so. Lastly, it ought to be said that this is written from a point of view (maybe it would be more correct to say bias) that is tentative and can perhaps be described as that of a humanist who is interested in science.

I I

G. P. Gooch's *History and Historians in the Nineteenth Century* makes unnecessary here an extensive retelling of the development of Victorian historiography. And while later historical thinking has given different significances to this development, none can deny the growth of English historical scholarship, even while admitting that the universities were tardy in recognizing the significance of contemporary German historical scholarship.

Without belittling the great influence of Gibbon, Hume, and Robertson, it can rightly be said that the Romantic movement gave a strong impetus to interest in history in England and on the continent in the first half of the century and that the most important figure in this respect is Sir Walter Scott. If Thomas Carlyle disparaged the historical value of the Waverley novels, and if Carlyle's contemporary, Leopold von Ranke, said that the differences between Commines and *Quentin Durward* led him to become a historian, Scott most deeply affected the mind of the French historian, Augustin Thierry, who as a boy had had his imagination fired by Chateaubriand.[5] (Gooch says that in France in 1802 Chateaubriand's *La Génie du Christianisme* was "an event in politics and religion, in historiography and literature."[6]) The antiquarianism associated with the Romantic movement in England and Germany paved the way to the reading public. The Romantic movement produced romantic historiography in England—that is, history written usually by men of letters who, though they did much research in preparation for their work, were unacquainted with the newer methods of scrutinizing historical evidence and who wrote histories with dramatic narratives, which bore a strong impress of the author's philosophy, and which espoused causes. Carlyle, Macaulay, and Froude are the outstanding historians of this type, historians whom Gooch calls amateurs and Trevelyan literary historians; and J. R. Green's *A Short History of the English People* can be termed the finest single volume. Of this book Gooch writes: "The publication of the 'Short History' in 1874 forms an epoch in historiography. The

[5] Gooch, *History and Historians in the Nineteenth Century* (London, Toronto, and New York, 1935), pp. 170-171. The gist of the book, which was first published in 1913, is to be found in Gooch's "The Growth of Historical Science," *Cambridge Modern History* (Cambridge, 1910), XII, 816-850.

[6] *Ibid.*, p. 162.

English-speaking world received the first coherent and intelligible account of its own past. The hero of the book was the people. . . . Dynasties come and go, battles are won and lost, but the people remain. . . . His work possesses the living interest of a biography and the dramatic unity of an epic. . . . Hundreds of thousands of all ages became for the first time intelligently interested in the history of their own country."[7] Green, however, might be called a beneficiary of the scientific school of historiography if he is not considered a happy fusion of both schools. He has been described as a "picturesque historian"; and though he was not a professional historian—he was a clergyman and, after his health failed, librarian at Lambeth—he was intimate with the professional historians at Oxford, where Stubbs was his great admirer.

The scientific method of studying history developed and flourished in Germany in the first half of the nineteenth century. Its pioneer was the philologist Niebuhr, who "raised history from a subordinate position to the dignity of an independent science."[8] The examination of historical evidence became progressively more rigorous, and the historian aimed at complete objectivity in the treatment of his material. (Ranke's phrase, *wie es eigentlich gewesen ist*—"as it actually happened," is a convenient and often quoted summary of this aim.) Philology provided the key to many locked rooms of man's recorded past, and it made brighter many rooms heretofore dimly lighted. Political history, which in its turn had been an advance over the compiling of annals, was augmented by legal, institutional, social, and cultural history; and through systematic study evidence of man's past was wrested from language, myth, archives, coins, inscriptions, and archaeological excavations. Germany produced a succession of brilliant historians, of whom the century considered Ranke and Mommsen the giants and to whom went to school the historians of France, the United States, and, somewhat belatedly in the latter half of the century, England. Giving powerful support to this historical method and its authority with the public

7 *Ibid.*, pp. 354-355.   8 *Ibid.*, p. 14.

was the work of the geologists—who vastly altered western man's temporal horizons—and of the biologists. (Darwin's work only set the keystone in the evolutionary thinking of his predecessors, and through Huxley it reached a greater audience than the scientists and philosophers had.) As the consciousness of history became more widespread and the historical method became more generally used, the study of history became a more popular but more specialized study at the universities, and the writers of histories began to be almost exclusively university professors. The indisputable achievement of greater objectivity did not, however, free the professional historians from bias: nationalism, for instance, appears in English, French, and German histories. Finally, as the century drew to a close, the professional historian was the recognized superior of the amateur, but his writings were less and less read by the general reader. Trevelyan comments on the situation thus: "What was wrong with the historical reaction at the end of Victoria's reign, was not the positive stress it laid on the need for scientific method in weighing evidence, but its negative repudiation of the literary art, which was declared to have nothing whatever to do with the historian's task."[9] And Rowse, perhaps with his eye more on contemporary developments of the same situation, says, "Of course, all this [the insistence that history is a science] made history much more difficult to write—at any rate, well—and much less interesting to read. On the other hand, since this point of view attached little importance to literary quality, it meant a great increase in the amount of history books turned out by people who did not know how to write. Never was there such a quantity of raw hunks of historical research, malformed, undigested, indigestible, as poured forth from the presses."[10]

For a variety of reasons the "literary" historians held sway longer in England than they did on the continent, but they did more to stimulate interest in history than did their European confreres. (Gooch says that, except for Macau-

[9] G. M. Trevelyan, *History and the Reader* (London, 1945), p. 11.
[10] *Op. cit.*, pp. 87-88.

lay, no one during the first half of the century had "given such an impetus to historical study as Carlyle."[11]) Unquestionably, one reason for this is that they wrote well, yet the professional historian's slow rise to preeminence was due in the main to the state of the study of modern history at Oxford and Cambridge. The Regius chairs of modern history at these universities were established in 1724; but "at Oxford in 1850, out of 1500 or 1600 students, the average attendance at the modern history course was eight."[12] Cambridge, which by the end of the century became the center of modern historical study in England, fared somewhat better. John Symonds was the first occupant of the Cambridge chair to discharge his duties (1778); and Seely, appointed in 1868, produced "the first important historical work written by a holder of the Cambridge Chair" and was "the first scholar of front rank to hold the post, and the first to realize the immense significance of German scholarship."[13] Besides, "the union of Church and State in England and the establishment of the Regius professorships to be filled by appointees of the Crown . . . [gave] rise to a very real cause of dissatisfaction among" the historians.[14] A novelist, poet, and clergyman, Kingsley could be professor of modern history at Cambridge; Stubbs, whose chief interests before being appointed Regius professor of modern history at Oxford had been medieval history and who had earlier been passed over for that chair because of his religious views, left his chair to become Bishop of Chester; and, lastly, each university preferred to appoint one of its own men. The English distrust of specialization has its weaknesses as well as its strengths. The appointment of Acton to the chair of modern history at Cambridge in 1895 marked

[11] *Op. cit.*, p. 323.

[12] J. W. Adamson, "Education," *Cambridge History of English Literature* (Cambridge and New York, 1917), XIV, 464.

[13] Gooch, *Studies in Modern History* (London, Toronto, and New York, 1931), p. 313 *et passim*.

[14] L. M. Salmon, *Why Is History Rewritten?* (New York, 1929), p. 118. Pages 118-123, from which the data of the next sentence were taken, give a full account of these difficulties. Miss Salmon's chapter on historiography in England is worth attention.

the accomplishment of a change, for he was not only a distinguished historian but a Roman Catholic.

The star of the "literary" historian apparently set with the bitter controversy over Froude's *History of England from 1529 to the Death of Elizabeth,* in which the professional historian Freeman led the attack. Though Stubbs, who had found fault with some of Froude's work as a historian, had praised its strong points in 1876, and though Trevelyan had taken up the cudgels for Carlyle in 1899,[15] the educated public came to think that the field was indisputably the scientific historian's. A succeeding generation of historians has begun to revise this view; and it is interesting to note that R. G. Collingwood, A. L. Rowse, and M. R. Cohen, who do not share the same philosophy of history, all three speak well of Macaulay, Carlyle, and Froude. This does not mean, however, that students of literature are barred from further work on these "literary" historians. For example, though Carlyle has fared better than most of them, it has recently been pointed out by a critic that he needs even closer scrutiny than the latest scholarship has given to his writing of history.[16] Froude and Macaulay await further treatment; Lytton Strachey's chapters on Froude and Macaulay in *Portraits in Miniature* and Professor Bald's article on Froude in *The Nineteenth Century and After* do not seem to me to have exhausted the field. Lytton Strachey, however, illustrates some of the pitfalls for one who would undertake new estimates. A beneficiary of the Cambridge school of scientific history, he had a strong Edwardian bias against the Victorians. And there is truth, I think, in Leonard Bacon's observation that "Strachey was really a novelist *manqué* and belongs in Thackeray's street —by no means in Gibbon's."[17]

15 Salmon, *op. cit.,* p. 110, n. 1, gives Stubbs's words. Trevelyan's defense of Carlyle is his "Carlyle as an Historian," *Nineteenth Century,* XLVI (1899), 493-503.

16 René Wellek, "Carlyle and the Philosophy of History," *Philological Quarterly,* XXIII (1944), 55-76.

17 "An Eminent Post-Victorian," *Yale Review,* XXX (1941-42), 324.

III

Besides the work of the "literary" and the professional historians in spreading an awareness of the past in Victorian England there were the historical societies, the historical study of literature, the museums, historical painting, and historical novels. The value of these as factors in the writing of social history has been amply proved by contemporary historians' use of them; what concerns us here is their bearing on literary scholarship and appreciation.

Since Elizabethan times there had been antiquarian and learned societies in England, but the second quarter of the nineteenth century witnessed an unparalleled flowering of historical societies which was characteristic of the Victorian period. The revival of interest in the medieval which the Romantics helped to create made Englishmen even more conscious than eighteenth-century scholars had been that much of Anglo-Saxon and Middle English literature was still unavailable; and it also produced a wave of bibliomania. These two forces joined with the renewed interest in history to bring into existence what R. H. Steeves[18] has called book clubs and general publishing societies, whose aims and scope testify to the widening concept of the historical. From the Roxburghe Club, an exclusive society for the publication of very limited editions of old English literature, evolved such societies as the Camden, Chetham, English Historical, Hakluyt, Parker, and Surtees which were less exclusive and dilettante than their prototype. Concerned with publishing pre-seventeenth century material bearing on civil and ecclesiastical as well as literary history, they made available a substantial body of Old and Middle English literature—among which were the *Towneley Mysteries*, Bishop Bale's *King John*, and the *Ancren Riwle*. At the same time arose philological and text societies particularly concerned with English literature considered from a scholarly and historical point of view. Though most of these sprang up in the forties, there is evident in them after

[18] *Learned Societies and English Literary Scholarship* (New York, 1913), p. 98. For the material of this paragraph I am greatly indebted to pages 98-203 of Steeves's book.

Furnival established the Early English Text Society in 1864
a wholly new scholarly tradition which was largely derived
from Germany. They became indispensable to contemporary scholarship, and with them were associated most of the
famous Victorian scholars of English.

These societies, however, reflect the growth of the historical mind among the educated. Other developments
show a diffusion of a sense of the past among the middle and
lower-middle classes, and they enable one to measure it.
The most conspicuous element in this connection is the
amazing increase of literacy in England during the century.
The product of many complex forces, this increase was
affected by mechanical developments. As an Irish literary
historian noted in 1878: "The influence of the great change
—the substitution of the steam *printing-press* for the hand-
worked *printing-press*—has been felt in every corner of the
land, where a cheap book or penny newspaper has found
its way."[19] Cheap books began appearing in 1823 when
"several London booksellers . . . commenced the publication of cheap weekly sheets, either containing portions of
some standard book; or a series of miscellaneous literary
articles, chiefly extracted from other works."[20] This led not
only to Brougham's Society for the Diffusion of Useful
Knowledge but also (through the practice of competition,
which was as common among publishers as among mill
owners) to the *Penny Magazine*, whose circulation of over
50,000 opened up the field of magazine publishing.[21] Among
the cheap books were selections from English literature, of
which perhaps the best known was Robert Chambers'

19 W. F. Collier, *A History of English Literature* (London, 1878), p. 440.
Collier is quoting J. Hamilton Fyfe's *Triumphs of Invention and Discovery*
(from a passage which describes the printing of *The Times* in 1872).

20 Robert Chambers, *History of the English Language and Literature*
(Edinburgh, 1837; 4th ed.), pp. 269-270. First published in 1836, this is the
first history to deal with all types of English literature and to be concerned
solely with them.

21 Chambers, pp. 269-270, has an account of the history of cheap books
from 1823 to 1835. He says (p. 270) that *Constable's Miscellany*, which
started publication in 1826, was "the first work actually to be published in
which original literature was made to depend for remuneration on a multitude of purchasers attracted by cheapness."

Cyclopædia of English Literature, which first appeared in 1844. On a far higher artistic level and even more famous is Palgrave's *Golden Treasury,* which "exercised a decisive influence from its publication" in 1861.

Histories of literature began appearing in ever greater numbers for increasingly wide and diverse audiences, which ranged from university students to those in mechanics' institutions. Professor Wellek's *The Rise of English Literary History* treats that subject up to the end of the eighteenth century. Of Thomas Warton, who is the culminating figure of the study, Wellek writes on page 201, "All the major problems of nineteenth-century literary history were formulated by Warton, even if his superstructure of ideas did not always properly control his materials." In a critique of literary history[22] Wellek has briefly commented on some of the major nineteenth-century writers of literary history; and he has pointed out, quite correctly, that some of these writers treated "literature as mere document for the illustration of national and social history" and that others, though recognizing that literature is first and foremost an art, "seem to be unable to write history."[23] Though, with the exception of J. A. Symonds, their use of the evolutionary concept was of dubious value, by the seventies they had —thanks to the labors of their predecessors—treated the full range of English literature. Certainly Arber was exaggerating when, in the preface to the first volume of *An English Garner* (1877), he wrote that "few of us adequately realize the immense literature which has descended from our ancestors." The histories aimed at large publics stress the pictorial aspects of the past; the more scholarly are organized around one or more ideas (Taine's history is a good example); and there is a development, parallel with that in historiography, from the romantic to the scientific.[24]

22 René Wellek, "Literary History" in *Literary Scholarship: Its Aims and Methods* (Chapel Hill, 1941), pp. 91-130. It is a pleasure to express my gratitude for Professor Wellek's help and generosity, which is all the more appreciated since he is working on a further study of Victorian literary history that will bring his study down through Hallam.

23 *Ibid.,* p. 116.

24 Cf. Norman Foerster, "The Study of Letters," *Literary Scholarship: Its Aims and Methods,* p. 9.

One does not hear again the note struck in 1835 by Chateaubriand in the preface to his *Sketches of English Literature*:

"In this Review of English Literature I have treated at considerable length of Milton, because it was written expressly on account of the Paradise Lost. I analyse his different works, I show that revolutions have approximated Milton to us; that he is become a man of our times. . . .

"I ought to premise that in this Historical View I have not stuck close to my subject. I have treated of everything— the present, the past, the future; I digress hither and thither. When I meet with the middle ages, I talk of them; when I run foul of the reformation, I dwell upon it; when I come to the English revolution, it reminds me of our own, and I advert to the actors and events of the latter. If an English royalist is thrown into jail, I think of the cell which I occupied at the prefecture of police. The English poets lead me to the French poets; Lord Byron brings to my recollection my exile in England, my walks at Harrow on the Hill, and my travels to Venice—and so the rest of the book."

Only rarely does one encounter such blatant moralizing as one finds in Chambers' *Cyclopædia of English Literature* (aimed at a middle-class audience) in this comment on Theodore Hook: "He obtained the distinction he coveted, in the notice and favour of the great and fashionable world; for this he sacrificed the fruits of his industry and the independence of genius; he lived in a round of distraction and gaiety, illuminated by his wit and talents, and he died a premature death, the victim of disappointment, debt, and misery. This personal account is the true 'handwriting on the wall,' to warn genius and integrity in the middle classes against hunting after or copying the vices of fashionable dissipation and splendour."[25]

Related to the increase of literacy and literary history is the teaching of English, which became more and more historical in approach. English became an important subject in the curriculum of nonconformist academies in the eight-

[25] Chambers, *Cyclopaedia* (Edinburgh, 1844), II, 534.

eenth century,[26] and after 1858 was increasingly important in the growing secondary schools.[27] From the early days of Oxford and Cambridge, rhetoric had treated literature, albeit mainly the classics; Sir Henry Spelman established the first lectureship in Anglo-Saxon at Cambridge in 1623;[28] and poetry and Anglo-Saxon were given chairs at Oxford in the eighteenth century;[29] but English did not become a pass subject at Oxford until 1873 and an honours one until 1893.[30] The universities and colleges in Scotland and Ireland and London University were ahead of Oxford and Cambridge in this respect.[31] The influence of the scientific approach in scholarship associated with Germany became evident in the increased study of philology.[32] Whether the increased teaching of English tended, as the decades passed,

[26] Stephen Potter, *The Muse in Chains* (London, 1937), p. 108.

[27] The Cambridge Local Examinations, instituted in 1858, made English a major subject to "provide an adequate test and stimulus for schools which lie between the great Public Schools and the National schools, and to raise their standard of instruction" (J. B. Mullinger, *A History of the University of Cambridge*, London, 1888, p. 214).

[28] Wellek, *The Rise of English Literary History*, p. 22. The lectureship lapsed on the death of the first incumbent, Abraham Wheelock, in 1653. (*D. N. B.*, xx, 1354.)

[29] The Chair of Poetry was established in 1708 (*D. N. B.*, article on Henry Birkhead). The Rawlinson Chair of Anglo-Saxon was established in 1795 (C. E. Mallet, *A History of the University of Oxford*, London, 1927, III, 127). It is worth noting here that Matthew Arnold was the first holder of the Chair of Poetry at Oxford to deliver his lectures in English, and that he held the chair from 1857 to 1867.

[30] Mallet, III, 453-454. At Cambridge the first examination for the Medieval and Modern Language Tripos was held in 1886 (Mullinger, *op. cit.*, p. 209). Cf. also Sir John Firth, *Modern Language at Oxford* (London, 1929).

[31] Chairs of history and English literature were established at the three Queen's Colleges in Ireland (at Belfast, Cork, and Galway) from their founding in 1845. The Chair of English at Trinity College, Dublin, was created in 1867; that of English Language and Literature at Glasgow, in 1861. The Merton Professorship of English Language and Literature at Oxford was established in 1885. Even at London, where English "occupied from the first [1836?] an important place in the examination, . . . except for the Quain Chair there was until recently [1920] a comparatively small provision of teaching posts in English." *The Teaching of English in England* (London, 1921), pp. 243-45.

[32] Potter, p. 172. Cf. also Raymond W. Chambers, *Concerning Certain Great Teachers of the English Language* (London, 1923) and *Man's Unconquerable Mind* (London, Toronto, and New York, 1939), pp. 342-408.

to create a finer or more general appreciation of English literature in England is, however, questionable.[33]

Museums and picture galleries played a larger part in diffusing a sense of the past among the urban middle and lower-middle classes than is generally realized. Outside of London, these classes usually had little to stimulate their consciousness of the past visually. There was not the royal and municipal pageantry which is the delight of Londoners; the collections of art which the aristocracy and the wealthy had acquired mostly in the eighteenth century were, even in London, rarely open to the public in the first half of the century;[34] and the Nonconformist chapels everywhere were, on principle, bare of paintings and statues. The Gothic Revival—itself an effect and a subsequent cause of historical awareness—was, I think, less influential in this respect than paintings because it was primarily architectural. (Old buildings, of course, induce a feeling of the past, but the beholder must have some knowledge of iconography or at least of the history of art to get the same sort of awareness of the past he can get from pictures—especially from the anecdotal historical painting of the nineteenth century.) Except for the British Museum, public museums were a nineteenth-century innovation in England; and their use as educational instruments, an American—and largely

[33] Potter maintains that the teaching of English decreased the appreciation of literature. *The Teaching of English in England*, pp. 252 and 256, comments on the indifference to literature prevalent among middle- and working-class people. Writing in the nineteenth century (and, of course, not thinking of England particularly), Jacob Burckhardt says in *Force and Freedom: Reflections on History* (New York, 1943; ed. J. H. Nichols), p. 152: "The greatest innovation in the world is the demand for education as a right of man; it is a disguised demand for comfort."

[34] Even a casual reading of Dr. Waagen's *Treasuries of Art in Great Britain* (London, 1854) and *Galleries and Cabinets of Art in Great Britain* (London, 1857) will quickly show that the average middle-class Englishman had small chance of seeing these private collections. Waagen was director of the Royal Galleries of Pictures in Berlin, knew Eastlake (president of the Royal Academy) and others prominent in art circles in England, and was thus able to get quick *entrée* to these private galleries. Cf. also Peter Cunningham, *London as It Is* (London, 1865), p. 11, for a list of the private galleries in London which were either closed entirely to the public or which required the owner's written permission for admission.

twentieth-century—practice.[35] London led the way here, but Manchester established a city art gallery even when its labor and housing conditions were beginning to cause concern among thoughtful people.[36] Most cities, however, did not acquire art galleries until the late eighties.[37] The lack of such galleries in the provinces is inferred in *Alton Locke* (chapter 25) when one of the laudable acts of Lord Ellerton was throwing "open his picture gallery, not only to the inhabitants of the neighboring town, but what (strange to say) seemed to strike the party [at Dean Winnstay's home] as still more remarkable, to the laborers of his own village."

In these museums and galleries were paintings which certainly reflect both the growing awareness of the past and the growing nationalism. By 1900 the National Gallery possessed twenty-three paintings by Englishmen of scenes from English history.[38] Fortunately the aesthetic quality of English nineteenth-century historical painting does not concern us here; its efficacy in helping people visualize the past does. This was a result of Benjamin West's innovation,

35 Most museums then could have been described in the words of a little boy I once knew: "You go in and you see 'em." For those interested in a segment of the sociology of art Ruskin's writings on museums might well merit a monograph. Cf. "On the Present State of Modern Art, with Reference to the Advisable Arrangement of a National Gallery" (1867), "The Opening of the Crystal Palace" (1854), and "A Museum or Picture Gallery: Its Function and Formation" (1880). But see also R. H. Wilenski, *John Ruskin* (New York, 1938), pp. 369-383.

36 The National Art Gallery was founded in 1824, the Manchester Corporation Gallery in 1829. The Soane Museum came to the city of London in 1835. The Dulwich Gallery, opened in 1814, was the chief public gallery in England in the early years of the century; it had no historical paintings. (Cf. *Catalogue of the Pictures of the Dulwich Gallery*, 1926.) Browning's connection with this gallery is well known; Ruskin used it; and Kingsley praised it in *Alton Locke* (ch. 6).

37 The Bristol Museum and Art Gallery was founded in 1835; the Walker Art Gallery in Liverpool, in 1877. The galleries in Birmingham, Leeds, Sheffield, and York were founded after 1885. (This latter is based on a comparison of Patterson's *Guide Book to the United Kingdom*, 1885, and Baedeker's *Great Britain*, 1890 and 1901.)

38 Cf. Sir Edward J. Poynter, ed., *The National Gallery* (London, 1900), III. Paintings of legendary subjects, like Millais' "The Knight Errant," or of scenes from historical fiction, like Yeames's "Amy Robsart," are not included in this figure. Scott and Bulwer Lytton supplied painters with subjects of this last named type.

painting historical scenes naturalistically rather than in conventionalized classic décor. The following, from a popular Victorian book about English painters, graphically illustrates the interest in this type of painting early in the century: "It [Eastlake's painting of Napoleon on the deck of the "Bellerophon," made while she was in Plymouth on her way to St. Helena] was nothing remarkable in the way of art, but it was a good likeness of the caged lion, with his uniform and decorations, also painted from the life, for they had been sent on shore for the painter's service. Five Plymouth gentlemen commissioned a large repetition of it, which was exhibited in London and all over the provinces, and brought the painter not only fame but £1000 in solid cash."[39] Lithography made possible the reproduction of historical paintings in color in secondary school history textbooks.

Whether paintings and galleries—especially through the constantly improved methods of reproducing pictures— affected literature by bringing about a decrease in the type of description so dear to Scott and his readers (and not so dear to the contemporary reader) is uncertain;[40] but there are interrelations between the two arts. The effect of the Elgin Marbles on Keats is well known; and though we are aware of the influence on Browning of the Dulwich Gallery, and of pictures elsewhere, it could stand further investigation. There is a field of study for students who have actual experience in both the arts, for I believe that there may be a close connection in method in the case of an artist who both writes and paints or plays a musical instrument. Thackeray, Ruskin, Rossetti, Morris, and Samuel Butler were painters; Hardy was an architect; and Browning and Hopkins were at least talented amateurs in music.

Most important, however, of all these media in spreading a sense of the past was the historical novel, which sometimes

[39] Allan Cunningham, *The Lives of the Most Eminent British Painters* (London, 1890), III, 314.

[40] I am inclined to think that the camera is a factor in the rise of abstract painting in our time and that the movie camera may have had an analogous effect—qualitative if not quantitative—on description in the work of serious writers.

did not share the opprobrium of the novel among the more strictly religious. Despite the admittedly great influence of the "literary" historians, I think more people got their knowledge of the past from historical novels than from histories. Certainly, English schoolboys often absorbed more history from Scott, Lytton, Marryat, and even Henty than they learned from their textbooks, though they had a guilty feeling that this was not "real" history. Gooch and Trevelyan have essays on the historical novel, but most historians have passed it by. In 1940, however, Sir John Marriot, a historian who admits to having had a prejudice against historical novels though he read novels as a diversion, published *English History in English Fiction*; and in his opinion the historical novelists come off rather well in their treatment of history. Where, in the seventies, Sir Leslie Stephen, a man of letters, could say "Sir F. Palgrave says somewhere that 'historical novels are mortal enemies to history,' and we should venture to add that they are mortal enemies to fiction,"[41] Sir John Marriot, a professional historian, says: "To the Temple of Clio are many different avenues. Constitutional and legal history obviously provides no appropriate material for the historical novelist. Would any novelist dream of making his story revolve around the origins of the English Parliament, or the evolution of the cabinet system? Shakespeare in *King John*, while making much play with the relations of the King and the Pope, never mentions Magna Carta. . . . The historical novel may on the other hand be an invaluable adjunct to the study of political, social, or even economic history. What historian would, for instance, write the Social History of the nineteenth century without reading Disraeli's *Sybil*, Mrs. Gaskell's *Mary Barton*, Kingsley's *Yeast*, or even Anthony Trollope's *Barchester Towers*, or John Galsworthy's *Forsyte Saga*?"[42]

41 *Hours in a Library* (First Series) (London, 1887; 2nd ed.), p. 240. To the second half of Sir Leslie's statement the contemporary historical novel would make one say, "Marry, and amen."

42 *English History in English Fiction* (London, 1940), p. 1. Sir John does not limit himself to novelists who portrayed an age earlier than their own

As A. T. Sheppard notes, "the Golden Age of the historical novel began with 'Waverley' and ended within a quarter of a century of Scott's death," and though an occasional novel of worth appeared, the historical novel fell into disfavor until the seventies, when it became fashionable for a time.[43] Other than Scott, no nineteenth-century English writer of major status confined himself to the historical novel, but studies of the lesser figures might be profitable. Professor Carl J. Weber has found "the shadow . . . of Ainsworth on many of the pages of the Wessex novels."[44] What might be even more profitable than a study of the historical novel in England during this century would be one that, not confining itself to a genre, examined many writers' use of the historical, especially in the light of more recent concepts of history. Almost every Victorian writer of note—Browning, Dickens, Thackeray, Eliot, Tennyson, and Hardy—made his *devoirs* at least to the current interest in history. Now, it is obvious that Scott and the romantic historiography of the first half of the century should find their reflections in Browning's historical dramas, Macaulay's *Lays of Ancient Rome*, Bulwer Lytton's historical novels, and even *A Tale of Two Cities*, *Henry Esmond*, and *The Virginians*, and also in the historical paintings of Turner, Stanfield, Maclise, Wilkie, Eastlake, and Huggins. But, without putting undue stress on mere correlation,[45] one might examine the possible relationships between the resurgence of historical painting in the eighties and nineties (Lady Butler, Gow, Orchardson, Pettie, Schetky, Waller, and Whitcombe), the popularity of the historical novel in the seventies which Sheppard notes, and Tennyson's historical dramas, Browning's "Hervé Riel," and "Clive," and Hardy's *The Trumpet Major* and

---

(a definition of a historical novel which seems valid to me), as is indicated from the novels mentioned in the quotation.

[43] *The Art and Practice of the Historical Novel* (London, 1930), p. 65. Sheppard carries further H. Butterfield's *The Historical Novel* (Cambridge, 1924).

[44] "Ainsworth and Hardy," *RES*, XVII (1941), 193-200.

[45] Cf. M. R. Cohen, *op. cit.*, p. 101, for a brief discussion of the limitations of repeated succession as a principle of causation.

The Dynasts (all of which were published between 1871
and 1904)—and this at a time when the romantic historian
was discredited. Had the Franco-Prussian War anything to
do with a resurgence of nationalism in England at this
time? Was it in some way related to Victorian satisfaction
over England's imperial greatness? One might also examine
whether there is any significance in various authors' choice
of historical material. The impact of Napoleon is noticeable
everywhere: even Meredith has a poem on him. Carlyle
made many references to Napoleon or his battles in *Frederick the Great*, quite forgetting that at least half his readers
did not share his boyhood memories; and *The Dynasts*
shows how long the impact was felt. The use of the Arthu-
rian material and of the Civil War might also bear examination in this connection as well as the influence of changing concept of history from the romantic to the more scientific (measured from *Waverley* to *The Dynasts*).

Nationalism was unquestionably an element in the progressive interest in the historical which is evident in the arts
and agencies treated here. Artists, readers, beholders, and
critics could hardly be expected to be exempt from an influence to which even some of the most severely objective historians succumbed. But nationalism is a broad term which
extends from patriotism to all that is evil in chauvinism.
And patriotism, as Virginia Woolf observed in *Three Guin-
eas*, begins with a love of a particular spot of land. Might
it, therefore, be possible that among relatively rootless city
folk in Victorian England the national past as they saw and
read it became a kind of substitute for the *lares* and *penates*
of the countryman and the dweller in a small town?

IV

Our indebtedness to historical scholarship is so great that
it is difficult to know where to begin an acknowledgment.
Perhaps all that is necessary to indicate the gains is to point
to the *New English Dictionary* and repeat the epitaph on
Christopher Wren's tomb in St. Paul's. Our editorial procedures, monographs dealing with limited aspects of a
subject, and cooperative scholarship are further evidences

of our obligations to the historians. The less happy effects would appear to arise from the almost inevitable slowness of one branch of scholarship in keeping abreast with even a cognate branch and from an unwise use of historical methods by literary scholars. Any consideration of these less happy effects, however, is proof of the secure place which history now holds in western thought.

The degree to which history is, or is capable of being, a science is as much a matter of debate today as it was in the nineteenth century, but the debate has taken on, quite naturally, aspects other than those it had earlier. So far as the procedures for examining evidence of the past, critically, are concerned, it is generally conceded that history is scientific—that is, subject to verification which is, so far as is humanly possible, free from the biases of the investigator. Here the value of the legacy of the nineteenth century to historical and literary scholars is not in question. The accumulation of fact by researchers of less skill than the great practitioners in both fields has justly drawn down on itself sharp criticism which is scarcely mitigated by the realization that it is a natural result of emulation (if not imitation) of procedures which were spectacularly successful in the natural sciences in the nineteenth century. There has, however, been a modification of the view of the method of scientific induction which Mill held. Modern thought no longer believes that the scientific investigator collects and examines data with an almost blank mind, and in circles outside those of the pure sciences there is increasing awareness of the use of hypotheses made by the scientists.[46] It appears to be generally agreed among historians that in the writing of history a historian, by having to select from among the facts which he has investigated and by having to give them some interpretation, uses procedures similar to those employed by artist and scientist—though in the interpretation the historian resembles the artist more than the

[46] Cf. *Theory and Practice in Historical Study: A report of the Committee on Historiography* (New York, 1946), pp. 31-32, and M. R. Cohen, *op. cit.*, pp. 76-82. The subject is more fully treated in Cohen's *Reason and Nature* (New York, 1931), pp. 115-125.

scientist. Some have held that a historian is objective if he is aware of the principle on which he selects and interprets his material. (The question of the responsibility of the historian for making and keeping his reader conscious of his principle is a moral one; and the related question of the reader's ability or willingness to keep in mind even a faithful discharge of this responsibility by the historian takes one into the subject of communication.) In practice, if not in theory, means are apt to combine with ends and to lead one into an area in which history, literature, science, and philosophy overlap. How far objectivity can or should keep clear of moral judgments, or even of moral presuppositions, is currently of interest to scientist and historian alike. The extent to which history can become part of a scientific study of man as some sociologists envisage such a study, is a question for historian, sociologists, and philosophers of history to venture into.[47] However these questions are viewed, it is obvious today that the "literary," or non-academic, historian is expected to have a more systematic and self-conscious grasp of his methods than his Victorian forebear.

The contemporary interest in examining the nature and limits of many kinds of specialized knowledge which the last two centuries have made possible, has brought about a vigorous examination of the theories of history. The vigor of the criticism is matched by the diversity of views, and the practising historian finds himself perhaps only less embarrassed by this activity than the literary scholar who strays into the arena. It would appear that the determinism which underlay eighteenth- and nineteenth-century scientific thinking rather naturally led some historians to accept a similar concept for their interpretations. And it led people who, like Spencer, wanted to remake society into an uncritical faith in materialistic determinism, a faith the best of

[47] Cf. F. J. Teggart, *Theory of History* (New Haven, 1925), and also *Theory and Practice in Historical Study*. This latter, a bulletin of the Social Science Research Council, has an excellent bibliography.

Here it is a pleasure to acknowledge my gratitude to my colleagues, Professors Mildred L. Campbell and Evalyn A. Clark of the Department of History at Vassar College, for many valuable suggestions about books on the theory of history.

the historians could not share. The importance of economic determinism in our day tends, however, to overshadow idealistic determinism (of which Hegel's is a good example). Monistic explanations are alluring, and the desire for them seems deeply imbedded in human nature. But beyond making one aware that no man can ever attain the complete objectivity he can conceive and in large measure apply in the natural sciences, the contemporary criticism of monistic theories of history by thinkers as different as Croce, M. R. Cohen, and Sidney Hook—to mention those I am acquainted with—is both an outgrowth of the nineteenth century's development of history and a liberation from dogmatism. Except among those who adhere to an uncritical economic determinism, there has come into existence a tempered and flexible use of determinism by historians, particularly when they are dealing with periods where there is ample documentation.[48]

How far some of the contemporary criticisms of the theory of history might serve to change or illuminate literary scholarship, I am not competent to judge; but I am inclined to think that it might repay us to become aware of some of the criticisms of the nineteenth-century concepts of progress and causation in terms of analogy with geology and biology. R. G. Collingwood's concept of the historical imagination[49] seems to me even more useful to the literary scholar than to the historian as a description of the process of arriving at a synthesis. M. R. Cohen's concept of "polarity and oscillation between opposite poles"[50] seems to me at least an effective corrective to the prevalent idea of evolution as it is applied to human events.

Useful and illuminating as any philosophy of history can be and is (whether in a limited study or in one that takes in a wide sweep of events), the historian must wrestle with what individuals or groups of individuals did. The expanded province of his field sends the historian to ever

[48] Cf. Sidney Hook, *The Hero in History* (New York, 1943), for a study of uncritical uses of determinism in history.
[49] R. G. Collingwood, *The Idea of History* (Oxford, 1946), pp. 231-248.
[50] M. R. Cohen, *The Meaning of Human History*, p. 273.

more complex and remote regions for explanations. His disciplines enable him to make interpretations which are as impersonal as the problems of his times permit. But since human beings are rather more complex than the entities which even the most abtruse contemporary science deals with, the historian confronts the age-old problems that have always confronted the poet and the philosopher— fate, free will, and the nature of man. Though here, unlike the poet, he cannot arrange the sequence of events to suit his pattern, he must, like the poet, rely on sympathy, imagination, and insight. And the literary scholar can do no less.

THE TRADITION OF BURKE

BY FREDERICK L. MULHAUSER

POMONA COLLEGE

THE study of Edmund Burke's influence upon the Victorian writers would be a contribution to the understanding of the intellectual climate of the Victorian period. Although it would be incomplete for a full appreciation of Victorian literature, it would extend remarkably our knowledge of the current of thought during the period, the particular problems which interested Victorian writers, and the kind of thinking which they applied to the problems. Ultimately, it would clarify certain aspects of Victorian social and political thought and lead to a fuller appreciation of the nature of certain authors' minds, the quality of their artistry, and the validity of their contributions to the current of thought of their time.

The Victorian era was an era very much concerned with the affairs of the world. The urgency of the immediate problems raised by the Industrial Revolution and the French Revolution roused the sympathetic interest of many Victorian writers. Some probed the problems more deeply and considered what came to be one of the central questions of the period: the nature of the relationship between the individual man and his institutions, the church, the state, the industrial enterprise, the Friendly Society, or the trade union. One of the central facts of the Victorian period is the growth of England's population from 1800 to

1900, for this growth in numbers complicated the social, political, and economic situations which compelled the attention of the writer. As the fruits of the Industrial Revolution became more and more clearly disappointing to most of the nation, and as the national polity grew so large and so complex that individual action became inadequate, men in England turned to the state for action in their interest. Thus, much of the writing of the Victorian period concerns itself with the nature and origin of the state, its proper and necessary function in society, the relation of the individual to that state, his relation to other institutions, and their relation in turn to the state. The web of eighteenth-century society had been broken open by the great economic and social revolutions, and all men felt the resulting confusion.

In considering their time the Victorians found the writings of Edmund Burke invaluable. Burke's prestige as a statesman, his jealous concern for the welfare of England, and the range and suggestiveness of his observations upon the nature and function of the state explain his attraction for the generations which followed him. His ideas spread like a dye throughout the century, for men turned to Burke for ideas and attitudes which helped them understand important tendencies of their times. Some Victorian writers were directly influenced by Burke's ideas. Disraeli's ideas of the relationship of the church and state, or Matthew Arnold's ideas of the function of the state, for instance, show unmistakable evidence of Burke's influence. In a more general way, certain characteristics of the Victorian times show parallels to concepts or attitudes developed by Burke. The conservative philosophy of gradualism and the appreciation of the importance of emotion in political affairs could be used as illustrations. It is most difficult to determine to what extent Burke influenced these developments, i.e., whether the force of his exposition brought them about, or whether they are the result of native English principles and attitudes, which he had expressed with clarity and force. Finally, perhaps the most tenuous yet most fruitful consideration of all is the nature of the effect of Burke upon the modes and forms of thought of the Victorians. The conservative tradition which he expressed so forcefully directed or colored the thinking of innumerable Victorians, and Burke's approach to national problems became one of the ways of considering contemporary perplexities.

Whether Burke's relation to the Victorian times was one of direct influence, similarity, or intellectual shaping does not call in question the value of the study of Burke to one interested in the development of Victorian England. A study of his works explains and illuminates much of the Victorian social and political writing and the temper of mind and methods of approach which produced that writing.

Although the evaluation of Burke's relation to the characteristic development of Victorian England or to the ways of thought of individual writers will necessarily require thoughtful discrimination, the study of influence is always a difficult and delicate undertaking. Even the study of Burke's direct influence upon nineteenth-century England, it should be pointed out, is complicated by several special difficulties which must not be underestimated. In the first place, Burke was no philosopher; he did not wish to build up a consistent philosophy of government and always developed his principles in terms of a particular problem at a particular time. The multiplicity of suggestions which may be found in his writings is bewildering and could be misleading. It would be very easy to overestimate the influence of Burke by overemphasizing brief suggestions, or principles developed for particular circumstances only.

The study of Burke's influence, moreover, is complicated by the intervening influence of the English and German Romantic writers. This difficulty is especially clear in the study of Coleridge, who felt the influence of both Burke and the German philosophers. In turn, it is generally accepted that Coleridge influenced Disraeli's Young England movement; yet Disraeli studied Burke's writings very carefully and may have found many of the tenets of Young England there. Thus, many sources for essentially similar ideas present themselves. The difficulty is also illustrated in some studies of the backgrounds of Fascism which confuse Burke's constitutional conservatism with continental doctrines of statism. Here deceptive likenesses must be carefully differentiated. In any consideration of Burke's influence, discrimination among the evidences is mandatory.

A third difficulty arises from the closer relationship of economics and politics which the Industrial Revolution brought about. This is not to suggest that Burke's political principles were unaffected by his economic principles, but certainly they were less affected than those of most Victorians. As will be seen later, the development of certain of Burke's political principles helped ultimately to overcome his economic principles of laissez-faire. It frequently happens, therefore, that Burke's followers among the Victorians show evidences of the influence of Burke's political and social principles at the same time that they show influences of economic facts and doctrines opposed to those he held, or even unknown to him. This apparent difference, however, is deceptive and should not be permitted to obscure the real relationship involved.

Finally, the study of economic and political thought is always hampered by the shifting meanings of certain terms. Not only do the labels *tory, conservative, whig,* and *radical* mean various things at various times and under various circumstances, but their emotional suggestions to the modern reader often color criticism of them. Burke has suffered from prejudiced interpretations of this sort when his opposition to the reform of the House of Commons or his excesses in his opposition to the French Revolution are overemphasized. It is even more important, however, to determine accurately the meaning of certain phrases which appear in political writing over and over again. Neither Burke nor any Victorian writer denied that the state existed for the welfare of the people. Yet an analysis of what kind of welfare the writer wished for the people, how it was to be attained and when, and what was meant by the phrase, "the people," will reveal startling and significant differences among the writers. The same variety is discoverable in the concept of education: Burke and the Victorian writers believed in education, yet there is wide variety of opinion as to who was to teach, what was to be taught, who was to be taught, and for how many years.[1]

I I

The critical study of Burke's influence upon his successors has been mainly directed toward the writers of the Romantic period. The importance of the French Revolution and the opposition to the revolution in the writings of the Romantic poets is obvious, and there has been a continued examination of the relation of Burke to Wordsworth, Coleridge, and Southey.[2] There has been also much excellent study of the political and social thought of Coleridge, the most important intermediary between Burke and the Victorians. Unfortunately, there has been a comparative neglect of the social attitudes of Sir Walter Scott. At least twice, once by Leslie Stephen and once by D. C. Somervell,[3] the close relation of Burke and Scott has been suggested, but no extended investigation has yet been published. Such a study is of paramount importance. A number of Scott's novels contain an imaginative presentation of Burkean ideas, and since their popularity was very great among Victorian readers of all classes, in them there may be one explanation of Burke's great influence in Victorian times.[4]

[1] Great service to the understanding of Victorian writers would be rendered by the study of what individual writers meant by such terms as "the people" or "education." The backgrounds of the Victorian vocabulary for the discussion of social and economic (as well as philosophical and theological) problems have been inadequately investigated. See the suggestive article by Robert M. Hutchins, "The Theory of Oligarchy," *The Thomist*, v (1943), 61-78, for an exploration of some of Burke's terminology.

[2] Alfred Cobban, *Edmund Burke and the Revolt Against the Eighteenth Century* (New York, 1929), is an indispensable introduction to the influences of Burke.

[3] Stephen, *Hours in a Library* (New York, 1894), I, 163-165; Somervell, *English Thought in the Nineteenth Century* (London, 1929), pp. 8-9.

[4] Note, for instance, the implications of Ruskin's well-known statement at the opening of *Praeterita*: "I am, and my father was before me, a violent Tory of the old school;—Walter Scott's school, that is to say, and Homer's."

The full force of both the Industrial Revolution and the French Revolution descended upon the Victorian period. The nature and extent of the consequences of the industrialization of society became increasingly apparent, and the ferment stimulated by French political doctrines had not been permanently suppressed by the deportation of agitators. Victorian writers, therefore, considered social and political problems, because such problems were inescapable and because they involved the most important questions of the time. In seeking for a solution to the multiplicity of problems many of them turned to Burke. Four of his ideas were of major importance, although in varying degrees, and directly influenced Victorian literature. The Victorians found in Burke a new conception of the past which led them to an attitude toward history completely different from that held by the eighteenth-century writers. They found a conception of the state and its function which helped them to reconcile progress and permanence in political affairs, and to build a new state within the framework of the old social order. Furthermore, Burke offered them a defense of the Established Church and an exposition of the relationship which ought to exist between church and state. And, finally, he offered them an ideal of colonial organization and management which guided them in building the second English empire.

In his consideration of political problems, the past was, for Burke, a reservoir of experience, a bank upon which the living were permitted to draw. It was the basis for judgment in contemporary affairs, a very much sounder basis than *a priori* theories untested in actual living. This reverence for the past which Burke bequeathed to the Victorians buttressed their unwillingness to change the traditional structure of English social life. It explains the paradoxical fusion of political democracy and social inequality and privilege which gradually came about during the Victorian era. One may discern, furthermore, in the *Reflections on the Revolution in France* anticipations of that respect

---

John Ruskin, *Works*, ed. E. T. Cook and Alexander Wedderburn (London, 1908), XXXV, 13.

for the feudal times which characterized many Victorians. As the bonds of custom and emotion which knit society together were strained by the economic degradation of the workers and the rise of a landless and socially untutored commercial aristocracy, Carlyle, Ruskin, and Disraeli re-emphasized the close relationship of each person in society. They contrasted Victorian and feudal times, and echoed Burke's insistence that the function of the aristocracy was to lead the nation and to alleviate the distress of the poor. Yet, as in Burke, privilege was not immune to criticism, and the exhortations of these Victorians to the landed aristocracy are anticipated by Burke's *Letter to a Noble Lord*. Some studies have emphasized continental philosophies as the sources of the Victorian's search into the past for guidance on contemporary affairs, but the native tradition, powerfully stated by Burke, and broadened by the Romantics, has not yet been fully evaluated.[5] Although students of historiography have accorded some notice to Burke, more investigation of the influence of his concept of the past and his defense of England's social pattern would be most useful.

Much more important for the Victorians, however, was Burke's concept of the state. Although this central idea in Burke's thinking has been closely studied, its implications for the study of Victorian literature have yet to be explored. In his concept, the Victorians discovered a possible resolution of two of their most pressing problems, the relationship of the individual and the state, and the relationship of progress and permanence in social institutions. They also found a basis for the most important political development in Victorian England, the social service state dedicated to the welfare of its members.

The state was built, according to Burke, upon spiritual

[5] "The belief that political values are to be judged in their relation with the historical community seemed to us the final teaching of Burke's political theory, and the lesson which the Lake Poets learned from him. Perhaps in this historic idea is to be found the ultimate explanation of what was original in the theory of Burke's followers as well as his own theory; perhaps a historical sense is the creative force in their revolt against the eighteenth century" (Cobban, *op. cit.*, p. 258).

foundations. It was an expression of the Will of God and performed its highest function in the moral development of its members. C. Crane Brinton has stated compactly the ethical assumptions underlying this belief: "Burke's fundamental ethical assumptions are at the opposite pole from those of his century. He fully accepts the pessimistic Christian doctrine of original sin. Man, the animal man of private sensations and emotions, is not, as Rousseau claimed, good, but, as St. Paul said, wicked. Left to themselves men are stupid, selfish, cruel, overreaching. Yet somehow these wicked men manage at times to live together on this earth without tearing each other apart, and life, if not joyous, is at least not death. Men in society are miraculously better than a knowledge of their attributes as individual animals would lead one to expect. Civil society—church, state, family, law, custom, even, Burke adds in defiance of a century which gave to the word a supremely dyslogistic sense, even prejudices—save man from himself. Civil society is thus of divine institutions, an essential part of God's rule."[6] In the *Reflections on the Revolution in France*, Burke makes the ethical nature of the state clear: "Government is a contrivance of human wisdom to provide for human *wants*. Men have a right that these wants should be provided for by this wisdom."[7] Also: "They conceived that He who gave our nature to be perfected by our virtue willed also the necessary means of its perfection: He willed, therefore, the state: He willed its connection with the source and original archetype of all perfection."[8] Finally, it is important to recall that in the well-known passage in the *Reflections on the Revolution in France*[9] Burke defined the state as a partnership "between those who are living, those who are dead and those who are to be born." A product of slow development and adjustment, it has become a miracle of delicate organization bound together by ties of emotion and habit. "It is a partnership in all science, a partnership

[6] *A Decade of Revolution, 1789-1799* (New York, 1934), p. 265.

[7] Burke, *Works* (Boston, 1894), III, 310.

[8] III, 361.

[9] III, 359-360. See also "An Appeal from the New to the Old Whigs," IV, 161-167.

in all art, a partnership in every virtue and in all perfection."

These concepts of the nature and aim of the state were of the utmost importance to the Victorians. Burke's definition of the state as an organism, a creation greater than the sum of its parts, offered an answer to the Benthamites and their philosophy of individualism. It asserted the interrelation of men in society and buttressed the impulses of humanitarianism. More important, it suggested the idea of the state as a body in which the elements but not the identity were always changing. Thus, it explained how it was possible to reform the government without violent upheaval; a method was indicated by which the old system of status and privilege might be preserved and the fabric of society maintained at the same time that necessary changes could be made. Tennyson's description of contemporary England is completely Burkean:

> A land of settled government,
>   A land of just and old renown,
>   Where Freedom slowly broadens down
> From precedent to precedent;

> Where faction seldom gathers head,
>   But, by degrees to fullness wrought,
>   The strength of some diffusive thought
> Hath time and space to work and spread.[10]

Burke's belief that the state is an organism formed for moral ends was, however, even more fruitful for the Victorians. In emphasizing the state as a means of satisfying the wants of men, Burke unconsciously laid the foundation for the modern social service state. If one extends the term "human wants" to include education, sanitation, social guidance, or protection from economic exploitation, one has in Burke's principle the apology for increasing state activity. It is ironic that Burke's laissez-faire economic principles were thus undermined by an extension of his beliefs about the nature and function of the state. The op-

10 "You Ask Me, Why, Though Ill At Ease," *Works* (Boston, 1898), p. 60.

position between laissez-faire economics and the principle of governmental interference is one of the most important in Victorian life and literature; Carlyle, Ruskin, Matthew Arnold, Disraeli, and Morris all sought governmental intervention. The importance of Burke's contribution to the development of the Victorian state which satisfied "human wants" is very great, and the nature and extent of that contribution warrants careful study.

Because the state was the means of the moral development of its members and because it was the complex product of the past, "The known march of the ordinary Providence of God,"[11] Burke emphasized the close relation of the church and state. Each was working toward the same end, and each buttressed the power of the other. The Established Church was valuable to the state because it consecrated the state and those who officiate in it, because it gave a sense of awe and reverence to the citizens of the state, and because it reinforced the sense of the transitoriness of individual life in the long tradition of the state. As a religious man, Burke had a personal feeling for the church; as a statesman who was always well aware of the emotional forces binding the state, he emphasized the close connection of church and state.

It is well known that Coleridge held beliefs similar to Burke's about the nature of the relationship between the church and state.[12] It is also noteworthy that Burke's views influenced Thomas Arnold and Benjamin Disraeli. Dr. Arnold followed Burke in emphasizing the close relationship of church and state, and he explored the meaning and possibilities of this relationship in his letters, and in the preface to the third volume of his edition of Thucydides.[13] Dr. Arnold was one of the first Victorians to understand that democracy and an orderly, creative state are not incompatible; he synthesized the principles of Burke and Coleridge with an untroubled belief in the machinery of democracy, which neither Burke nor Coleridge could ac-

[11] "Letters on a Regicide Peace, II," v, 349.
[12] Cobban, *op. cit.*, pp. 238-249.
[13] See A. P. Stanley, *The Life and Correspondence of Thomas Arnold* (New York, 1903).

cept. Too little attention has been paid to the social thinking of Dr. Arnold; a thorough study of his beliefs and their
relationship to Burke and Coleridge would be most valuable. Disraeli's defense of the Established Church is apparent everywhere in his writings. Although Disraeli followed
Bolingbroke and not Burke in his condemnation of the
Whig oligarchy, he praised Burke in *Sybil* and, especially in
the *Vindication of the English Constitution,* showed inescapable evidences of having studied him closely. A careful
comparison of the relationship of Disraeli to Bolingbroke
and to Burke would illuminate Disraeli's novels and his
political pamphlets.

In their thinking on political problems, however, the
Victorian writers did not concern themselves solely with
the nature and function of the state, for with swifter means
of communication, faster ships and expanding markets, the
relation of England to the rest of the world became increasingly important. Whether colonies were to be regarded
as lands of opportunity by which England's domestic problems of population could be solved, or as symbols of power
from which the English might derive self-satisfaction, or as
trading posts and coaling stations by which English trade
might flourish, they formed a part of every Victorian's
thinking, from Carlyle to Kipling. The building of England's empire during Victoria's reign at once heightened
English nationalism[14] and internationalism. Tennyson, Disraeli, and Kipling all felt a pride that the sun never set on
the British flag, and a responsibility for the satisfactory
management and development of the colonies.

A careful comparison of the principles of colonial relationship held by Burke and the Victorians would be fruitful. In his speeches on America, India, and Ireland, Burke
developed ideas of expediency, trusteeship, humanity, and
reconciliation. It has been suggested that Burke developed

---

14 The rise in the feeling of nationalism in Victorian England and its relation to the literature of the period is worthy of more attention from literary students. Burke's contribution to national feeling needs to be explored; it is clear that in his writing on the French Revolution he had
roused English nationalism. Wordsworth was especially influenced by this
aspect of Burke's thought. See Cobban, pp. 133 ff.

principles which ended the Mercantilist theory of colonial management and opened the way for the doctrines of duty and trust which, however debased they became in commercial and jingoistic minds, motivated Victorian colonial policy.[15] It need not be recalled that Macaulay shared Burke's attitude on India, that Burke's American speeches were quoted during the debates on Canada and Jamaica, and that Matthew Arnold reprinted Burke on Ireland as "the greatest of our political thinkers and writers," the value of whose political thinking and writing "is at its highest when the subject is Ireland."[16] Furthermore, Burke anticipated the sense of the moral unity and the interdependence of the members of the late-Victorian "Commonwealth of Nations." He looked upon the empire as a "mysterious whole," and in the first *Regicide Letter* points out that nations are joined "by resemblances, by conformities, by sympathies," rather than "papers and seals."[17]

These four ideas of Burke, his concept of the past, the organic nature of the state, the moral function of the state, and the doctrine of trusteeship in colonial affairs, were the most vital influences which the Victorians inherited from him. There are, however, similarities between Burke and the Victorians which may be profitably studied, but with greater difficulty. Other forces such as the lessons learned from the political events abroad, especially in France, the distinctive thought of the English Romantic writers or the continental philosophers, and the interplay of economic and social forces within England itself also influenced the Victorian climate of opinion so markedly that it is hard to evaluate Burke's influence accurately. Yet the extent and significance of these characteristic Victorian beliefs, and their undoubted similarity to those Burke held, make the investigation of Burke's part in them all the more necessary.

The most important of these similarities is that the structure of English society during the Victorian period devel-

[15] See R. Coupland, *The American Revolution and the British Empire* (London, 1930).
[16] *Edmund Burke on Irish Affairs* (London, 1881), p. vi.
[17] "Letters on a Regicide Peace, I," v, 317.

oped according to Burke's conservative concept of change. The governing power of Victoria declined, yet the monarchy rose in prestige. Suffrage was extended and political democracy triumphed; yet the process was gradual, and status and privilege were maintained. Socially, inequalities were recognized, accepted, and even defended on the Burkean grounds of tradition. In making reforms the Victorians, like Burke, "heaved the lead every inch of the way they made," for they believed fundamentally in his definition that "Reform is not a change in the substance or in the primary modification of the object, but a direct application of a remedy to the grievance complained of."[18] It is exactly this attitude which explains in part the limitations and inadequacies of the social and political reforms suggested by Victorian writers. This attitude also explains the piecemeal quality of reform throughout the period, and the damaging tendency of considering each social problem in isolation.

Further, the Victorian writers were not socially democratic, and many of them were not politically democratic. In Carlyle, Disraeli, Ruskin, and Tennyson there is praise of social inequality, and even the concept of the leader in society in the writings of Mill and Matthew Arnold is essentially Burkean. Trollope, in his novels, offers an accurate picture of a Burkean society, yet Victorian society sat for the portrait. The sources and ramifications of this major characteristic of Victorian times need to be carefully investigated, not only for what would be revealed about Burke's influence but for what might be added to our knowledge of the Victorian writers' beliefs and their methods of thought about social problems.

Another similarity of Burke to Victorian social and political writing occurs in the importance accorded in both to the anti-intellectual forces in society. His recognition of expediency, emotion, prescription, and prejudice as not

18 "Letter to a Noble Lord," v, 186. Compare Tennyson's definition of a Conservative:

> That man's the true Conservative
> Who lops the mouldered branch away.

Hallam Tennyson, *Alfred, Lord Tennyson, a Memoir* (London, 1898), I, 345.

only desirable but necessary elements in society anticipated Disraeli, Bagehot, and later political theorists. It also parallels the Victorian belief in the importance and power of emotion in life. Their interest in the feudal system, which was not so much an attempt to turn back history as to reassert the importance of the emotional and spiritual bond in society, and their feeling about the empire, are two political parallels to their humanitarianism, sentimentalism, and religious feeling. Much of the Victorian's emotionalism was an inheritance from the Romantic movement and the Wesleyan revival, but Burke's part in this characteristic of Victorianism must not be overlooked.

Finally, in addition to these direct influences, and similarities of Burke to the thought of the Victorian age, there is another relationship which merits the close and careful study of literary historians. A large and fruitful field of investigation lies open to those who examine the Victorian modes of thought: the way in which a problem was attacked, the channels through which thought characteristically flowed. Too often students of the period forget, in approaching such complicated problems as municipal housing and sanitation, or the relation of the government to education, or the techniques of organizing labor and bargaining collectively, that Victorian thinkers did not have the benefit of modern experience or theory. The Parliamentary Blue Books impress a modern reader with the honesty and good will of the investigating committee rather than with the excellence of the committee's techniques of investigation, or with their capacity to synthesize the raw material into generalizations which are as meaningful as the evidence from which they came.

Carlyle, or Arnold, or Mrs. Browning, or any other of the host of Victorian writers who addressed themselves to any aspect of the social problem about them, lacked the penetration, the insight of modern specialists in economics, sociology, social psychology, or public administration. No matter how brilliantly they may occasionally "anticipate" Marx or Sumner, Frazer or the Lynds, in their analyses of their time, anticipation was not enough nor was it necessarily characteristic or general.

But in understanding and appraising the Victorians one must do more than enumerate the tools which they lacked and the effects of this lack. It would contribute immeasurably to our understanding to investigate carefully not only the ideas which a given author held, and the sources for those ideas, but also the way his mind seems to have worked, what kind of evidence he was sensitive to, what kind of preconceptions or prejudices he seems to have held, and what process of reasoning he characteristically employed.

In such a consideration of the modes of thought of the Victorian writer, it seems likely that the influence of Burke would be found to be most important. Loyal always to the welfare of England, unquestionably conservative and even aristocratic in his thinking, and admired as one of the great statesmen of the recent past, Burke and his writings naturally commanded the attention of Victorians who were interested in social and political affairs. The mark of this reading appeared not only in direct and indirect influences in which *what* the Victorian thought showed evidence of contact with Burke, but also in a third way, in *how* he approached a problem and how he "solved" it.

I I I

In his essay, *The Function of Criticism at the Present Time*, Matthew Arnold, having pointed out that ideas are the elements with which the creative power works, praises Burke because, "almost alone in England, he brings thought to bear upon politics, he saturates politics with thought. It is his accident that his ideas were at the service of an epoch of concentration, not of an epoch of expansion; it is his characteristic that he so lived by ideas, and had such a source of them welling up within him, that he could float even an epoch of concentration and English Tory politics with them."[19] But Burke's ideas were at the service of more than his own epoch of concentration; they were at the service of all those who succeeded him—government

[19] *Works* (London, 1903), III, 15.

officials, political theorists, philosophers, and writers. So forcefully had Burke stated the English conservative tradition, so stimulating and suggestive were his ideas that they became an inescapable part of the intellectual atmosphere of the Victorian period. Whether one ultimately agreed or disagreed with Burke's thought, it always had to be reckoned with, studied, absorbed, and then accepted or rejected.

It is not astonishing, therefore, to find evidences of the influence of Burke in Wordsworth's *Convention of Cintra*, and Matthew Arnold's *Culture and Anarchy*, in Trollope's novels, and Tennyson's *In Memoriam*, in Carlyle's *French Revolution*, Thomas Arnold's letters, and Disraeli's *Sybil* and *Coningsby*. Whether by direct quotation or paraphrase, by parallel expressions of similar ideas, or in the methods of approach to social problems and the modes of thought employed to solve those problems, the Victorian age demonstrates inescapably its knowledge of Burke's ideas and attitudes. It is hardly too much to say that in some fashion Burke influenced all who followed him in their consideration of social and political affairs.

It would be untrue to imply that the influences of Burke upon Victorian letters have been ignored, but much investigation remains yet to be done. A thorough critical appraisal of Burke's relationship to the Victorian age would help modern readers to understand better some of the central problems of the period and the intellectual background of the writers, and thus it would contribute to a sounder appreciation of Victorian literature.

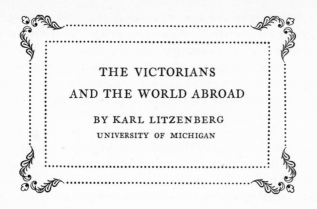

THE VICTORIANS
AND THE WORLD ABROAD

BY KARL LITZENBERG
UNIVERSITY OF MICHIGAN

DESPITE the fact that it is often misused and frequently misapplied, Arnold's well-worn metaphor of *two worlds* remains a reasonably accurate figure for the several pairs of nineteenth-century forces which, in opposing each other, assailed the tranquillity of the Victorian mind and demanded resolution. The world within the British Isles and the world without represent such a conflict. While the struggle for supremacy between the tradition of insularity and the tradition of cosmopolitanism was not so violent as the conflict precipitated between mechanism and the soul of man, it is nevertheless of considerable importance to an understanding of the Victorian mind, and represents a field which might well be cultivated with greater care.

Critics unfriendly to the age have usually centered their attacks on certain proverbial *bêtes noires*: Victorian provincialism, narrowness of outlook, complacency, and false morality.[1] Consequently, misconception and misinterpretation of the place actually occupied by parochialism have caused the adjective *Victorian* to take on tones and colors highly distressing to admirers of the nineteenth century. Still, the practice of finding the best light to walk by was

[1] See Howard Mumford Jones's merry treatment of incorrect definitions of Victorianism in the present volume. Cf. also H. E. Bannard, "The Real Victorians," *Spectator*, CLXVIII-CLXIX (1942), 228-229, and comments thereon, pp. 281, 306.

more common in the age of Victoria than the prevalence of "moral earnestness," "restricted vision," and the reverberations of "glory-in-empire" may suggest.

A congress of forces gradually mitigated the strength of Victorian insularity; and among these none was of more significance and none exerted more constant pressure upon the Victorian intellect than the external force which was constituted by the culture of the world abroad. Students have learned a great deal about the Victorian mind from studying the impact of foreign ideas upon nineteenth-century English literature, but have not yet made more than reasonably satisfactory progress toward a total understanding of this impact. Much that the Victorian period stands for was natively British; and much that was actually foreign was converted by Victorian writers into something resembling the native—witness certain of Browning's Italian poems, Arnold's "Balder Dead," FitzGerald's *Rubáiyát*, and the *ragna rök* concept in Morris's theory of revolution. The fact that two of the great long poems of the age were based upon foreign materials does not make the *Ring and the Book* or *Sigurd the Volsung* any less valuable to the student of Victorianism in Browning and Morris. It is true that Browning's love for Italy might trouble the literal Victorian mind; it is true, as well, that Morris had no little difficulty in convincing his countrymen that they should interest themselves in Scandinavian heroes. But the Victorians ultimately accepted the infiltration of foreign subject matter and foreign ideas into their literature, and accepted foreign literature itself—after the embargo of first objection had been raised.[2] This statement need not de-

---

[2] See C. R. Decker's valuable papers on the reception of certain foreign worthies in England: "Balzac's Literary Reputation in Victorian Society," *PMLA*, XLVII (1932), 1150-1157; "Zola's Literary Reputation in England," *PMLA*, XLIX (1934), 1140-1153; "Ibsen's Literary Reputation and Victorian Taste," *SP*, XXXII (1935), 623-645. Mr. Decker's treatment of mutations in Victorian taste vividly illustrates the changing fortunes of foreign writers in Victorian England. Realism and Naturalism were furiously resisted, but not seriously impeded. See W. C. Frierson, "The English Controversy over Realism in Fiction, 1885-1895," *PMLA*, XLIII (1928), 533-550; C. R. Decker, "Victorian Comment on Russian Realism," *PMLA*, LII (1937), 542-549; and "The Aesthetic Revolt against Naturalism in Victorian Criticism," *PMLA*,

pend for its support upon the influence of the Germans on Carlyle and Carlyle's campaign to popularize German literature and philosophy; upon Browning and Italy; upon Swinburne and France; upon Borrow and Spain, Doughty and Arabia, Burton and Africa, or Morris and Scandinavia. The anglicizing of "The Ballad of Dead Ladies," the *Rubáiyát*, and the translation of hundreds of German, French, Italian, Scandinavian, Spanish, and Slavic works into English during the nineteenth century are also indices to the popularity of foreign literature among the Victorians; nor may we neglect the incidental and sometimes purely literary uses which Arnold, Kingsley, Elizabeth Barrett, George Eliot, Dickens, Thackeray, Hood, Meredith, Tennyson, Mill, and countless other Victorians made of non-English materials in their original English writings. A mathematical approach to the matter would show that the body of Victorian literature would be disastrously reduced if only that which is *British* in a reasonably strict sense were allowed to remain in the Victorian canon.[3]

LIII (1938), 844-856. An interesting interpretation of the Victorian critical tendency to approve that which was similar to British literature, and to reject foreign elements such as Realism and Naturalism, is to be found in A. R. Favreau, "British Criticism of Daudet, 1872-1897," *PMLA*, LII (1937), 528-541, with the conclusions of which the present writer does not entirely agree. It is important to bear in mind that hostile reviews by no means kept Englishmen from buying and reading foreign importations, as booksellers' catalogues, circulating library lists, and publishers' sales records unequivocally prove.

[3] Because of the limitations of space, no attempt has been made to turn this chapter into a complete bibliographical essay. For general bibliographical materials covering Anglo-foreign literary relations, the following partial list may be found useful: "Literary Relations with the Continent," *CBEL*, Vol. III; annual *PMLA* bibliographies; current "Anglo-French and Franco-American Studies," *Romanic Review*; current "Anglo-German Bibliography," *JEGP*; C. F. Harrold, "Recent Trends in Victorian Studies," *SP*, XXXVII (1940), 667-697 (a most comprehensive bibliographical essay); Brian W. Downs, "Anglo-Danish Literary Relations: the Fortunes of Danish Literature in Great Britain," *MLR*, XXXIX (1944), 262-279; Remigio Pane, *English Translations from the Spanish: 1484-1943: a Bibliography*, Rutgers University Studies in Spanish, No. 2 (Rutgers University Press, 1944), corrected and greatly supplemented by E. G. Mathews, "English Translations from Spanish: a Review and a Contribution," *JEGP*, XLIV (1945), 387-424; Clarence Gohdes, *American Literature in Nineteenth-Century England* (New York, 1944), an excellent book to which further reference is made in

Casual and occasional uses of foreign material in native English literature show how, in one fashion, continental culture exerted its influence upon Victorian thought currents and art forms. In general, the non-English ideas and motifs which actually became a part of the main stream of the thought and literature of the Victorian age were changed or adapted in such a manner as to make them part of the British tradition. In varying degrees, this type of assimilation can be observed in English versions of Positivism, political liberalism, and Naturalism. The tendency to anglicize or to "Victorianize" is also well illustrated in the uses to which Carlyle adapted German thought; it may be observed equally well in Carlyle's interpretation of the hero concept and in his corruption of the *Heimskringla* in *The Early Kings of Norway*. Ruskin's history of Venetian architecture, Arnold's carrying the agnostic's burden into a foreign setting in "Stanzas from the Grande Chartreuse," Browning's attack on narrow views of art in "Fra Lippo Lippi," and Mill's analysis of democracy in *Representative Government* all demonstrate effectively that, when Victorian purposiveness was superimposed upon non-English subject matter, the borrowed substance might lose some of its alien character. There were exceptions: The advocates of Symbolism and Naturalism, and the art-for-art's sake circle tended, in general, to resist traditional influences— not always with complete success. Not infrequently, however, a foreign concept was incorporated into English literature with the definite purpose of strengthening some particular approach to the "Condition of England Question." This is not to say that Victorian culture suffered thereby.

I I

For the most part, nineteenth-century scholars have treated specific literary relations and influences more frequently than they have dealt with the comprehensive aspects of the foreign impress on the Victorian intellect.[4] We

---

this chapter. Other bibliographical materials are cited below, where pertinent.

4 See, for example, William J. Courthope, *A History of English Poetry*,

have a satisfactory understanding of such relations and influences in the works of Carlyle, D. G. Rossetti, William Morris, James Thomson, and Swinburne, for example; and the annals of comparative literature contain a great quantity of published materials designed to illuminate the relationship of Balzac, Zola, Ibsen, Turgeniev, Kant, Goethe, Leopardi, Baudelaire, and Mallarmé to individual English writers or to English literary forms or movements in the nineteenth century. Studies and bibliographies of German and French literature in English translation are available, along with books and monographs on the Italian influence on the English novel, the French drama in England, Poe's literary reputation in England, the influence of the Völsunga Saga and the Nibelungenlied on Morris's *Sigurd the Volsung*, Browning's use of the "Old Yellow Book" in *The Ring and the Book*, Walt Whitman's reception in England, Wagner in Great Britain, and the rise of colonial literature. These impressive and admirable contributions to the understanding of Victorian literature—and scores of others

---

6 vols. (New York, 1895-1910); Georg M. C. Brandes, *Main Currents in Nineteenth Century Literature*, tr. Diana White and Mary Morison, 6 vols. (London, 1901-05); John T. Merz, *History of European Thought in the Nineteenth Century*, 3 vols. (Edinburgh, 1903); Frédéric A. Loliée, *A Short History of Comparative Literature from the Earliest Times to the Present*, tr. M. Douglas Power (London, 1906); Fernand Baldensperger, *Études d'Histoire Littéraire*, 2 vols. (Paris, 1907-10); Oliver Elton, *A Survey of English Literature, 1780-1880*, 4 vols. (New York, 1920); Laurie Magnus, *English Literature in Its Foreign Relations* (London, 1927); George Saintsbury, *The Later Nineteenth Century*, Periods of European Literature, Vol. XII (Edinburgh and London, 1907); Paul Van Tieghem, *La Littéraire Comparée* (Paris, 1931); Emery Neff, *A Revolution in English Poetry, 1600-1900* (New York, 1939). For a fine example of the comprehensive treatment which may be given to Anglo-foreign intellectual relations, see René Wellek, *Immanuel Kant in England, 1793-1838* (Princeton, 1931). Professor Wellek shows how foreign material was changed and adapted upon being imported, and yet establishes conclusively the importance of Kant's contribution to English philosophy. The relations between English and foreign formal philosophic systems are outside the realm of the present chapter; however, the complete story, when it is told, will include this broad field as well as some others which receive bare mention here, or are omitted entirely. Future researchers into foreign literary and philosophical relations can do worse than follow Professor Wellek's approach. It may be remarked that in this chapter we are primarily concerned with Victorian attitudes toward foreign *belles-lettres*.

which are equally useful—constitute a tremendous collection of valuable scholarly work. The special section of the *Cambridge Bibliography of English Literature* devoted to nineteenth-century English literature and its foreign relations, in spite of specific omissions, and in spite of its failure to include certain important aspects of these relations, represents a monumental assemblage of materials. Available scholarship, and the areas yet untouched, both suggest that a cooperative project, undertaken by Victorian scholars interested in all phases of the foreign influence upon English letters, would produce a work of great usefulness. In an essay of limited length one can only invite attention to certain phases of the larger problem. It is therefore necessary that the present discussion be concerned chiefly with types of Anglo-foreign literary relations and with a few of the ways in which such relations were stimulated and carried on.

III

The Victorian reader, both through such active campaigns on behalf of continental literature as Carlyle's insistence that the English understand the Germans and such occasional adaptations of non-English material as are found in Arnold's "Balder Dead," Elizabeth Barrett's "A Curse for a Nation," and Swinburne's "Hertha," was exposed to an impressive amount of foreign thought and culture. Despite the persistence of parochialism (to be observed, for example, in the vicious attacks on Balzac), and the lingering "American cousin" attitude, Carlyle's interpretation of *Entsagen*, Morris's treatment of *The Laxdæla Saga*, Browning's reproduction in verse of the Italian Renaissance, and Swinburne's zeal in the Italian cause attracted partisans and defenders who were numerous and faithful, even though they may have been less vociferous than were those who objected to foreign importations on insular grounds. It is true that the Victorians strenuously resisted Flaubert, Daudet, and French Naturalism; it is also true that they were inclined to think of the Norse sagas as proper subjects for scholarly investigation rather than as materials for polite literature. They professed shame, unbounded admiration, or simple amazement when they read Whitman;[5] they liked Cooper because they thought him similar to Scott; they looked upon Baudelaire as an evil genius; and, even late in the century, some of them took seriously the statement which Sydney Smith had made in 1818: "But why should Americans write books . . . ?"[6] They laughed Ibsen[7] off the stage, and debated the subject of Zola's "pernicious" novels in the House of Commons.[8] But before the century was over, rising interest caused Ibsen's works to be reprinted often, and Zola to be lionized, though enemies of both still walked abroad.

In the end, the Victorians received and assimilated much more from the outside world than their first reactions to Carlyle, Baudelaire, Daudet, and the sagas had promised. The first translation of a work by Tolstoi was done into English;[9] and Emerson went to England in 1847 as a lecturer.[10] Oliver Wendell Holmes was given credit in 1886 for cementing Anglo-American relations;[11] Trübner pub-

[5] For a very interesting explanation of Swinburne's attitudes toward Whitman, see W. B. Cairns, "Swinburne's Opinion of Whitman," *AL*, III (1931), 125-135. The treatment of Whitman in America should not be forgotten when his fortunes in England are under discussion.

[6] "But why should Americans write books, when a six weeks' passage brings them, in their own tongue, our sense, science and genius, in bales and hogsheads?" *Works of the Rev. Sydney Smith*, 4th ed., 3 vols. (London, 1848), II, 27.

[7] Cf. Decker, *op. cit.* ("Ibsen"); Miriam A. Franc, *Ibsen in England* (Boston, 1919); William Archer, "Ibsen and English Criticism," *Fortnightly Review*, n.s. XLVI (1889), 30-37.

[8] *Pernicious Literature. Debate in the House of Commons. Trial and Conviction for the Sale of Zola's Novels. With Opinions of the Press* (London [National Vigilance Association], 1889), a pamphlet reprinted from *Hansard*. The Society for the Suppression of Vice was engaged in similar unenlightened activities.

[9] Cf. Antonia Yassukovitch [assisted by Abraham Mill], "Tolstoi in English, 1878-1929," *New York Public Library Bulletin*, XXXIII (1929), 531-565.

[10] However, Alexander Ireland took pains to get Emerson a "good press" in advance of the tour. See Townsend Scudder III, "Emerson's British Lecture Tour, 1847-1848, Part I, The Preparations for the Tour, and the Nature of Emerson's Audiences"; "Emerson's British Lecture Tour, 1847-1848, Part II, Emerson as a Lecturer in Britain and the Reception of the Lectures," *American Literature*, VII (1935-1936), 15-36; 166-180.

[11] Edward Delille, "Oliver Wendell Holmes," *Fortnightly Review*, n.s. XL

lished his *Bibliographical Guide to American Literature* in 1855 and 1859; and both Garibaldi and Mazzini were warmly received by English writers on their visits to London.

Carlyle and Swinburne—to name two Victorians who were as different as possible—possessed British patriotism in common as well as great love for English tradition and history. Both were extensively influenced by non-English literature and non-English thought. It may be that Carlyle was constricted by his background and by congenital Calvinism in a manner and degree beyond his own awareness; yet he explored German philosophy and literature, French literature and history, and Scandinavian history and myth more deeply than many of his contemporaries. Dickens composed several novels which are hyper-British, albeit critical of English abuses; he also wrote *American Notes*—an emphatically provincial document—and *A Tale of Two Cities*. George Eliot, in *Middlemarch, Mill on the Floss*, and *Adam Bede*, consciously lifted the provincial novel to a new artistic level; she also wrote an essay on the wit of Heine, and translated Strauss and Feuerbach. Morris was active in the work of the Society for the Preservation of Ancient Buildings ("The Anti-Scrape"), and wrote *The Fostering of Aslaug*, as well as many other pieces based on foreign sources. Cosmopolitanism is found in the Victorian period in strange places even though insularity is often co-existent with it. The stubbornness of custom and the survival of tradition must not be construed, however, as forces which seriously impeded the natural processes of cultural evolution. Such an evolution asserted itself in the Victorian period as it has in every literary epoch in history, Thomas Gradgrind and Bishop Wilberforce to the contrary notwithstanding. Indeed, a most effective antidote to the view of life represented by the Victorian squire in his country seat, by Mr. Bounderby and the Duke of St. Albans, by the hom-

---

(1886), 234-243. A splendid treatment of Holmes and the English is presented by Eleanor M. Tilton, *Amiable Autocrat, A Biography of Dr. Oliver Wendell Holmes* (New York, 1947). See particularly Chapter 23, "Celebrity in England."

age paid to Mrs. Grundy, and the pride-without-conscience
in an empire on which the sun never sets, is the knowledge
that in intellectual matters—and not in applied literature
alone—the Victorians did not "Buy British" exclusively.
The widespread incorporation of non-English or non-Brit-
ish elements into the general literature of the period offsets
to some extent the extreme Britishness of a host of Victorian writers, and should most emphatically destroy the
notion that insularity and provincialism wholly won the
day. To be sure, several foreign philosophers and men of
letters failed to gain Victorian audiences; but it serves no
useful purpose to associate such failures with the spectacular hostility which greeted Ibsen, Balzac, and Zola.[12]

I V

While ample evidence of the Victorians' interest in the
outside world can be adduced from the history of nineteenth-century *belles-lettres*, the relationship of this interest
to cosmopolitan contacts which were provided in other
fields and by other agencies may not be ignored. The tales
related by professional travelers and explorers, the increase
of tourist travel on the continent, the intercourse between
English and foreign scientists, formal philosophers, artists,
and musicians, the expansion of empire, and reports on the
progress of America all contributed to the widening of the
Victorian cultural horizon.

Such travelers as Lord Dufferin, du Chaillu, Doughty,

---

[12] The hostility to Zola was more complex than at first appears; nor was
prudishness or false morality always at the bottom of it. It should be noted
in connection with the treatment of Zola, and other foreign writers, that
what the critics advised and what the public bought were not always in
agreement. Quite naturally, while the controversy over "Pernicious Literature" was at its height, Zola was enjoying a tremendous volume of sales. His
books also sold well before the controversy reached a formal stage. By
separating the evidence, one can establish: (1) that Zola was the most hated
foreign writer ever to invade the English world of letters; or, (2) that his
popularity was greater for a time than that of all native British novelists.
Zola's case shows pretty well that one cannot evaluate a writer's reputation
or general popularity by using reviews alone. In connection with *popularity*,
it may be pointed out that the actual sale of foreign novels in England is
a field which might be more deeply explored.

Morris, Borrow, Sir Richard Burton, Alexander Kinglake, and Anthony Trollope, as well as scientists like Lyell, Darwin, and Huxley, brought into the Victorian drawing room strange and wondrous tales of a world remote from the British Isles. The high peak of interest in the hardship and adventure of exploration was reached, of course, when Stanley was despatched (news value guaranteed) in search of Livingstone. The popularity of the historical novel and the novel of foreign setting is an obvious and appropriate corollary to the Victorian interest in books of exploration and travel. *First Footsteps in East Africa, Arabia Deserta, The Bible in Spain*, and the *Voyage of the Beagle* may well belong to the same general areas of interest and culture as *Henry Esmond, The Virginians, Hereward the Wake, Rienzi, A Tale of Two Cities, The Cloister and the Hearth, Romola*, and *Vittoria*.

Exchange of information and opinion between English scientists and their colleagues on the continent, while directly affecting a limited number of individuals, played no inconsiderable part in the development of Victorian thought. Cuvier's relationship to pre-Victorian geology and the controversy over Lamarck's theory of transmutation were still argued by scientists in the age of Victoria. Huxley translated Kölliker and wrote a famous interpretation of Kölliker's teleological arguments. The remarks of "Darwin's Bulldog" on the "Perpetual Secretary of the French Academy"—though scarcely designed to improve diplomatic relations between the French and English—indicate that British scientists were not inclined to be hemmed in by international borders even in their quarrels. Huxley also calculated the monetary value of Pasteur's researches in immunology in terms of the war indemnity of 1870. Helmholtz attracted his share of opponents and supporters in England; and at the end of Victoria's reign Koch made his famous pronouncement on tuberculosis in men and cattle at the Congress of London, thereby causing a royal commission to be appointed to study the matter.

Of all the Victorian's interests in and reactions to the world abroad, however, his attitude toward the expansion of empire is perhaps the most difficult to analyze and to comprehend. Pride in the magnitude and wealth of empire —a pride possessed by thousands of Victorian Englishmen— cannot always be interpreted as chauvinism, or explained as greedy worship of acquisition, however cruel or unjust. It is of no small importance, in this connection, that one of the early Victorian essayists, despite the inaccuracies of his Indian papers and the confused aims of *Warren Hastings,* was among the first critics of the methods of imperialism; and that one of the last Victorians, himself the laureate of the empire's foot-sloggers, wrote a Jubilee poem which by implication argued for reform in the government of empire —reform in which humility and obeisance to the will of God would take precedence over the *White Man's Burden* and the *Majesty of England.*

Between the time of Macaulay and the time of Kipling, Englishmen had become well acquainted with the far-flung and ever-expanding empire which was governed from London. Younger sons were "sent out" to find their careers on other continents and scions of established colonials came home to be educated. It was not from news accounts of the Indian insurrections and the Crimean War, nor from Australian wool and beef or Canadian furs alone, that the Victorian learned about life in the colonies and was made aware of their significance to England. In the last part of the century every section of the British Isles had its share of men who had "been out."

It may be remarked in passing that—except, perhaps, for Anglo-Irish literature and the Irish Revival—the growth of English literature in the dominions throughout the nineteenth century has not received the attention it deserves from literary historians. The Irish Revival, on the contrary, has been treated by many hands and has a peculiar interest here in that it produced a literature which was not "colonial."[13] With their self-conscious nationalism, their refusal to be engulfed in English culture, and their patent declaration of insularity and cultural autonomy, the sponsors of

[13] See "The Literatures of the Dominions," *CBEL,* III, 1045-1098.

the Irish movement actually stimulated the development of a literature in the British Isles which was in many ways *foreign*.

The Victorian interest in and attitude toward America, its progress, its literature, and its general culture, have likewise drawn the attention of numerous literary historians. Several highly illuminating studies have been written in the field of Anglo-American relations, literary and otherwise, though many phases of the nineteenth-century intercourse between the two nations have yet to be examined.[14] The periodicals of Victorian England contain hundreds of articles on American matters, and many on American literature, though it is virtually impossible to discover in these writings on America any "typical" Victorian attitude toward the American scene. In general, one can mark two points of view, or variations on two themes. On the one

[14] A few important titles may be listed here: W. B. Cairns, *British Criticism of American Writings, 1815-1853*, University of Wisconsin Studies in Language and Literature, No. 14 (Madison, 1922); Robert E. Spiller, *The American in England during the First Half Century of Independence* (New York, 1926); Robert B. Mowat, *Americans in England* (Cambridge [Mass.], 1935); Howard M. Jones, "The Influence of European Ideas in Nineteenth-Century America," *AL*, VII (1935), 241-273; Mitford M. Mathews, "Notes and Comments Made by British Travelers and Observers upon American English, 1770-1850," *Harvard University Summaries of Theses* (1936), pp. 341-344; Frank L. Mott, "Carlyle's American Public," *PQ*, IV (1925), 245-264; E. P. Laurence, "An Apostle's Progress: Matthew Arnold in America," *PQ*, X (1931), 62-79; H. W. Blodgett, *Walt Whitman in England* (New York and London, 1934); W. S. Vance, "Carlyle in America before Sartor Resartus," *AL*, VII (1936), 363-375; James P. McCormick, "Robert Browning's Reputation in the Nineteenth Century in England and America," *Northwestern University Summaries of Doctoral Dissertations* (1937), pp. 10-14; Bertha Faust, *Hawthorne's Contemporary Reputation: A Study of Literary Opinion in America and England, 1828-1864*, University of Pennsylvania Dissertation (privately printed, 1939); Max Berger, *The British Traveller in America, 1836-1860*, Columbia Studies in History, Economics and Public Law, No. 502 (New York, 1943). There are many more including several studies of American literary relations with countries other than England, of which Andrew Hilen's *Longfellow and Scandinavia* (New Haven, 1947), is a recent and an impressive example. Several of these investigations suggest others which remain to be done. Professor Gohdes's book is a veritable mine of research projects in the Anglo-American literary field. It may be suggested that a comprehensive bibliography of Anglo-American cultural relations would be welcomed by scholars working in both the American and the Victorian fields.

hand, there was a tendency to consider America as one of the colonies, and American literature as a fairly insignificant (and sometimes contemptible) offshoot of the mother literature; and on the other, an earnest desire to understand the Americans and to give them credit for attempting to create—if not always to produce—a significant literature. An illuminating contrast in attitudes is represented by Sydney Smith's "Who reads an American book?"[15]—a remark which was current before the real English successes of nineteenth-century American writers had been made—and by Emerson's "We have listened too long to the courtly muses of Europe," which was proclaimed in the very year of the Queen's accession to the throne. The same Emerson was said by a reviewer in 1885 to look "less American than most Americans."[16]

It has been held that American literature did not come into its own until it was emancipated from servile dependence upon British critical opinion, until American writers no longer felt obliged to measure their successes by the stamp of approval grudgingly bestowed by Edinburgh and London. If American literature did triumph in the face of early antagonism toward it, and in spite of the toadying of American authors and publishers to British reviews, it should also be observed that the support of an author from one country by a writer in the other strengthened Anglo-American literary relations, and particularly advanced the cause of American literature in England. The association and correspondence of Carlyle and Emerson is a case in point here, as is the publication of *Sartor Resartus* in book form in America (with Emerson's assistance) before it appeared as a book in England.

Many Englishmen were vitally interested in the general

[15] "In the four quarters of the globe, who reads an American book? or goes to an American play? or looks at an American statue?"—*Edinburgh Review*, XXXIII (1820), 79.

[16] Critical notice of O. W. Holmes, *Ralph Waldo Emerson*, in *Time*, I (1885), 248. For an interesting treatment of American attitudes toward a national literature, see John C. McCloskey, "The Campaign of Periodicals after the War of 1812 for a National American Literature," *PMLA*, L (1935), 262-273.

affairs of the United States during the Victorian age: democracy, the Civil War and the slave question, industry and transportation, and American life and manners in general. It is unfortunately true, however, that *Domestic Manners of the Americans, American Notes*, and *Martin Chuzzlewit* presented pictures of contemporaneous American civilization which many Victorians regarded as completely authentic and were only too willing to accept. In some quarters the views of Dickens were still credited at the end of the Queen's reign, while Cobbett's enthusiasm for America was apparently disregarded or forgotten shortly after the Victorian age commenced.

The most popular American writers in England during the first part of the nineteenth century appear to have been Irving, whose *Bracebridge Hall* and *Sketch Book* were widely read during the forties, and Cooper, who was taken up with great interest several years before 1837. "By the time the Victorian Age began, a generation was growing up in England that knew its *Last of the Mohicans* almost as well as it knew its *Ivanhoe* or its *Pickwick*. . . ."[17] As time passed, American books appeared in England in ever-increasing numbers, with Emerson, Longfellow (who was attacked by Lockhart), Hawthorne, Lowell, and Holmes reaching a large English public. Dickens admired Bret Harte, and Tennyson approved of Longfellow though he said little about him; Whitman was championed by W. M. Rossetti and Symonds (among others); N. P. Willis had become a fixture in the dandiacal body (and one of its favorite writers) just before Victoria's accession; and *Uncle Tom's Cabin* enjoyed sensational sales in the early fifties. Mark Twain's works and humorous writing in general achieved great popularity, while both Holmes and Longfellow were spoken of by English reviewers at various times as the most popular American writers in nineteenth-century England.[18]

---

[17] Amy Cruse, *The Victorians and Their Books* (London, 1935), p. 237.

[18] Professor Gohdes has made a complete examination of Longfellow's fame in England in "Longfellow and His Authorized Publishers," *PMLA*, LV (1920), 1165-1179, and in Chapter 4 of his book on American literature in England. It goes without saying that various American writers were popular at various times in England. Gohdes has concluded, on the basis

The controversy over Walt Whitman drew many participants; but the native quarrel over the "Fleshly School of Poetry" and the skirmishes over Zola created more excitement than did the fortunes of Whitman.

Holmes's success in England is the more remarkable because of his mixed feelings about England. He was said by one reviewer to be "as much known and loved in this country as in his own," and was scolded by another because he "twits us with our 'insular limitations.' "[19] The popularity of Holmes came chiefly from the *Autocrat of the Breakfast Table*; and it is noteworthy that English reviewers applauded his geniality, his humor, and his common sense, and at the same time criticized Holmes for not being another Carlyle. There was general agreement, however, that Holmes had done a great deal to give Englishmen and Americans respect for each other.

American men of letters who visited England were cordially and often enthusiastically received. The later Victorians did not generally assume an attitude of condescension towards the visiting Americans, though early in the century Mary Russell Mitford had said of Willis that he was "more like one of the best of our peers' sons than a rough republican."[20]

When Emerson made his English lecture tour in the late forties, he was already well known as a writer. Longfellow was honored by Oxford, where he received the degree of Doctor of Civil Laws, and by Cambridge, where he received the degree of Doctor of the Laws. He was no less honored by the courtesies extended to him by the Poet Laureate and the Queen. Lowell, who either outgrew or sublimated his early antipathy for England, became a highly regarded member of English literary and intellectual society after accepting the appointment as Minister to the Court of St.

---

of his comprehensive investigations, that from an overall point of view, "Emerson was pretty generally regarded in the better circles as the outstanding writer of America, but Hawthorne was proclaimed the leading artist. . . ." (*op. cit.*, p. 139.)

[19] Delille, *op. cit.*, p. 235; *Time*, I, 248.

[20] A. G. L'Estrange, *The Friendships of Mary Russell Mitford as Recorded in Letters from Her Literary Correspondents*, 2 vols. (London, 1887), I, 265.

James. As a speaker and lecturer he was in demand in every section of England, and proved to be an ideal ambassador of good will, both as an individual and as an author and editor.

Charles Eliot Norton's correspondence with the Brownings, with Ruskin, the pre-Raphaelites, Thackeray, and Carlyle, and especially his editing of Carlyle after the Froude controversy, entitles him to a high place in the history of Anglo-American literary relations in the nineteenth century. His services to literature were of as much importance to England as to America; and their ultimate approval by Englishmen is an excellent example of the acceptance of American literary scholarship by the late Victorians.

The Englishman at the beginning of the nineteenth century was by no means convinced that America was a civilized nation, or a nation of sufficient maturity to produce a significant independent culture. The idea that American literature was and should be derivative has not been entirely dissipated even today. But throughout the Victorian age we can trace a growing interest in American culture, and a growing respect for its value as well. Dickens's interpretation of the American scene is one index to the British attitude; the lecture tour of Matthew Arnold is another; the British explanation of Cooper's popularity, the tendency to admire Longfellow, and yet to consider him to be generally inferior to the great Victorian poets, and the strong resistance of Kingsley and Ruskin are still others. But, in spite of divergences of opinion, the strength and vigor of American life, the magnificence of American scenery and the wealth of American resources, the independence of her people, and the potentialities of her literature were no longer unknown in England—and were not always dispraised—at the time of the death of the Queen.

V

The long-standing relationships which had existed between England and France, and England and Italy, were strengthened during the Victorian period, and the cause of

German thought and literature was advanced greatly.[21] Interest in Italy was stimulated not alone by Browning, but also by political sympathy for the cause of Italian liberty (as reflected in the poetry of Elizabeth Barrett and Swinburne, for example); by the Italian expatriates, the rediscovery of Dante, and the presence in England of Mazzini and Garibaldi.[22] The early nineteenth century regard for Italy was cast in the Byron-Shelley-Trelawny tradition; but the Victorian Englishman's sympathy for the Italians was strengthened by the events of 1848-1849—Clough witnessed the defense of Rome in 1849—and Italian became the cultured Englishman's third foreign language (after French, but before German). The Italian *belles-lettres* contemporaneous with Victorian literature, however, were not nearly so important in nineteenth-century England as were the literature and art of earlier times.[23]

Literary relations between England and France during the Victorian period have a strange and somewhat unsavory history, though the uncertain career of the French novel in England was crowned with ultimate success. Literary intercourse between the English and the Spanish, the English and the Dutch, the English and the Portuguese, and the English and the Czechs was not of prime significance during the period,[24] but the literatures of Scandinavia and Russia

21 See Wellek, *op. cit.*, and C. F. Harrold, *Carlyle and German Thought: 1819-1834*, Yale Studies in English (New Haven, 1934).

22 Anglo-Italian relations have received considerable attention from scholars. A comprehensive survey of politico-literary relations is to be found in Harry W. Rudman, *Italian Nationalism and English Letters. Figures of the Risorgimento and Victorian Men of Letters* (New York and London, 1940). The bibliography lists and classifies "Friends of Italy" in England.

23 Cf. G. M. Trevelyan, "Englishmen and Italians," *Proceedings of the British Academy*, IX (1919-20), 91-108.

24 See Brian W. Downs, "Anglo-Dutch Literary Relations, 1867-1900," *MLR*, XXXI (1936), particularly Section B, pp. 337-346; Dr. Fran Paxeco, "Relations between Portugal and Great Britain," *MLR*, XVIII (in four parts, of which parts II, III, and IV are pertinent here): Part II, 56-63; III, 110-114; IV, 149-155; E. A. Peers, "The Literary Activities of the Spanish 'Emigrados' in England (1814-1834)," *MLR*, XIX (1924), 315-324, 445-458. See also *CBEL*, Vol. III; note 3, above; note 22, above; and H. C. Barrows, Jr., *Main Stages in the Development of the English Literary Traveller's Experience of Italy: 1750-1860*, unpublished Ph.D. dissertation, Harvard University, 1948.

became ever more important as the Victorian age advanced. These revived, continuing, and new historical relationships should not be our only concern, however, as we attempt to evaluate the impact of the external world upon Victorian culture. Certain phases of this impact suggest that any such evaluation will force one to deal with highly diverse and exceedingly complex considerations.

Browning's use of Italian materials, it may be pointed out, was quite different from Carlyle's use of those of Germany. Browning interpreted the art and culture of Italy, past and present, and the actual Italian scene; Carlyle attempted to synthesize German thought—with such idiosyncrasies as have been often discussed—and with the avowed purpose of making such a synthesis a part of Victorian dogmatic literature. The Italian influence on applied literature resulted almost entirely from English political sympathy with the Italian *cause*. So far as Germany, France, and Italy were concerned, "The imports decidedly exceeded the exports,"[25] whether the imports took the form of translations and explications of Kant and Goethe, Comtism, Symbolism, or the patent belief that the determination of the Italian people to be free was legitimate material for Victorian verse. To chart the reactions of the Victorian reader to each direct importation or to each adaptation of foreign material in native English literature would be futile; but certain general conclusions concerning these reactions may be drawn.

The fact that many English writers borrowed heavily from foreign literatures indicates that not all their readers were so busy with insular matters—for example, the "Condition of England Question"—that they neglected the culture of the continent, imported chiefly from Italy, Germany, France, Russia, and Scandinavia. This is an incomplete statement of obvious historical fact, the implications of which may be explored with considerable profit. It is true that during recent years many important aspects of England's literary relations with Europe in the Victorian

---

[25] Elton, *op. cit.*, IV, 365.

age have been carefully examined; but no comprehensive judgment of the historical import of these relations has been made, nor have we reached any agreement concerning what the rediscovery of the continent actually signifies. The reactions of the Victorians to the Russian novelists, the literature of the Old Norsemen, the French dramatists, Ibsen, and Zola are of great artistic, intellectual, and sociological importance; the meaning of these reactions is clear to us, but we too often regard them as isolated commentaries on Victorian taste. In synthesis with other aspects of foreign influence they would constitute a remarkable chapter on the development of Victorianism. The present investigation does not involve aims so ambitious; it may be well, however, to suggest certain adjuncts to such a synthesis by considering briefly a few of the many forces which stimulated interest in the world abroad, in foreign *belles-lettres* and general culture during the Victorian age.

The most obvious stimulus, and probably the least trustworthy, is the Victorian equivalent of the Grand Tour which, although it had lost its significance as an aristocratic institution after the French Revolution and the War with France, permitted thousands of Victorians to come into direct contact with the world across the Channel. Paris, from the time of the Battle of Waterloo, attracted English visitors in large numbers; and later in the century the Latin Quarter and *la vie de bohème* vied with the Riviera in popularity among English tourists. The journey up the Rhine, the "cures" in Switzerland and Germany, and the winter *giro* through Italy increased in popularity throughout the century. The inexpensive "Circle Tour," the Peninsular Cruise, and the Iceland voyage—often taken by Victorian sportsmen because of the excellent hunting and fishing in Iceland—enabled the Victorian to see for himself the world outside the British Isles. Travel became democratic —that is to say, less expensive than it had been—and was no longer reserved to the affluent. But the fact that the Browns, the Robinsons, and the Tuppers were enabled by the improvement of transportation facilities and the lowering of travel rates to descend upon Paris and Rome like locusts does not prove necessarily that the cultural level of middle class England was thereby perceptibly raised. The Browns, the Robinsons, and the Tuppers were probably no different from the gentleman from Middletown who spends fifteen minutes in the Louvre, and devotes the rest of his day to sitting in a *bistro* meditating upon the mysteries of art. It does not follow that English interest in the French drama was greatly strengthened during the Victorian period because a particular week-end Circle Tour of Paris and environs included, in its over-all cost, a ticket of admission to the comedy of the day.

Of obviously greater importance to the Victorian acquisition of continental and American culture were the English men of letters who sponsored foreign writers; the cosmopolitan reviews; continental scholars resident in England; native scholars and translators; the very considerable use of foreign material in native English literature; and the commercial promotion of foreign works by legitimate publishers such as Henry Vizetelly,[26] and by innumerable literary pirates.[27]

Carlyle is recognized as the first great Victorian to become an indefatigable sponsor of continental literature and philosophy. Morris's love for the Norse sagas and Eddas made him equally insistent that the British become acquainted with the literature of Iceland. Gosse and Archer placed their own reputations in jeopardy by supporting the cause of Ibsen, while Swinburne's enthusiasms for Victor Hugo and other foreigners, though perhaps not representative of

[26] Vizetelly rightfully claimed to have been among the chief sponsors of foreign literature in England: "I also introduced to English readers hundreds of volumes from foreign authors whose writings until then had been sealed to the multitude, when my publication of the works of M. Zola, and the persecution of a band of fanatics, brought about my pecuniary ruin"— *Glances Back through Seventy Years*, 2 vols. (London, 1893), II, 432.

[27] The "pirating" of continental and American authors by English publishers in some cases reached scandalous proportions. For a specific example of the popularizing of a non-English author in England, and the effect of unauthorized editions of his work upon his reputation, see Gohdes, *op. cit.* ("Longfellow and His Authorized British Publishers"). Gohdes has established that Longfellow's popularity in England owed as much to pirated editions as to legitimate publishers.

sponsorships as effective as those of Morris, Carlyle, Gosse, and Archer, were no less well known. Championing a foreign worthy or a foreign idea was a popular and significant pastime during the eighteenth century; but in the nineteenth, with such men as Carlyle and Morris, it took the form of evangelism.

Periodicals such as *The Foreign Quarterly Review, The British Foreign Review or Quarterly European Journal, The Foreign and Colonial Quarterly Review,* as well as those of longer life and wider interest (*The Westminster Review, The Academy, Fraser's Magazine, The Fortnightly Review, The Cornhill Magazine, Temple Bar, et al.*), contain important reflections of cosmopolitan interests in the Victorian age and, in varying degrees, may be counted among the stimuli here under discussion. Investigation of (1) the critical attitudes adopted by various major nineteenth-century magazines in dealing with foreign literature, and (2) the relative amount of space given over to foreign matters, literary and otherwise, should produce information of considerable interest to students of the Victorian era. The incidence of foreign titles in the circulating library lists indicates that further study of Mudie's and Smith's would also repay the effort.

The presence in England of influential continental scholars, many of whom were expatriates because of their political sympathies, further stimulated interest in the world across the Channel. Blanco White's activity in early Victorian England is a case in point; and not the least of Blanco's services to international intellectual relations was his translation into Spanish of Paley's *Evidences.* A number of Spanish liberals came to England as émigrés between 1814 and 1834, among the most distinguished of whom was Antonio Alculá Galiano, who became Professor of Spanish in the University of London. The presence of the *emigrados* in England caused a surprisingly large number of Spanish periodicals to appear in London before 1830. *Ocios de Españoles Emigrados,* for example, was established for the distinct purpose of disseminating Spanish culture in England; but most of the Spanish publications had ceased to exist by the time the Victorian age commenced. The activity of the *emigrados* in the twenties and thirties, however, may have had some influence on later Anglo-Spanish relations.

The senior Rossetti and the Italian circle which surrounded him after 1824 contributed much to the English interest in Italian culture, especially in Dante; and of course Rossetti's sphere of influence was somewhat enlarged when he became Professor of Italian at King's College. Dante Gabriel Rossetti was heir to the transplanted Italian culture nourished by the expatriates; his services to the Dante revival and other Anglo-Italian interests, therefore, have most obvious connections with the Italian intellectuals who were among the émigrés in his father's coterie.

Karl Blind, who came to England as a political refugee, soon established himself as an important influence in Victorian cultural and political life. It was he who entertained Mazzini and Garibaldi on their visits to England, visits which in themselves advanced Anglo-Italian relationships; and Blind is given credit as well for introducing Swinburne to Mazzini. Max Müller went to England in 1846 to edit the Rig Veda, established himself at Oxford, and remained to become a naturalized British citizen and to have a chair of comparative philology created for him.

Two distinguished Icelanders, Eríkur Magnússon and Gudbrand Vigfússon, spent a considerable amount of time in Victorian England, the former working with William Morris on various Norse translations, the latter collaborating with Frederick York Powell in the production of three of the most important Scandinavian works of scholarship which have been published in England: the 1878 edition of the *Sturlunga Saga* (with its *Prolegomena* on Old Icelandic literature), the *Corpus Poëticum Boreale*, and the *Origines Islandicæ*. The extensive contribution which was made to the study of continental literature in England by Gabriele Rossetti, Magnússon, and their many compatriots has already received considerable attention, but is worthy of further investigation.[28]

[28] See Oliver Elton, *Frederick York Powell*, 2 vols. (Oxford, 1906); and

The activity of native English scholars in the study of continental language and literature and in the preparation of translations was greater in the Victorian age than it had been at any other time in the history of English letters. In the field of Scandinavian study alone, Victorian England produced such accomplished scholars as Samuel Laing, Edmund Gosse, Benjamin Thorpe, Richard Cleasby, Sir Edmund Head, Sir George Webbe Dasent, William Archer, and F. Y. Powell. Equally imposing catalogues could be compiled for each of the great European literatures; and the names of several major professional and non-professional scholars of the age—Carlyle, Arnold, Browning, G. H. Lewes, D. G. Rossetti, Morris, and Swinburne— would appear in such lists with frequency.[29]

Victorian translations and various reactions to them cast many interesting sidelights on Victorian cosmopolitanism. It would serve no purpose here to attempt a description either of the number or the variety of such translations. They show in general that much of the important and representative literature of the major languages of Europe was available to English readers in their own language by the end of the Victorian age. Perhaps the most notable advance (after the German) was made in the field of Old Norse. Between the time of George Webbe Dasent's version of the *Prose Edda* (1842) and the publication of the Morris-Magnússon *Saga Library* (1891-1905), most of the great

Stéfan Einarsson, *Saga Eiríks Magnússonar í Cambridge* (Reykjavík, 1933), both excellent examples of the value of investigation in this field. See also E. R. Vincent, *Gabriele Rossetti in England* (Oxford, 1936), a detailed and useful work. The affiliations of Marx and Engels in Great Britain should be noted in passing.

[29] The large number of pieces written on foreign worthies by Carlyle, Arnold, and Swinburne is especially noteworthy. The attitude of formal critics toward the status of literary criticism in mid-Victorian England was at least related to the interest which Arnold and G. H. Lewes found in French criticism. See Arnold's remarks on the *Revue des Deux Mondes* in "The Function of Criticism at the Present Time" (the section on "Disinterestedness"); the many references in Arnold's critical works (*passim*) to Sainte-Beuve, Renan, and other continentals; and Lewes's apostrophe to Sainte-Beuve in a review written in 1853. Lewes's "European outlook" has been interestingly treated by Morris Greenhut, "George Henry Lewes and English Classicism," *RES*, XXIV (1948), 126-137.

literature of the medieval Norsemen had been made available to English readers either in translation or in paraphrase. The body of translations from the Old Norse completed during the Victorian age includes both Eddas, the *Heimskringla*, four of the five great sagas, several minor sagas, much of the poetry, and a considerable amount of scholarly and antiquarian material.[30] This strenuous activity in the field of Norse translation is the more remarkable when one observes that the documents which were rendered into English by Morris and Magnússon, Vigfússon and Powell, Dasent, Head, and others deal with life in an age which, in Victorian terms, was barbarous and uncivilized. Yet strangely enough, the Victorian *interpretation* of the Old Norse spirit did not usually resemble that of the late eighteenth century when—through egregious mistranslation—Norse lays were sometimes connected with the ghoulish phases of early Romanticism, and were highly esteemed as authentic representations of the "Gothick."

VI

To epitomize the Victorian reception of translated foreign contemporaneous literature, we may examine the fortunes of Balzac, Zola, and Ibsen, for their cases illustrate the Victorian proclivity for expressing violent first objection followed by friendly tolerance, and often by warm approval.[31] Early critics apparently recognized Balzac as the father of French Realism and greeted him with appropriate vituperation.[32] But the original indignation over Balzac, than whom no "baser, meaner, filthier scoundrel [ever] polluted society," gave way to eulogy at the end of the century for, in the passing of time, he had become one of those "divine spies, from whom the world has no secrets. . . ."[33]

---

[30] See the present writer's monograph, *The Victorians and the Vikings: A Bibliographical Essay on Anglo-Norse Literary Relations*, University of Michigan Contributions in Modern Philology, No. 3 (Ann Arbor, 1947).

[31] There are a few notable exceptions. Certain reviews, over a long period of years, vociferously represented the insular tradition in their criticism of foreign importations. This appears to be a fertile field for investigation.

[32] Decker ("Balzac"), p. 1150.

[33] *Ibid.*, p. 1157.

Swinburne defended Hugo while he attacked Zola;[34] and Andrew Lang, with tongue in cheek, attributed the English dislike of Zola to unfortunate Puritanism.[35] The notorious debate held in the House of Commons on May 2, 1888, brought out the fact that Zola's novels were selling at the rate of a thousand copies weekly. "Nothing more diabolical had ever been written by the pen of man," declared Samuel Smith, Esq., of Flintshire, who opined further that France was corrupt and dying as a result of such writing as Zola's.[36] The Secretary of State for the Home Department supported Mr. Smith, contending that in Zola, "French romantic literature of modern days . . . [has] reached a lower depth of immorality than it [has] ever known before."[37] As a result of this official condemnation of Zola, Henry Vizetelly, publisher of the Zola translations, was fined £100 at the November session of the Central Criminal Court, in 1888, having been convicted of publishing an obscene libel: namely, *La Terre*. Instruments of invective were sharpened, and the adjectives "filthy," "immoral," "base," "sottish," "obscene," "lascivious," and "lewd" were brought out of temporary retirement for special application to Zola—and to others.[38]

The bitter division of opinion over the worth of literature from abroad presented some most peculiar critical attitudes and, in several instances, dichotomy in the judgments made by one individual.[39] Swinburne's dislike of Zola is incompatible with his early worship of Baudelaire, and for that matter, incompatible with the tone of *Poems and Ballads*.[40] Saintsbury was a loyal supporter of French

[34] A. C. Swinburne, "Note on a Question of the Hour," *Athenaeum* (June 16, 1877), p. 768.

[35] Decker ("Zola"), p. 1142. Tennyson's unhappy comments on "Zolaism" in "Locksley Hall Sixty Years After" should be noted.

[36] *Pernicious Literature*, pp. 1, 6.   [37] *Ibid.*, p. 12.

[38] The laws of obscene libel are of interest in this connection. See Alec Craig, *The Banned Books of England* (London, 1937).

[39] Robert Buchanan's unpredictable attitudes are well illustrated in his treatment of Rossetti, Whitman, and Zola. Buchanan's changes in taste and opinion, and those of some of his contemporaries, will bear further examination and analysis.

[40] Even more inconsistent is Buchanan's defense of Whitman, in the light of his "Fleshly School" attack.

writers, especially of Baudelaire, but he treated Ibsen with a coolness which may pass for contempt.

The opposition to Ibsen, while grounded on a base quite different from that on which the attacks on the French writers were made, was both violent and vicious. William Archer, Ibsen's second English sponsor, was willing to prophesy that Ibsen's modern plays would probably never enjoy permanent success on the English stage.[41] But in answer to the Victorian objection to Ibsen's didacticism (*sic*), Archer asked, "What really great art is not didactic?"[42] The Ibsen argument resolved itself into a stage controversy, but Ibsen's popularity among readers cannot be reconciled with the protracted refusal of the Victorians to attend productions of his plays until very late in the century: Victoria herself witnessed the performance of *Ghosts* in 1897. The *Academy* stated: "If a decisive proof is wanted of the judicial separation between the reading and the play-going public in England it may be found in the fact that two collected editions of Ibsen's prose dramas have been issued in eleven years. Ibsen is the supreme pariah of the English stage, while by English bookmen he is honored beyond any living dramatist, native or foreign."[43] Saintsbury said of Ibsen at a still later date: "He is parochial, and not of a very large or a very distinguished parish."[44]

Most of the foreign writers who attempted to establish themselves in England, and whose cases are represented in hyperbole by the early rejection and later approval of Balzac, Zola, and Ibsen, found admirers and supporters: publishers who commercialized their successes at home, or English champions who introduced and explained them to a fairly willing and a reasonably receptive public, after acrimonious controversy had reduced itself in some quarters to stubborn, moralistic objection, and in others to academic debate.

[41] "Ibsen and English Criticism," *Fortnightly Review*, n.s., XLVI (1889), 37.
[42] Archer, *op. cit.*, p. 31. [43] *Academy*, LX (1901), 244.
[44] Saintsbury, p. 326. Ibsen was not the only foreign writer who suffered from Saintsbury's indifference and occasionally grotesque judgments. Cf., for example, the remarks on Dostoievsky and Tolstoi in *The Later Nineteenth Century.*

By the end of the century, scholars and translators had made available to the Victorian reader a magnificent library of foreign literature in English. The constant increase in the quantity and variety of translated materials throughout the period is *prima facie* evidence of the fact that the Victorians were buying and reading the literature of Europe. Though they did not always read it with pleasure and approbation, the ultimate Victorian approval of continental and American literature was never in real doubt. The changing attitude of the Victorians toward foreign importations may have been conditioned by an inherent and perhaps unconscious feeling that the new must be resisted until it has become seasoned with age; it may represent that unpredictable reform in taste and judgment which may appear within any given decade or year; it may have had its origin in the gradual disintegration of militant insularity. It is not necessary to decide here what produced the change: the important fact is that it occurred.

VII

The nineteenth-century Englishman's reactions to foreign elements in the literature of his time should be of considerable importance whenever the meaning of the adjective *Victorian* is under consideration. The use of this much abused term as an epithet suggestive of complacency, smugness, false morality, and stolid provincialism can most easily be defended if one assumes that the conscience of Albert the Good established the authentic pattern of Victorian behavior, or that the portraiture of manners and the social philosophy of certain minor female novelists constitute eclectic representations of Victorian life. It is far more accurate, however, to define the temper of the age in terms of intellectual and physical expansion, social consciousness, philosophic conflict, and cosmopolitanism. Yet we may ponder with profit the amazing circumstances which placed the parochial view of British infallibility, self-righteousness, jingoism, and the White Man's Burden in juxtaposition with the rise of science, the extension of empire, the growth of liberalism, and the assimilation of foreign culture. From a point of vantage in the twentieth century, it is convenient, if not entirely satisfying, to remark that so strange a concomitance merely illustrates the complexity of the times; that the age of Tennyson was, after all, the age of Darwin, the English Omar, Thackeray, Borrow, and Richard Burton; of Ibsen, Tolstoi, Emerson, Hawthorne, Victor Hugo, Baudelaire, and Abraham Lincoln. To conclude that it was so recognized by every thinking Victorian would not accord with the canon of evidence which can be adduced; but in the same canon one may trace the decline of the insular attitude and the rise of cosmopolitan interest.

It cannot be argued that the literary relations of England with the outside world in the Victorian age brought a complete and final end to narrow concepts of nationalism, or to that parochialism which was nurtured on false pride. It is manifestly clear, however, that Englishmen looked across the English Channel, across the North Sea, and across the Atlantic Ocean with ever-clearer vision and with ever-greater understanding of what their eyes beheld as the decades of Victoria's reign passed; it is equally apparent that, in so doing, they developed a deeper, wider, and more intelligent interest in the world abroad than has sometimes been credited to them by critics hostile to their age.

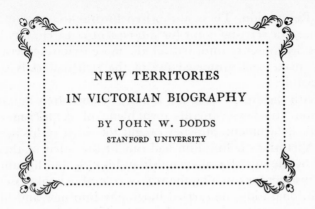

NEW TERRITORIES
IN VICTORIAN BIOGRAPHY

BY JOHN W. DODDS
STANFORD UNIVERSITY

THE field of biographical research offers unusual entice-
ments today to literary scholars interested in the Victorian
age. Many influences are converging to make desirable not
merely an extension into a number of by-paths but also a
careful re-examination of many of the major figures of
Victorian literature. It is abundantly clear, moreover, that
the most important tasks at hand are not those for the antiquarian but for the writer of constructive scholarly imagination. It is time for Victorian biography to come of age,
and there is need, not of mere task-workers, but of biographers superior in perceptive and in creative scholarship.
It is not the purpose of this chapter to survey the entire
field of *desiderata*, but rather to indicate certain lines of
approach and to suggest some of the kinds of tasks which
need to be done.

Victorian biography has gone through a series of clearly
marked stages. Until well beyond the turn of the century it
suffered, with notable exceptions, from what Carlyle called
"the Damocles Sword of Respectability." Hence the dismal
series of "official" *Lives*, reverent, discreet, commemorative
—not so much hiding the wart as denying that warts ever
existed. Writers were Great Men to their children, who
either wrote pious accounts of the paternal glories or appointed the biographers who were to be the custodians of

the Reputation. These authorized biographies remain, of course, the starting-point for subsequent research, for they are storehouses of information, the more irritating because they make such distorted use of the rich materials then accessible.

With the 1920's came the inimitable and often imitated Lytton Strachey, with his own blend of skepticism and ironic detachment. Strachey caught the spirit of his age as the Victorians before him had caught the spirit of theirs; and by the superb craftsmanship of his style and his unerring instinct for catching the real or colorable weaknesses of traditional idols, he carried biography into new and hitherto uncharted waters. Strachey, if he did not always tell the whole truth, told truths different from those of his Victorian predecessors. The trouble came not so much with Strachey himself, for his distortions had a certain therapeutic value and were in healthy reaction against idolatrous sentimentalities. Like so many masters, he was ruined by his disciples. The shoals of little Stracheys who swam in his wake instituted the new school of "debunking" biography —concerning which, fortunately, one is now able to write historically. The practice of this school ranged from an amiable subacidity to shrill sensationalism. Little writers shook the coattails of Victorian titans, dragging their subjects into the laboratory of the psychoanalyst and subjecting them to clinical post-mortem examination. Such biographers believed that the only corrective to a false reverence was a hostile irreverence. The Victorian who could be discovered to have departed from the codes of his generation was the man for them. They took in vast quantities of dirty linen and smirkingly washed it in public. But like all fads this wore itself out, or sickened from surfeit. It marked an age; that is its sufficient epitaph.

As everyone knows, this new school delighted in fictionizing biography—interpolating long imaginary conversations and pretending to crawl inside an author's mind to tell us what went on there. A little later there were some manifestations of a still newer fashion in popular biography. This used many of the techniques of the Strachey-

esque writers, but found it amusing to patronize its subjects rather than to satirize them. The method here was
that of a jocular familiarity, affectionately condescending.
The sneering satire of the 1920's was an irritating distor-
tion; the offensive condescension of the 1930's was mere
misbehavior. Fortunately it was recognized by most sensible
people as a public nuisance.

Fashions in biography aside, the time has come now for
reappraisals. We are far enough away from the Victorians
to have a new perspective and a fresh objectivity. Hagiog-
raphy is not likely to be revived, but there is no penalty
now for honestly liking your author. New materials have
been accumulating, and as pious descendants progressively
disappear the biographer will be troubled less and less by
the fearful withholding of important letters and documents.
Just as importantly, the explorations which have been
made into the thought-currents of the Victorians, the documentation and exposition of intellectual and social backgrounds, give the biographer access to the age and bring
into focus much which was previously confused and contra-
dictory. We are accumulating the materials for complete
and veracious portraiture, for that re-creation of personality against the background of its times which is the essence
of intelligent and truthful biography.

Even a brief survey of the field makes one realize the
clear need for extended reconsiderations of many Victorians.[1] Biographies have continued to appear, of course, and
not a few of them have been suggestive and useful. Many of
them have been concerned with an aspect of the man and
his work or have been brief and factual accounts of his
career. There is almost no major Victorian who would not
benefit from the right kind of "full-dress" treatment, which
uses new biographical discoveries, incorporates the findings
of the monographs that treat special aspects of his career,
assimilates social and intellectual backgrounds, and em-
ploys, in many cases, the new tools of scientific psychology.

[1] For a valuable summary and criticism of modern Victorian studies up
to the war years, see C. F. Harrold: "Recent Trends in Victorian Studies:
1922-1939," *Studies in Philology*, XXXVII (October, 1940), 667-697.

We need more of the complete kind of study which will do for the major Victorians what A. H. Quinn did for Edgar Allan Poe, Stanley Williams for Washington Irving, and N. I. White for Shelley. We need the amplitude of the "official" *Life* (not its sentimentality or its reticences) plus a modern awareness and incisiveness and a structural plasticity. "Life and Times" sounds old-fashioned today, but it it not far off the point, if "times" is interpreted to mean an integrated presentation of the influence of an age upon an author, and not mere chunks of history hauled in to give a semblance of background.

It may be assumed that such reappraisals would be neither eulogistic nor acidulous. They must be what Harold Nicolson calls "pure" biography, the essential of which is historic truth used, as Sidney Lee put it, to "transmit a personality." This postulates more than an assemblage of facts, however well documented. We can do with a minimum of laundry lists and canceled checks. The new biographer must not merely be complete, he must translate experience by means of his constructive and shaping power. He must be objective, but not merely literal. He must, if his biography is to be a proper synthesis, present not a thesis but a coherently satisfying point of view which embraces all the known facts and interprets them without special bias. The reappraisal of the Victorians can never be made merely by standing upon library stepladders. It must be as scholarly as a meeting of the Modern Language Association and as human as—well, Lockhart or Froude. Clearly this is a call for paragons.

I I

There are few major Victorian authors who do not stand in need of full, amplified reinterpretation. Thomas Carlyle is a good case in point. No one will ever be able to do for Carlyle quite what Froude did, but Froude's necessary limitations and the discovery of new materials point the need for a *Life* complete in its scope and acute in its interpretation. This need has not been filled by Emery Neff's admirable brief study of the socially and economically "prophetic" Carlyle, and most decidedly not by D. A. Wilson's amorphous six-volume compendium of special pleading—useful as the latter must always be as a quarry of anecdotal information.

In like manner Matthew Arnold waits a biographer, and, it is to be hoped, will soon find one. Howard F. Lowry's editing of Arnold's letters and notebooks has been preparing the way for such a work. It is strange that this really great Victorian, whether because of the reticence of his descendants or because his life lacked the pungent dramatic quality infusing everything which Carlyle, for example, said or did, has never had even reasonably adequate biographical attention. Certainly Hugh Kingsmill's book (1928), which reared a whole biographical superstructure upon the dubious references of the Marguerite poems, will not do. Lionel Trilling has given us the keenest critical study to date (1939); but until Arnold's biography is properly written a perceptible gap in our knowledge of Victorian men of letters will remain unfilled.

Walter Savage Landor has been interestingly though by no means definitively placed by Malcolm Elwin's biography (1941). Walter Pater is badly in need of a biographer; it is strange that no one has properly addressed himself to the task of correcting Wright's official *Life* (1907) and re-evaluating Pater's career. Newman, in spite of the attention that he and his group have received in recent years, still awaits a full-dress *Life* which will make use of the materials which have accumulated since Wilfred Ward's two-volume biography in 1912. Macaulay was objectively treated by Richmond C. Beatty in his *Lord Macaulay: Victorian Liberal* (1938), but the book which will supplement Trevelyan and give us a complete critical and biographical appraisal of Macaulay is still to be written.

A monumental task awaits the biographer, too, who will write a comprehensive *Life and Times* of John Ruskin, making use of the multifold Ruskin materials which are continually turning up, and submitting Ruskin's career to an analysis beyond the scope either of Collingwood or Cook. R. H. Wilenski's *John Ruskin* (1933)—though it ventures into realms of psychopathology which are full of shoals for anyone except the trained specialist—has perhaps pointed the direction which a study should take. Wilenski's subtitle: "an introduction to further study of his life and work" is an indication that the field is clear for subsequent exploration.

Among the major novelists, there are many important figures to be treated. In the long years since J. W. Cross's *George Eliot* (1885) a great deal of information has come to light which not only supplements but changes the standard verdicts and makes imperative a complete revaluation. Blanche Colton Williams did much to clear the ground in her *Life* (1936), but the last word is by no means in. This is shown, for example, in Gordon Haight's *George Eliot and John Chapman* (1940).[2]

Dickens is another subject for future biographical study. It may be that Forster's great work, as well as the mere volume of accumulated and accumulating evidence, has deterred some otherwise courageous writer from attempting the *Life* which the elapsed years make necessary. There has been no dearth of "interpretations" of Dickens in recent years: from Ralph Strauss's useful *Portrait* (1928) through Leacock's distressingly thin treatment (1933), Kingsmill's journalistic sketch (1934) and Thomas Wright's adequate but unimpressive *Life* (1935) up to Una Pope-Hennessy's latest treatment (1945). Ley's annotated edition (1928) of Forster's *Life* is one of the most important contributions to Dickensian scholarship in this generation. Here again, however, the field is open to the biographer who can do for modern times what Forster, by the very limitations of his period and his sympathies, was unable to accomplish. There is a place for a long, comprehensive, careful study of Dickens, written on the basis of new knowledge and relating the man to his perturbed times. The truly "definitive" life of Dickens is yet around the corner.

[2] Professor Haight some time ago announced that he is at work on a biography, which we can hope will fill in the complete picture. Meanwhile we can be thankful for Gerald Bullett's excellent short biography (1947), which is based on much scholarly material, and is both objective and appreciative.

If this is true of Dickens it is true to a greater extent of Thackeray. Thackeray is the most considerable Victorian literary figure of whom there has not been an even approximately satisfying or complete biography. By his own wish he was spared the pious genuflections of an "official" eulogizing biographer after his death. Ironically enough, a reverent family interpreted his wish to mean no biography at all, and as a result the letters and journals which would have made possible the complete interpretation of Thackeray's intricate personality were for long strictly withheld. As any one would have known, the family ban could not prevent people from writing about Thackeray, and there has been a series of fragmentary and necessarily inadequate *Lives*. Of these one of the best was that of Malcolm Elwin (1932). More recently, Lionel Stevenson's *The Showman of Vanity Fair* (1947) has brought fresh perceptions to the study of Thackeray's career. And still more recently the decks have been cleared for possible definitive work. Gordon N. Ray, with the approval of the heirs, has published a massive edition of Thackeray's letters. The materials are now at hand for the long overdue biography of one of the most important Victorians.[3]

There is an acute need, too, for comprehensive resurveys of the major poets. The curious unanimity with which scholars have failed to come to grips with Tennyson is hard to explain. Certainly problems are there to be solved, and plenty of them. It is a strange commentary on "the most typically Victorian" poet that the dull filial biography by Hallam Tennyson in 1898-1899 should still be the standard work in the field. Harold Nicolson's penetrating little book (1923) is the only reasonably perspicuous treatment we have of a man who was not, providentially, quite the pattern of perfection his worshipers wanted us to believe him. But Nicolson's book is brief and incomplete. The bibliography of critical writings about Tennyson is sufficiently long; why has no one taken it upon himself to do an honest and comprehensive modern *Life*? Sir Charles Tennyson's

[3] Since this was written, Mr. Ray has announced that he is midstream in the writing of a *Life* of Thackeray.

Tennyson (1949) does much to fill in the picture of the young Tennyson, but this book should stimulate rather than deter future treatments.

In like manner the work upon Browning is distinctly out of date. Since Griffin and Minchen published their *Life* in 1910 a great deal of information has been gathered, and as William DeVane says, "The whole life of Browning needs to be set forth more completely and with some very different emphases." Here again the lack is not that of material—sentimentalists, pedants, and capable scholars alike have been adding steadily to the already tremendous Browning bibliography—but of someone to do the proper synthesizing and interpreting.

III

These, then, are some (by no means all) of the biographical *desiderata* for the major Victorians. When one reaches the second flight of Victorian authors even more inheritors of unfulfilled renown are found. Here the need is just as often for exploration as for definition. We can have no adequate picture of the whole *mise-en-scène* of Victorian literary life, for which scattered materials have steadily been piling up, until a whole range of fresh biographical studies has been made. Such a considerable person in his own time as William Harrison Ainsworth, for example, has been neglected. Michael Sadleir made a brilliant beginning with Bulwer Lytton in *Bulwer: A Panorama* (1931), but we have no satisfactory study of Bulwer's career after the age of thirty-three. And to know Bulwer and his popularity is to begin to understand certain distinct areas of the Victorian mind. Arthur Hugh Clough, another forgotten figure, needs careful and full delineation.

The list can be continued. John Forster and J. A. Froude, two great Victorian biographers, have themselves lacked adequate biographical attention. The most considerable study of Francis Jeffrey is Lord Cockburn's *Life*, published in 1852! J. G. Lockhart has been pretty well ignored since Andrew Lang's *Life and Letters* in 1897. John Wilson, whose career illuminates many by-paths in English letters, has been the subject of just one biography since 1862.

Still further toward the periphery of Victorian letters are many writers whose careers we must have in some detail if we are to understand the Victorian literary world. Until we know more about the by-paths of Victorian taste and accomplishment our record of the age will continue to be fragmentary and two-dimensional. Dion Boucicault and Tom Robertson—to take two important figures of the moribund Victorian theater—were men of great importance in the contemporary scene. Neither has been adequately considered, either for himself or by way of reflecting an important area of Victorian life. Samuel Lover was not a great novelist, but he deserves better than the official *Life* by W. B. Bernard in 1874; for to know how and why Lover was popular is to know more about the intellectual background of a century. Such a considerable person as Marryat was interred by his daughter in a *Life and Letters* in 1872 and, although resurrected in Hannay's *Life* of 1889, he has never been properly considered. Yet Marryat is an important index of his age.

Alexander Smith needs to be rediscovered; as does Sir Henry Taylor, of whom a proper study (beyond that of his autobiography) would also reveal much about mid-Victorian England. Most surprising of all, in these peripheral considerations, is the neglect accorded one of the liveliest and most provocative of early Victorian writers: William Maginn. He would have made an excellent subject for one of the "new" biographers, for his career was reasonably lurid. He was also a profoundly important influence in journalism and criticism, and he deserves better than the rapid treatment he has received in books devoted to larger subjects.

The ease with which such recommendations as these can be extended indicates the very real opportunities at hand for Victorian biographical scholarship. Much valuable critical work has already been done. Bit by bit we are acquiring the studies of Victorian society and thought necessary to bring the age into focus. But accomplishment in biography has lagged behind the critical consideration of Victorian social and literary ideas. The charting of the intellectual cross-currents should before this have given point to new biographical interpretations. There are, to be sure, explicable reasons for this biographical lag. Fundamental has been the difficulty of getting at definitive materials. But it is to be hoped that in post-war England many family archives hitherto unbreachable may now be reached by energetic workers. In recent years many valuable collections of letters and papers have been finding their way into libraries where they await the uses which this paper has been urging.

There is scope here for varying abilities of honest scholarship. We need to know all that can be known about nineteenth-century England. No one man's reading of any person worth writing about is enough. Yet the clear need is for a series of major biographical works by men of deep learning who are yet masters of that learning, who have in addition to sympathy and critical acumen a firm creative imagination. I see no very good reason why these biographers, however vast their erudition, should not present truth palatably and submit their synthesized material in readable form. Felicity of style need not in itself be suspect, and if we are to have more than a series of academic exercises the writers must combine lucidity and precision—the first fruits of good writing—with a sense of pictorial and dramatic values. They must be at once astringent and good-humored, sympathetic and critical. The point would not need laboring if publishers' lists were not so full of biographical studies which are either smart and thin or dull and pedantic. Sir Charles Firth once said, "I think Lytton Strachey's a very bad style in which to tell the truth." It would be more accurate to say that Strachey used a very good style in which to tell something less than the truth. Nevertheless good style and truthfulness are not mutually exclusive.

The fullness of the years is bringing rich opportunities to Victorian scholarship. As I said earlier, the demand is for paragons of biographical skill. If we can't get them we shall of course have to be content with something less. Yet the tasks are there, and need doing.

OUR NEW
HELLENIC RENAISSANCE

BY JOSEPH E. BAKER
UNIVERSITY OF IOWA

"I know of no body of literature, except perhaps that of
Ancient Athens, so well adapted as the Victorian to giving
the modern American—student or layman—a lively understanding of what we mean by a civilized society, or for
raising into his own consciousness those remnants of civilized tradition which have been shouted down but not yet
obliterated by contemporary ballyhoo." That sentence concluded my essay, "Victorian England and Modern America";[1] it may stand as the beginning of a series of considerations that seem to me to promise greater riches the deeper
we penetrate. The association of Athens and Victorian
England suggests certain significant observations. We speak
of Florence and Athens together because fourteenth-cen-
tury Florence gave us a revival of Classical studies and consequently a more humane philosophy of life; future centuries may associate Athens and nineteenth-century Oxford
for the same reason.

Now that it no longer seems paradoxical to speak of the
Carolingian Renaissance, and the "Renaissance of the
Twelfth Century," in addition to *the* Renaissance which extends from the fourteenth to the seventeenth century, we
may as well recognize that a revival of humanistic culture,
nourished on ancient Classical literature, but expressed in
fresh creative art and thought of its own, is likely to occur

[1] *American Review*, v (Sept. 1935).

whenever western man has got lost, has forgotten the Greek discovery that he is primarily a human being, and then, after a number of generations, has found that other paths are blind alleys. It is just barely possible that we might have a Renaissance superior to that of the sixteenth century, as the latter was superior to the one four hundred years earlier; but I am not engaged in prophecy. I wish to disentangle a certain thread of cultural development from the tangle of the last century, a thread which is still unbroken, that we may pick it up and follow it as a clue, perhaps to find our way out of a labyrinth. As the Renaissance of the sixteenth century led us out of a decadent Medieval emphasis upon externals, back to an emphasis on the human spirit, so our own Hellenic revival might lead us back to human reason, away from our subjection to the inhuman standards of numbers, material wealth, natural force, and uncritical emotion. It is difficult to establish our values by the constant use of reason, in the dry light of ever vigilant criticism. It is much easier to say that our values (such as justice, or beauty) can be determined by the mechanical process of counting, or by simply giving way to our feelings. But the deadly absurdity of the easier way is clear by this time. We have been swept into a quagmire in the flood of four great movements which rose in the eighteenth century, triumphed in the nineteenth, and are likely to destroy us in the twentieth, unless reason can moderate them for human ends. I refer to the triumph of industrialism, of science, of romanticism, and of "democracy," using or misusing this latter word to include not only the anarchic ideals of Shelley but also the rise of the "mass men" with their criterion of popularity.

As we read nineteenth-century literature, awake to its twentieth-century implications, we can see that these movements were essentially noble, but each had a tragic flaw. Their overweening hybris now threatens a tragedy in which civilization itself will be destroyed. Watching this historical spectacle we have found it easy to adopt a fatalistic attitude, or at least the attitude of a spectator at a play, experiencing a certain catharsis from the contemplation of one disaster after another. But to do so is to let a figure of speech become a guide of life. For in actuality we are *not* observing a drama, in which everything is predestined in a pattern to an inevitable conclusion. A dramatist creates figures that can do nothing except what the author makes them do, and the historians (especially those claiming to be "scientific") often assume the author's privilege of showing us figures who lack independence. As Guedalla says, in *The Hundred Years*, "There is always a temptation to assign ineluctable causes to chance happenings, since history is infinitely more impressive when it is inevitable." But fortunately humanity is not bound to lie down and let the juggernaut of "progress" or regress run over it. We are free to disobey the "scientific" historians and to have a Renaissance on our own terms. In spite of the current of modern events, in spite of the assertions of men like Spengler and Berdyaev, there is no necessary impossibility in the conception that we might find a revival of rational Hellenic culture in the modern world.

But even those who are not fatalists may say, "Granted that we *might* revive the Hellenic life of reason today, is there any sign that it is being done? In the nineteenth and twentieth centuries we admirers of classical enlightenment seem to be defenders of a lost cause, of an old form of culture that is being liquidated, however much the truly educated may regret it. A new Dark Ages of specialization, force, and superstition, has been closing in upon us. Whatever we may do tomorrow, don't we stand today at the end of a dying civilization which flowered in the sixteenth century?" Now the importance of research along this line in nineteenth-century literature is that it shows this analysis to be false. The humanistic culture was not bound to go under, and it did not go under. What the nineteenth century shows us, closely examined, is a dying down of the Latin Renaissance—so much is true. But it shows also the rise of a new Hellenic Renaissance. Obviously the Latin language has been losing its place in the schools. But it is also true that there is much more interest in the Greek view of life today than a century ago. Chesterfield could say, "Plato,

Aristoteles, Demosthenes and Thucydides, whom none but adepts know." Today our journalists recommend Thucydides as "required reading"[2] for the understanding of current events, the radio sends practical politicians to Demosthenes, and we have been shown, by Adler's *Art and Prudence*, that Aristotle said the last word on the principles governing the movies as an art.

It is important to remember that in spite of the catalysis supplied by the Greeks, the Italian Renaissance was predominantly Latin, partly even a nationalistic revival of Roman traditions. Petrarch, enthusiastic about Roman political ideas, a Latin poet himself, could not read Greek. In the sixteenth century "Humanist" came to mean "Ciceronian" more often than "Platonist." North of the Alps, Erasmus recognized the importance of Greek, and he probably recovered the Socratic spirit better than any modern— but Erasmus himself is one of the glories of *Latin* literature, the greatest Latin author since Augustine. Shakespeare, close as he was to the humane spirit of Greece, thought of himself as on the side of Rome more than Greece, and owed his debt to the Greeks largely through Latin middlemen. As Hardin Craig says, "It must be remembered also that in England we have to do not only with an imperfect and mixed classicism, but mainly with a Latin classicism."[3] On the other hand our modern Renaissance is not Latin but Greek. And when those two overlap, one can often dissociate the Latin culture from the Greek: of the receding Latin tradition one could name Voltaire, Chesterfield, Gibbon, Thackeray; of the rising Greek culture, Goethe, Emerson, Arnold, Maritain. As the one Renaissance was especially indebted to Italy, this was especially indebted to Germany, though both were destined, perhaps, to reach their supreme literary expression in English.

2 The title of a leading article by Elmer Davis, *Saturday Review of Literature*, xx (Oct. 14, 1939), 3 ff. See Chesterfield, *Letters*, ed. Dobrée (London, 1932), IV, 1610 (1750).

3 *The Enchanted Glass* (N.Y., 1936), p. 215.

II

Before pursuing this idea further, it is necessary to remove another of those stumbling blocks that obstruct our intellectual progress in exploring the nineteenth century. And that is the popular fallacy that poetry leads the way, and criticism comes lagging after, merely formulating what has been done. But criticism usually comes first, in our different literary epochs. The earlier Romantics like the Schlegels wrote philosophic criticism; the younger Romantics like Heine put their theory into practice. Emerson's formulation of Transcendentalism preceded the flowering of New England literature with its Transcendental orientation. When Sidney's *Apologie for Poetrie* was written it was the most important piece of original literature in the modern English language, except for Spenser's *Shepherds Calendar*, and Sidney had the critical acumen to praise the *Shepherds Calendar* as poetry of the quality one had a right to expect of the Renaissance. For in spite of the dearth of great literature, Sidney could see that England was ready for a literary outburst. Of Chaucer he says, "I know not whether to marvel more, either that he in that misty time could see so clearly, or that we in this clear age walk so stumblingly after him." In his comparison of the possibilities of the two periods Sidney was proved to be right; within the next two generations appeared two-thirds of the greatest English poetry. The next distinct movement of English literature, the Neo-Classical, had its greatest critic, Dryden, at the very beginning. And, to skip to the present, the critic who may still seem to have the wisest understanding of the social and intellectual values of the twentieth century is Matthew Arnold. As H. V. Routh says, "He prepared the way for our own age."[4] This of Arnold, the great Classicist.

In early nineteenth-century criticism there is a phenomenon that puzzled me for a long time, and it has evidently puzzled others. I once argued at length that our Romantic poets were Classical critics—often better classical critics

[4] *Money, Morals and Manners as Revealed in Modern Literature* (London, 1935), p. 124.

than the eighteenth-century Neo-Classicists. This is a paradox; but with proper modifications it is generally true. And that is strange. In a conscious revolt, one expects the statements of theory to be even more revolutionary than poetic practice. But there is, I think, a solution to this problem, in the conception of an Hellenic Renaissance. These Romantic poets were not, in their criticism, merely the last of the Neo-Classicists, for they were disagreeing with their predecessors. We have, here, not evidence that criticism is more conservative than creative art, but a proof that criticism, dealing as it does with general principles, really leads the way for later poetry, fiction, drama, education, and statesmanship. I am speaking now only of the greatest criticism written in the Romantic period, and in England, where the best criticism has nearly always been written by leading *poets*.[5]

To understand the direction of currents in a literature so recent as the Victorian, it is necessary to observe what preceded as well as what followed. Almost everything that grew to maturity in the mid-century had its roots in the first quarter of the century; and had there not been a dearth of great books between 1825 and 1835 we probably would be treating the whole of the nineteenth century as a unit, at least as homogeneous as the Neo-Classical period. It has long been recognized that this is true of the elixir of Romanticism itself, so that we speak of "the Victorian Romantics" of the mid-century and of the Neo-Romantics of the *fin de siècle*. It is equally true that Victorian Hellenism is the daughter of a less pure Hellenism of the Romantics. This fact has been obscured by the unwillingness of twentieth-century Hellenists like Paul Elmer More to admit their own descent from Romantic grandfathers. To think of Paul Elmer More as a spiritual descendant of Shelley may be surprising, but it is impossible to read More's series, *The Greek Tradition*, without recalling Shelley's statement that Plato taught "a moral and intellectual system of doctrine, comprehending at once the past, the pres-

[5] The more romantic critics in England were prose writers: Edward Young, Hazlitt, Lamb, DeQuincey, Pater.

ent, and the future condition of man. Jesus Christ divulged
the sacred and eternal truths contained in these views to
mankind, and Christianity, in its abstract purity, became
the exoteric expression of the esoteric doctrines of the
poetry and wisdom of antiquity." Reading More, one is
reminded of Shelley more often than of any eighteenth-
century Neo-Classicist, and the reason is this new Hellenic
Renaissance. Who wrote the following—Shelley or More?
"But whilst the sceptic destroys gross superstitions, let him
spare to deface, as some of the French writers have defaced,
the eternal truths charactered upon the imaginations of
men . . . [beware] . . . an unmitigated exercise of the cal-
culating faculty."

It has always been the characteristic of Humanists to
treat poets as "unacknowledged legislators of the world."
Shelley can speak more classically than "typical" eighteenth-
century critics. In his "Essay on . . . the Athenians," he
writes: "As a poet, Homer must be acknowledged to excel
Shakespeare in the truth, the harmony, the sustained
grandeur, the satisfying completeness of his images, their
exact fitness to the illustration, and to that to which they
belong." In Arnold's "Literature and Science" (a lecture
which begins with praise of Plato and concludes with an
assertion of the "necessity for Greek") when Arnold quotes
the statement that love is the "desire in men that good
should forever be present to them" he is quoting, word for
word, *Shelley's* translation—not that of his master Jowett—
and he is quoting it so casually that I believe he had been
reading the *Symposium* not in Greek but in Shelley. Or
consider this fine bit of Humanism from the *Defence of
Poetry*: "never was blind strength and stubborn form so
disciplined and rendered subject to the will of man, or that
will less repugnant to the dictates of the beautiful and the
true, as during the century which preceded the death of
Socrates." It would be hard to find a stronger statement of
Hellenism, except perhaps Shelley's own

> Greece and her foundations are
> Built below the tide of war

Based on the crystalline sea
Of thought and its eternity;
Her citizens, imperial spirits,
    Rule the present from the past,
On all this world of men inherits
    Their seal is set.

These are lines 696 to 703 of *Hellas,* and this is from the preface: "We are all Greeks. Our laws, our literature, our religion, our arts have their root in Greece." Cicero himself was not more Classical when he spoke, in *Pro Flacco,* of "Athens, the source whence civilization, knowledge, religion, agriculture, justice, and law have sprung and spread into all lands."

I have quoted extensively from Shelley because this is one way of defining Hellenism, in words which the Victorians had read, and also because Shelley seems at first glance the least Victorian of the Romantics. As to Keats, I will merely say that while scholars disagree on how much philosophic thought we may ascribe to him, it is absurd to think that Keats was philosopher enough to have discovered, independent of the Greeks, that "Beauty is truth, truth beauty." Clearly Keats did not originate this; the only question is whether he fully understood it, and his failure to add the third member of the Platonic trinity makes us suspect that he did not. *Goodness* did not appear as a central concern in the fake Paganism and the fake Medievalism that can be traced back through Swinburne and the Pre-Raphaelites to Keats. The relation of Wordsworth to the Victorians is more obvious. He was almost one of them. When he died, Carlyle was fifty-five years old and had written his best work. Wordsworth is not, in the Continental sense, a Romantic. In Germany, he would have been included with Schiller and Goethe as one of their "Classical" authors; and to the French he seems—Victorian! A great deal of confusion has arisen from the transfer of French and German meanings to the English word "Romantic." Stuart Sherman, an Arnoldian Humanist, said, "All Arnoldians tend to become Wordsworthians as they grow older" and he includes Arnold himself in this generaliza-tion.[6] Yet I once knew a graduate student who had been so far led astray by the conventional contrast made between the greatest "Romantic" and the greatest "Classicist" of the nineteenth century that he quoted the following passages to show a contrast between Wordsworth's primitivism and Arnold's Humanism (Which is which?):

"What actions are the most excellent [for poetry]? Those, certainly, which most powerfully appeal to the great pri-mary human affections: to those elementary feelings which subsist permanently in the race."

"What confessedly constitutes the most valuable object of all writing, whether in prose or verse [is] the great and universal passions of men, the most general and interesting of their occupations, and the entire world of nature."

The writer of the first of these passages proceeds to recom-mend "the contemplation of some noble action of a heroic time" (which betrays perhaps a romantic desire for flight into the imaginary past), while the latter expresses a deep conviction "of certain inherent and indestructible qualities of the human mind, and likewise of certain powers in the great and permanent objects that act upon it." Unfortu-nately for our conventional contrasts, the first of these authors is Arnold, the second Wordsworth. Our modern Classicists can find in Wordsworth the best poetic expres-sion of their advice "to control Rebellious passion: for the Gods approve/ The depth, and not the tumult, of the soul"; of their Sophoclean admiration for "the just Gods whom no weak pity" moves; and of the "principles of truth,/ Which the imaginative Will upholds," in aspiration towards the "central peace, subsisting at the heart/ Of endless agita-tion."[7]

One may contrast Wordsworth's avowed endeavor at all times "to look steadily at my subject," with the really Ro-

---

[6] *Shaping Men and Women* (N.Y., 1928), p. 275, thinking perhaps of the statement in Arnold's *Letters* (N.Y., 1895), II, 186.

[7] *Laodamia*, lines 73-75, 160; *Excursion* IV, 1127-28, 1146-47.

mantic critical dictum of Pater on "Style": "In proportion
as a writer's aim . . . comes to be the transcribing . . . not
of the fact, but of his sense of it, he becomes an artist, his
work, fine art." Wordsworth's critical theory is broader and
deeper than his own practice; it is best regarded as the beginning of a movement that becomes clearly defined in
Arnold. Wordsworth's recommendations as to diction have
been exemplified not so much by his verse as by that of
Browning and all important poets since Browning. In
theory and practice this has sometimes swung over to ex-
cessive naturalism (as Coleridge feared). But insofar as it
was a demand for "a selection of language really used by
men" Wordsworth was advocating genuine classical directness and simplicity, against the hopelessly unclassical ba-
roque diction that has been misnamed "Neo-Classical."
Browning's translations and imitations of Greek poetry
show what profoundly classical effects could be achieved
with the kind of diction he used and Wordsworth defended.
Professor Rouse argues in favor of this kind of simple and
natural language as the appropriate English for a prose
translation of Homer, and it is significant that Rouse once
edited Arnold's *On Translating Homer*. Chesterfield, ad-
miring Neo-Classical "poetic diction," speaks contemptu-
ously of "the porter-like language of Homer's heroes."[8]
Curiously enough, hostility to a classical directness of diction has held out longest in the field of Homeric translation, and one still finds those who prefer the "poetic diction" of Butcher and Lang, or of Lawrence. But outside
the classroom, Wordsworth's classical revolution against
classicism's opposite, "neo-classical" diction, has triumphed
completely. Arnold's objection to modern poets, that they
use "exuberance of expression" instead of the needed
"great plainness of speech" like "the poetry of the an-
cients," no longer applies.[9] Arnold did consider "parts of
Wordsworth" Grecian. And it is to be noted that Wordsworth was taken as the example of *pure*, as distinguished

[8] *Letters*, ed. Dobrée (London, 1932), IV, 1610 (1750).
[9] *The Letters of Matthew Arnold to Arthur Hugh Clough*, ed. H. F.
Lowry (Oxford Univ. Press, 1932), letter of Oct. 28, 1852, p. 124, 97, n.d.

from ornate, art in English poetry, by the Victorian follower of Aristotle, Walter Bagehot.

Byron and Scott made their contribution to revitalizing
classical attitudes in literature, but these I must omit. I
have been able only to touch upon the beginnings of our
Hellenic Renaissance among the great Romantic poets.
The prose writers and minor poets should also be studied
for other seeds of this movement. Perhaps Jane Austen's
unromantic art was not so anachronistic after all. Her diction might be described as "a selection of language really
used by women." She is the feminine counterpart and natural predecessor of Trollope, who was so deeply admired
by such a Hellenist as Paul Elmer More. There was in the
Romantic period an adequate critical preparation for Victorian Hellenism. We may begin to see the past century
and a half not as a period of dwindling Romantic inspiration, a period whose best mental energies were more and
more absorbed in natural science and the pursuit of material gain, but rather as a century and a half when critical
thought achieved an increase in clarity and wisdom, with
natural science as merely one aspect of the revival of the
Hellenic spirit.

III

"Hellenism is a far more powerful force today than when
the classics held an undisputed sway in higher education,"
says Sir R. W. Livingstone, in *Greek Ideals and Modern
Life*, and he proceeds to defend this generalization in a lecture pertinent in our study of Victorian culture. He finds
the germ of what he prefers to call "a second Renaissance
of Hellenism" in Shelley, and he illustrates it from Goethe,
Gladstone, John Stuart Mill, Arnold, Ruskin—deliberately
selecting men of a variety of views and interests. Classicism
is obviously a counterweight to Romanticism, but Livingstone finds it significant rather as a reaction against the
other three nineteenth-century movements whose triumph
I have mentioned: industrialism, democracy, and science.
For example, under the impact of science and Biblical
"Higher Criticism," "Those who ceased to be Christian

217

found themselves without a philosophy. . . . Hence men
began increasingly to find a great philosophy of life as well
as a great literature in Hellenism." Meanwhile, among
those who remained Christians, "a second Christian Platonism was born. . . . Jowett and Inge are its chief representatives in the Anglican Church; in the Roman Communion
its influence can be seen in von Hügel."[10] Livingstone, himself president of Corpus Christi, has failed to show how
important Oxford was in this movement, giving us Shelley, Newman, Thomas Arnold, Matthew Arnold, Ruskin,
Jowett, Pater. (Nor does he show the American participa-
tion in this Renaissance—Emerson, Lowell, Babbitt, Santayana, to mention some of the leaders that Harvard alone
may claim.) Can we say that Oxford Platonism has succeeded in a Hellenic Renaissance, where Cambridge Platonism (including Spenser and Milton) was doomed to take
second place in a Latin Renaissance? Are we avoiding this
time the hostility to Aristotle which gave us some of the
most dangerous fruits of the earlier renaissance? Livingstone does not show us how various movements, so different at the beginning, have converged. He does not define
to what extent this is a Platonic Renaissance, and to what
extent it is Neo-Platonic, or pre-Socratic, or even Sophis-
tical. He tells us almost nothing about the Aristotelian
revival.

Innumerable questions invite discussion as soon as we
begin to consider the ubiquity of Hellenism in Victorian
literature. There are the Brownings with their praise, ad-
vocacy, and imitation of Euripides—balanced by the Arnoldian admiration for Sophocles. Professor Harrold has
written of "Newman and the Alexandrian Platonists,"[11]
but no one has evaluated the debt to the same school of
Newman's opponent, Kingsley. There is the whole subject
of translations, no mere pedant's problem. I have already
mentioned the change of style used in translating Homer.
There are semi-translations, like Browning's *Balaustion's*

[10] *Greek Ideals and Modern Life* (Cambridge: Harvard Univ. Press, 1935),
pp. 14, 36-37.
[11] *Modern Philology*, XXXVII (Feb. 1940).

Adventure, probably more significant than a straight translation. Meredith has this in common with the Greeks, that Naturalists (like Joseph Warren Beach) speak of his Naturalism while Humanists (like Stuart Sherman) speak of his Humanism. Mention of these men, of Bagehot, of Swinburne, shows how widely diffused was Victorian Hellenism, how men came to it independently. It is not merely one school or clique or even one unified current of thought like Medievalism. Hellenism meets us in unexpected places: "in essentials Macaulay's is the metaphysic of Herodotus . . . essentially they view the stream of time from the same standpoint, and see in history . . . [assertions] . . . of a timeless rationality," says G. M. Young, and "the poetry of the fifties comes back to the memory best . . . with not a little of the fresh, instinctive perfection of the Greek lyric," and, "In its many-sided curiosity and competence, its self-confidence and alertness, this Late Mid-Victorian culture is Greek. In its blend of intellectual adventure and moral conservation, it is really Athenian. I doubt if any lines of Tennyson were more often quoted by contemporaries than these:

> Let knowledge grow from more to more,
> But more of reverence in us dwell;
> That mind and soul, according well,
> May make one music as before,
> But vaster.

No words could express more perfectly the Victorian ideal of perpetual expansion about a central stability. But would anyone guarantee that they are not a translation from Sophocles?"[12]

Indeed, so numerous are the similarities that we must recognize the real parallel between nineteenth-century England and fifth-century Athens. Both were leading commercial states whose coin was standard throughout the civilized world; but both succeeded in keeping the trader

---

[12] *Daylight and Champaign* (London, 1937), pp. 19-20, 175-176, 263-264. Young also discusses the "Attic revival" in English prose style, and traces it through Newman to Oriel College (pp. 119-123).

"in his place" because they preserved the older tradition of the cultivated gentlemen of leisure. Their maritime empires, held by powerful navies, were subordinated to the preservation of a rich civilization at the capital city, but this culture was not subordinated to commercialism. The keenest intellectual activity did not serve, but rather fed upon, material prosperity. Athenians too were familiar with the conflict between aristocratic tradition and middle-class libertarian "democracy," between "science and religion," between convention and instinct. Religion, art, and morality underwent much the same changes in Athens and England. Both had their breakdown of age-old traditions, the "radical" assaults of sophistic relativists, the philosophic reconstruction on a basis not of convention or of instinct but of reason. The Victorians naturally found themselves at home with Greek minds, and made fruitful use of the work of their predecessors.

I V

Rather than take up in a hit-or-miss way the relation of Victorian literature to various Greek thinkers and artists, I shall use, as an example, one aspect of this Renaissance, the revival of Plato. Victorian Platonism has usually received the merest mention towards the end of books on the Platonic tradition, and the effect is tantalizing. It would be tempting to follow up some of the hints. A. E. Taylor remarks that Ruskin's social ideal is "thoroughly Platonic" and his *Fors Clavigera* "the best of all commentaries on the *Laws* and *Republic*" of Plato.[13] More surprising, John Stuart Mill is cited as "perhaps the greatest of nineteenth-century Platonists," by Paul Shorey.[14] Still another scholar has mentioned Victorian Platonism as an expression of the "revulsion" *against* "the empirical trend in English philosophy," that is "the Lockean tradition which culminated in John Stuart Mill." This revulsion, according to Roth, took the form of "turning to German idealism" and also "the constant re-study of ancient Greek texts," the latter

[13] *Platonism and Its Influence* (N.Y., 1927), p. 91.
[14] *Platonism, Ancient and Modern* (Berkeley, 1938), p. 231.

illustrated by "Jowett's translation of Plato." All these
anti-empirical movements "soon concentrated themselves"
around "the study of Hegel."[15] But we must observe that
Jowett himself was deeply influenced by Hegel. Can it be
that his translation is itself Hegelian and less empirical
than, say, Mill's Plato? Fortunately, in *The Platonic Legend* Professor Fite has criticized Jowett's translation at
length, though not in these terms. Worthy of the best
efforts is the problem of disentangling the German from
the Platonic—and both from the direct Neo-Platonic—
strands in nineteenth-century idealism. It is unfortunate
that Muirhead, in *The Platonic Tradition in Anglo-Saxon
Philosophy*, does not distinguish between the influence of
Plato and Hegel on the "Anglo-Saxons" (by which he
means those who speak English). According to Roth, "that
aspect of Hegel which . . . exercised a permanent impression on English thought was that part which derives from
Spinoza." Now we have here a complication indeed, since
Spinozist philosophy has been a prominent influence opposing Platonic dualism and the Graeco-Christian assertion of human freedom. This complication can be illustrated in Matthew Arnold, a Platonist whose religion is
dedicated to something very like Spinoza's *Deus sive
Natura*. In "Spinoza and the Bible" Arnold ascribes much
to Spinoza that might seem to be Platonic. The increasing
influence of Spinoza's monism and Plato's humanism in
Victorian England may explain Arnold's Stoicism, for the
Stoics held something of the same bifurcated philosophy.
This illustrates how such research can proceed step by step.
After demonstrating Arnold's Stoicism (which has been
done very well in an Iowa dissertation by John Hicks) the
next step is to relate this to both the current of Platonism
and the influence of Spinoza. Then one can find to what
extent other Victorians were making use of these two philosophic traditions. The question presents itself: What in
the history of Victorian civilization brought about this
search for guides that would once have been considered
un-English?

[15] "Spinoza in recent English Thought," *Mind*, xxxvi (1927), 205.

What is the connection between the rise of Science, and the nineteenth-century revival of Platonism? Shorey praises Plato and Platonism for their genuine contribution to science,[16] and Michael Roberts in *The Modern Mind* has shown the favorable relations between the Platonic (or Augustinian) tradition and science, both, he thinks, especially British in their practicality. A. E. Taylor says, "Platonic conceptions have re-emerged at the critical points in the history of modern science."[17] F. S. C. Northrop has pointed out that "One of the most interesting things in contemporary scientific thought is the returning interest in the Platonic conception of science."[18] John Burnet says "Galileo, Kepler, and Copernicus were all perfectly aware that they were building on a Platonic foundation," but he recognizes that in the Latin Renaissance there was an unnatural conflict between these two Hellenic traditions: he speaks of "the folly of any estrangement between science and Humanism. That is a survival of the time when Humanism was mainly Latin in character; for it is true, of course, that the Romans were almost without scientific interests. . . . There are signs that twentieth-century Humanism is learning a better way."[19] It was the Victorians who taught us this better way. In the eighteenth century, as in the sixteenth, an unnatural separation was preserved between the two streams of culture: abstract "Classicism" on the one hand, and empirical observation on the other. It took one touch of Plato to make these two akin, and this marriage took place in the nineteenth century.

The adventures of Plato in Victoria's England include curious misinterpretations, for example by the aesthetes, whose deep perversity tempted them to pervert everything

[16] *Platonism, Ancient and Modern*, pp. 16-17; and also in the *American Philosophical Society Proceedings*, LXVI (1927).

[17] *Platonism and Its Influence*, pp. 26-27. Cf. also his *Plato* (N.Y., 1936), especially the last chapter. See Constantin Ritter, *The Essence of Plato's Philosophy* (N.Y., 1933), pp. 274, 278-279.

[18] In the *Saturday Review of Literature*, VII (Dec. 27, 1930), 481; "contemporary physics makes the philosophy of Plato take on a new life and a more pressing importance" (p. 483).

[19] *Essays and Addresses* (London, 1929), pp. 274, 124.

they handled. Pater, in better prose than usual, wrote an excellent book on Plato, and yet he got about as far away from Plato as one could get when he wrote that "the *formula* of Plato's genius" is his "sensuous love of the unseen."[20] Among the various false Platos that appeared to the Victorians was the superstitious one. "From Bacon, Macaulay, and Lange, this conception of Platonism as antiscientific passed into the popular writings of Huxley and Tyndall, and so became a commonplace."[21] And there is also the ambiguous Platonism—or Augustinianism without Platonism—of the super-subtle thinker, Newman, whose essay on Aristotle's *Poetics* manages to present Christianity as a flight from the facts, Poets as men whose "habits of mind" do not lead them especially to "communication with others," and Aristotle as an idealist more romantic than Shelley's Plato.[22]

Romantic Platonism was often Neo-Platonism, as we can see in Shelley or Emerson—and to what extent among the Victorians? Neo-Platonism carries in solution genuinely Platonic ideas that often crystallize unexpectedly into wisdom, but on the whole it is too mystical to be an example of Classical Hellenism. In Shelley, in Emerson, and in the German Romantic thinkers, distinctions are blurred between Self and God and Nature. And this confusion is the very quintessence of that Romanticism which awakens the suspicion of all Classicists. Carlyle retains much of the Germanic confusion, transmitting it to Emerson; and their conception of poetry is sometimes close to Shelley's. But,

[20] *Plato and Platonism* (London: Macmillan, 1925), pp. 140-143.

[21] Shorey, "Platonism and the History of Science," *American Philosophical Society Proceedings*, LXVI (1927), 181. Bacon did not recognize his own "immense debt to Plato" (p. 180). (Shorey elaborates this in *Platonism, Ancient and Modern*, p. 182.) Coleridge wrote to Gooden Jan. 14, 1820, that Bacon "Taught pure Platonism . . . and abuses his divine Predecessor for fantastic nonsense, which he had been the first to explode." I see a cause for Bacon's unfairness in the false separation of Humanism and science in his age.

[22] For other aspects of Newman's relation to Classical culture, see Alvan S. Ryan, "Newman's Conception of Literature," in *Critical Studies in Arnold, Emerson and Newman* (University of Iowa Studies, Humanistic Studies, VI, Iowa City, 1942). This volume contains also John Hicks' "The Stoicism of Matthew Arnold."

on the whole, Ernest Barker is right when he says, "Carlyle is of modern thinkers the most akin to Plato, because he has the most vivid sense of the spiritual reality of the universe"—besides being a critic of democracy.[23] It is this combination which shows how close Carlyle is to Plato. One seeks far and wide among the Victorians for another great literary artist who combines some form of philosophic idealism with the political views of Plato; the other idealists are liberal; the other authoritarians are not Platonic. Carlyle rejects the dream world of romantic escape (which Newman had found even in Aristotle[24]) and substitutes a genuinely Platonic ideal of public service: "The hour of Spiritual Enfranchisement is even this: When your Ideal World, wherein the whole man has been dimly struggling and inexpressibly languishing to work, becomes revealed, and thrown open; and you discover" that it "is here or nowhere," that every situation has "its Duty, its Ideal."[25] The Platonic idealism that lies at the foundation of Carlyle's social and ethical thought is even clearer in his *Chartism* when, speaking of the need of a scheme to educate the English people, he says, "The *thing* lies there, with the facts of it, and with the appearance or sham-facts of it; a plan adequately representing the facts of the thing could by human energy be struck out, does lie there for discovery and striking out."[26]

Emerson said of Carlyle, "his guiding genius is his moral sense, his perception of the sole importance of truth and

[23] *Political Thought in England from Herbert Spencer to the Present Day*, Home University Library (N.Y., n.d.), p. 189. And in his *Political Thought of Plato and Aristotle* (London, 1906) Barker also says (p. 162) "it is with an English writer, Thomas Carlyle, that one may best compare Plato."

[24] Contrast Carlyle's conception with this from Newman on Aristotle: "Poetry, according to Aristotle, is a representation of the ideal . . . ; poetry . . . delineates that perfection which the imagination suggests . . . it recreates the imagination by the superhuman loveliness of its views, it provides a solace for the mind broken by the disappointments and sufferings of actual life."

[25] *Sartor Resartus*, ed. Harrold (N.Y., 1937), p. 196. Carlyle gives a grave moral twist to words that in Goethe are blithely complacent.

[26] *Works*, Centenary ed. (N.Y., 1899), XXIX, 198.

justice."[27] And this is equally true of Plato. Justice and truth—with beauty. For both were also great artists, achieving beauty in prose literature far beyond those who pursued art for its own sake. Carlyle's purpose is more intellectual than has usually been recognized; indeed, he carried on into the Victorian age some of the work of the eighteenth-century Enlightenment: "That there should one Man die ignorant who had capacity for Knowledge, this I call a tragedy, were it to happen more than twenty times in the minute."[28] Platonism has been aptly described as "not a 'body of results,' but a 'mode of life';—an implacable crusade against ignorance."[29] Closely related to this is the ideal of the "implacable" rule of the philosopher-king: "The man of intellect at the top of affairs: this is the aim of all constitutions and revolutions, if they have any aim. For the man of true intellect, as I assert and believe always, is the noblehearted man withal, the true, just, humane and valiant man. Get *him* for governor, all is got; fail to get him . . . there is nothing yet got!"[30] When Carlyle later elaborated his political proposal for a modern society, he came even nearer to Plato's *Republic*. The spiritual leaders rule the "guardians," but both together form one upper class. "For indeed the Wiser and the Braver are properly but one class; no wise man but needed first of all to be a brave man."[31] Here, and elsewhere, Carlyle recognizes the basic importance of the Classical virtue of courage.

Carlyle did not know that he was a follower of Plato and did not recognize any marked agreement until very late in his career. (This, doubtless, explains why the connection has been overlooked.) Emerson says, "When I saw him in

27 *Journals* (Boston, 1909-14), VII, 347, in 1847.
28 *Sartor Resartus*, p. 229.
29 H. Gauss, *Plato's Conception of Philosophy* (London, 1937), p. xxii; cf. pp. 204-207: "The first 'hall-mark' of Platonism, . . . is, that, by regarding philosophy as a lifelong devotion to the Idea of Truth, it makes an end of the self's central position in it. . . . Secondly . . . the Platonist thinks preponderantly in social terms. In his eyes such a solitary wisdom as that conceived by the Stoics is not an ideal at all."
30 *Heroes and Hero-Worship*, ed. MacMechan (Boston, 1901), p. 195.
31 *Past and Present, Works*, X, 242.

1848, he was reading Wright's translation of some of Plato's dialogues with displeasure. I was told by Clough, in 1852, that he has since changed his mind, and professes vast respect for Plato."[32] In 1853 Carlyle told him this himself, having noticed at last that Plato wrote "Latter-Day Pamphlets" "refined into empyrean radiance and lightning of the gods!"[33] Carlyle, like Shakespeare,[34] got his Platonism at second hand, largely through Christianity. "Our creeds are the formulae of victorious Platonism,"[35] and Christian thought has preserved a Platonism more genuine than that of the Neo-Platonic poets. Perhaps for this reason Carlyle is close to Plato in an attitude on which most Platonists correct their master, that is, in his unwillingness to accept literature on merely literary grounds. "Poetry? It is not pleasant singing that we want, but wise and earnest speaking. . . . Our Aristos, well meditating, will perhaps discover that the genuine 'Art' in all times is a higher synonym for God Almighty's Facts . . . that all real 'Art' is definable as Fact, or say as the disimprisoned 'Soul of Fact' ";[36] and in Carlyle this elevation of the social and philosophic above the aesthetic in the judgment of literature is found in conjunction with a very Platonic theory of poetic inspiration. Plato, Augustine, and Carlyle would stand together in their attitude towards the stage. Not to carry this further now, let me turn aside to remark that no one has set forth Carlyle's relation to Augustine, "the Christian Plato," his predecessor in the application of a religious "philosophy of history" to the downfall of earthly cities.

Why do we find Victorians who are closer than earlier writers to Plato? The answer is to be found in their parallel social situation, which I have already sketched, and in the

[32] *Journals*, VII, 442 (written in later).

[33] *The Correspondence of Thomas Carlyle and Ralph Waldo Emerson* (Boston, 1894), II, 254 (May 13, 1853).

[34] Shakespeare used Platonism, whether he believed in it or not. See J. E. Baker, "The Philosophy of Hamlet" in *Essays in Dramatic Literature: The Parrott Presentation Volume* (Princeton, 1935).

[35] W. R. Inge, *Personal Idealism and Mysticism* (N.Y., 1907), p. 67.

[36] *Works*, XXX, 24-25. Though this is from "Shooting Niagara," 1867, similar statements are made in his earlier works.

threat of a breakdown in traditional religion. Joseph Warren Beach has shown one "substitute" for religion adopted
by the intellectuals, the "concept of Nature" in which they
put their trust.[37] But this is a better key to Romantic than
to Victorian literature. For Nature was not the only refuge
in an age of doubt. This was not merely a two-sided conflict, Naturalism *versus* Supernaturalism, or "Science *versus*
Religion" as it was popularly called. Many Victorians were
not willing to reduce everything to the laws of Nature,
"even though the preternatural," as Arnold was willing to
grant, might "have to be given up."[38] With his classic statement that "Man hath all which Nature hath, but more,"
Arnold is properly recognized as neither a Naturalist nor a
Supernaturalist, but as the formulator of modern Humanism. And he owed much to Carlyle, whose relation to
Humanism has not been properly recognized. Few realize
the truth in A. Wyatt Tilby's statement: " 'What is man,
that thou art mindful of him?' is common ground to David
and Darwin. But Carlyle, for all his protests and prophesy-
ings of the Eternal, was a pure humanist. Man was the
measure of his universe, and absolute truth for him must
therefore be expressed in moral values and none other."[39]
In his *Latter Day Pamphlets* Carlyle wrote, "Not because
Heaven existed, did men know Good from Evil. . . . It was
because men . . . knew through all their being, the difference between Good and Evil, that Heaven and Hell first
came to exist."[40] Likewise, Plato's *Euthyphro* had raised the
question that eternally divides the East from the West:
whether something is holy because it is loved by the gods,
or is loved by the gods because it is holy. Carlyle's demand
for a Christian idealism without any "Jew old-clothes" or
churchly trappings—what does this leave but naked Platonism? Carlyle was willing to grant that men like Voltaire

[37] *The Concept of Nature in Nineteenth Century English Poetry* (N.Y.,
1936).
[38] *God and the Bible* (N.Y., 1895), p. x. In 1882 Arnold wrote "supernatural Christianity . . . is certainly going." *Letters* (N.Y., 1895), II, 234.
[39] *The Great Victorians*, ed. H. J. and Hugh Massingham (N.Y., 1932),
p. 115.
[40] *Works*, XX, 334.

and Gibbon had succeeded in their work, so that the old "Mythus of the Christian Religion looks not in the eighteenth century as it did in the eighth." But what he wanted now was "to embody the divine Spirit of that Religion in a new Mythus, in a new vehicle and vesture, that our Souls, otherwise too like perishing, may live."[41] No one in England was more important in the secularizing of religion. Unfortunately, living alone there at Craigenputtock, he turned for his new vehicle and vesture to the Germans, who never really succeeded in building up a satisfactory "Mythus." His theories are confused. "Natural Supernaturalism" does not really say what he wanted to say. By the time he realized that these theories did not really formulate his intuitions, it was too late, and he simply turned away from the task. He wrote to Emerson, "I grow daily to honor Facts more and more, and Theory less and less," and soon after finishing *Sartor Resartus*, "From Germany I get . . . now no tidings, no influences, of moment."[42] It would have been natural to turn to Platonism, which "might indeed be called the intellectual side of Christianity,"[43] but as Emerson said of Carlyle on his first visit in 1833, "Plato he does not read, and he disparaged Socrates."[44]

We should not disparage Carlyle. No Victorian had a greater influence on modern thought. Yet Carlyle was not "Attic." He lacked one of the Hellenic virtues—moderation. He did not appreciate the side of Hellenism one finds in Latin culture and Aristotle. His *Heroes and Hero-Worship* is a sympathetic survey of the main elements in the spiritual history of western culture, omitting only the

[41] *Sartor Resartus*, p. 194.

[42] *The Correspondence of Thomas Carlyle and Ralph Waldo Emerson* (Boston, 1894), I, 93 (April 29, 1836) and 25 (Aug. 12, 1834).

[43] J. H. Muirhead, *The Platonic Tradition in Anglo-Saxon Philosophy* (London, 1931), p. 26.

[44] Emerson, "English Traits," *Complete Works*, Centenary ed. (Boston, 1903-4), V, 16. This is followed by a sentence which would apply not only to the history of Europe after Marcus Aurelius, but also to the development of modern thought among men who, like Carlyle, accepted the positive achievements of the Enlightenment: "Gibbon he called the splendid bridge from the old world to the new." Carlyle (and Emerson) overestimated the capacity of the Germans to establish a bridgehead at the opposite end.

Greeks and Romans! Close as he was to Plato, Carlyle was even closer to Aeschylus—but that is another story.

I have not tried to outline the history of Victorian Platonism but to suggest some of the different types of problems, each of which demands investigation at length: the various interpretations of Plato's meaning; the use of Platonism, conscious, unconscious, indirect; the relation of Platonism to other movements like science; the value of Platonism in contributing wisdom and beauty to Victorian literature. And for this Hellenic combination of wisdom and beauty, I think no period of English literature offers us more, not even the Latin Renaissance—with the single exception of Shakespeare himself. One would suppose, from recent listings of advanced courses in literature, that Marlowe and Donne offer us more "wisdom and delight" than Arnold and Thackeray and Carlyle, but this seems to me false.

The influence of the Greeks over the Victorian mind was reinforced by that astonishingly Hellenic spirit, Shakespeare. He had been misunderstood in the Latin Renaissance and the Neo-Classical period as an untutored natural genius, one who warbled "his native wood-notes wild."[45] Romanticism carried on this interpretation, simply shifting the tone from one of condescension to adulation, using him to justify irregularity and capricious impetuosity. It took the Hellenic Renaissance to see that Shakespeare was a delicate *artist*, that his works were the creation of a vigorous reason, though not of mere logical calculation. This is one of the contributions of the Germans to criticism, and in coming to these conclusions they turned to Plato as, in A. W. Schlegel's words, "the best ancient guide to the arts." But Schlegel made the mistake of turning against Aristotle, who is not really the enemy of Shakespeare. One of the other achievements of nineteenth-century Hellenism was

[45] Milton's critical position was Neo-Classical, from the time he wrote this obtuse phrase concerning one of the most civilized products of European culture, until at the end of his life he published, without any mention of Shakespeare but with some innuendoes, the preface on "That Sort of Dramatic Poem Which Is Called Tragedy," introductory to *Samson Agonistes*, the greatest of the Neo-Classical imitations that fail to produce the effect of Greek tragedy.

the salvaging of Aristotle, and the demonstration that his *Poetics* is applicable to the greatest drama of any age. (Butcher's commentary on Aristotle's theory of poetry is a Victorian example of this work.) Coleridge reached much the same conclusions as Schlegel, more or less independently, but he succeeded in holding on to Aristotle, whom he calls "the parent of science" and "the master of criticism."[46] And here we are back to Coleridge, the greatest Platonic philosopher of the past two centuries. Almost any study of the Victorians, if it goes deep enough, can be carried back to Coleridge. For example, he was a forerunner of the Anglo-Catholic revival, which later found itself by finding Platonism, as we can see in the novel *John Inglesant* by Shorthouse.[47] And Anglo-Catholicism in the twentieth century has included in its fold some of our leading Platonists, like A. E. Taylor, T. S. Eliot, and Paul Elmer More, who almost ascribes his own Anglicanism to *John Inglesant*.[48] But Coleridge was also (through Dr. Arnold, John Sterling, *et al.*) a leading force in that other current of Platonism, Broad Church and Liberal, which gave us Jowett, Matthew Arnold, and Paul Shorey. It is only recently that these two streams, which took their rise in Coleridge, and seemed to be going in different directions during the Victorian age, have flowed back together. There is hardly any important movement in Victorian thought that did not owe a debt to Coleridge, or at least to some general development he represents. As a *prose* writer, he is not a Romantic but a pre-Victorian.

Lucas deplores Coleridge's "fondness for general principles"—which he calls "Germanic"—in Coleridge's criticism of the excesses in Wordsworth's discussion of poetic diction.[49] Yet Coleridge's criticism of Wordsworth is not Germanic but Aristotelian; he adopts "with full faith the prin-

---

[46] *Table Talk*, July 2, 1830, in *Complete Works*, ed. Shedd (N.Y., 1853), VI, 336.

[47] I have tried to show this in Chapter xv of my *The Novel and the Oxford Movement* (Princeton, 1932).

[48] More, "Marginalia. I," in *The American Review*, VIII (Nov. 1936), 7-8.

[49] Lucas, *The Decline and Fall of the Romantic Ideal* (N.Y., 1936), pp. 191, 199, 180.

ciple of Aristotle, that poetry is essentially *ideal*, that it avoids and excludes all *accident*; that its apparent individualities of rank, character, or occupation must be *representative* of a class"; following probability, not mere possibility. He objects to Wordsworth's "matter-of-factness": "To this *accidentality* I object, as contravening the essence of poetry, which Aristotle pronounces to be σπουδαιότατον καὶ φιλοσοφώτατον γένος, the most intense, weighty and philosophical product of human art."[50] It is this phrase which Arnold quotes from Aristotle as the equivalent of "a higher truth and a higher seriousness." Irving Babbitt thinks that Arnold in using this was following Goethe; is it not just as likely that he had read the *Biographia Literaria?*[51] Babbitt's Aristotelianism, so different from that of the eighteenth-century Neo-Classicists or the twentieth-century Neo-Scholastics, goes back, like so many of Babbitt's main ideas, through certain mid-century writers, to Coleridge.

In *The Spirit of Medieval Philosophy*, Gilson makes the general statement that "The philosophy of Christians was indeed, and could be nothing else than, a continuation of Greek philosophy."[52] Our thinkers who have picked up again the Scholastic link in the Hellenic tradition usually trace this revival back to Pope Leo XIII and his encyclical in 1879. But two generations before that, Coleridge, declaring his allegiance to the same chain of thought, had come to the defense of "not only Plato and Aristotle, but even Scotus Erigena, and the schoolmen from Peter Lombard to Duns Scotus."[53] To the secretary of the new Royal Society of Literature Coleridge wrote, on March 16, 1824, that "the particular department of Letters, to which (relatively at least to the Society)" he could be considered attached was double, namely:

[50] *Biographia Literaria*, ed. Shawcross (Oxford, 1907), II, 33, 101; then he goes on to quote a letter that sounds like Arnold on the advisability of choosing to portray "actions" from "a former age" rather "than the present."

[51] *On Being Creative* (Boston, 1932), p. 12.

[52] *The Spirit of Medieval Philosophy*, tr. Downes (London, 1936), p. 418.

[53] "Appendix E" to "The Statesman's Manual" in *Complete Works*, ed. Shedd (N.Y., 1853), I, 478.

"1. The reciprocal oppositions and conjunctions of Philosophy, Religion, and Poetry (the heroic and dramatic especially . . . comprizing both the homeric and hesiodic species, and . . . the lyric) . . . in early Greece . . . [and also the] Religion of civilized Paganism.

"2. The influences of the Institutions and Theology of the Latin Church on Philosophy, Language, Science and the Liberal Arts from the viith to the xivth Century."

Platonism when it gets too far from Aristotle gives us the vagaries of Neo-Platonism and "Romantic Platonism." On the other hand, such rigid "Aristotelianism" as we find sometimes in the eighteenth century, or in the works of our Neo-Thomists, is far below Aristotle, who was, after all, a follower of Plato. These two Hellenic traditions when they are at their best stay quite close together. And this is the happy thing about Victorian Hellenism—it was not rigid and exclusive. Plato would ban Homer; Aristophanes assailed Euripides and Plato's idol Socrates; the great Athenian Democracy killed Socrates, was hated by Plato, and exiled other Greeks of surpassing genius. But the Victorians were eclectic; they were charmed by the spirit of all Hellas; and in this sense Victorian Hellenism is more comprehensively Hellenic than that of any one Greek. They must be counted among the worshipers of the Goddess of imaginative reason—among those "Happy, who hearing obey her, the wise unsullied Athene."[54]

V

Since the most recent past literature we read in English is Victorian, and since America is today where England was in the days of Carlyle and Arnold, what is theirs is, in a double sense, ours. If we wish a Hellenic Renaissance of our own, we cannot do better than study the Hellenic spirit and its modern development in Victorian England. We should have a number of studies of the sort which would help our own world cope with its problems by turning attention to modern Hellenism—beyond the well-known manifestations in science and athletics. We should build

[54] Kingsley, "Andromeda," last line.

bridges from Victorian to contemporary literature. Many problems of this sort are awaiting investigation; for example, Platonism in the novel from Shorthouse to Santayana. We need not only scholarship in this field, but also criticism, and the more Hellenic it is, the more critical it will be. Indeed, the crying need of our literary criticism today is to rediscover the critical intelligence of Greece. If scholarship and criticism can keep this tradition alive, it should flower in appropriate creative art. O'Neill's imitation of Greek tragedy was not genuinely Hellenic, but it suggests the opportunities that are open. We are already witnessing a vigorous Hellenic revival in religious thought, but how many of our "intellectuals," or our clergymen, are aware of it? Toynbee's *Study of History*—the first thoroughly worked out philosophy of history offered in opposition to the deterministic systems of Marx and Spengler—should be studied in the light of this tradition. The world needs a few statesmen as imbued with Hellenic culture as Jefferson, Mill, Arnold. If we cannot hope for philosopher-kings, we might at least educate the kind of public men that came from Victorian Balliol and Rugby. Dr. Arnold is said to have lived with Thucydides, Plato, and Aristotle as if they were his own contemporaries. Whoever wants to understand our intellectual life would do well to keep his eyes on the leaders of this Hellenic revival, Victorian and contemporary, for every step forward begins with a glance backward, and every great movement in history has aimed at the revival of some past attitude towards life, purged, of course, of its evils, its temporary accidents.

It may be objected that in the nineteenth and twentieth centuries most men have not been interested in the spirit of Hellas, and that in the nature of things and of human psychology only a few could ever cultivate the reason or possess the leisure necessary to do so. But a Renaissance is always carried on by a few—I am not talking about a Reformation. A Reformation, like a Revolution, requires active mass support, requires a Bible, a Koran, a *Das Kapital*, a *Mein Kampf*. Matthew Arnold understood well enough that a small "remnant" is enough to save even a democratic nation. A study of the sixteenth century, or a reading of the *Apology of Socrates*, should remind us that cultural movements are not necessarily mass movements. A Renaissance is so different from a Reformation that when both arise at once there is danger of a head-on collision. Luther might have been speaking for certain nineteenth-century extremists when he said, "There is no greater enemy of grace than Aristotle's ethics." As an illustration of the attitude some of our modern reformers have developed towards Victorian Hellenism, I may quote Upton Sinclair's explanation, in *Mammonart*, that Homer secures his effect by making his heroes the center of interest to gods and men, and "above all else, by portraying them as unrestrained in their emotions and limitless in their desires. These are the familiar devices whereby aristocracy signifies itself. And that explains why such men as Matthew Arnold and Gladstone write volumes of rhapsody over Homer. There is in England a class which has invented ways of setting forth to the world the fact that it does not have to work for a living. There are things this class can do which the vulgar herd cannot do; and one of these things is to read and appreciate Latin and Greek literature." Upon reading that Arnold rhapsodized over Homer because he liked to see aristocrats "unrestrained in their emotions and limitless in their desires," one is tempted to say, "Shades of Arnold!" Now it is obvious that such hostility to Hellenic culture is in direct descent from the *Edinburgh Review* attacks on Oxford which were effectively answered in Newman's *Idea of a University*. (The very title of that book is Platonic.)

The new Renaissance has been paralleled by a new Hebraism. And in reaction, men of culture have been tempted to seek refuge under the wings of a counter-reform insistent on obedience, institutionalism, authority, and the suppression of free thought. But in spite of extremists with their appeal to mass support, the Hellenic spirit has never died out of the West, and after every Renaissance some of the gains have been retained. After a fanatical interlude, darkened by hatred of the classical culture of the "leisure class," we come back to the central conviction that "the proper study of mankind is man." Probably the new Renaissance will survive, even in the United States, even in Germany, in spite of our naturalism, our emotionalism, our mass movements, our abject subordination of humanity to machinery. It should be noted that Germany's Hellenism has been more primitive than ours, leading to a Spartan, rather than Athenian revival. I know of no Victorian Hellenist who admired Sparta so highly—except Pater, fascinated by corpse-like "beauty," and ready to indulge himself in the contemplation of arrested decay wherever he could find it. And Pater was even closer to the *fin de siècle* Byzantine revival that had its capital in cosmopolitan Paris, and its devotees among the decadents in all western nations. The chapter "Byzantium" in Mario Praz's *Romantic Agony* might serve as a starting point for a number of investigations into the unclassical use of Greek antiquity by the aesthetes. But Sparta's *Kultur* was too primitive to be called "culture" in the sense the Victorians gave the word; and in Byzantium the Greeks at last abandoned their Hellenism. Primitivism and decadence do not constitute that culture which has nourished the minds of those who have read literature in English until we take certain Hellenic attitudes for granted. Since the fading away of our "Hebraism" in the early nineteenth century, the English-speaking peoples, in addition to their Hellenic encouragement of science and athletics, have had a kind of healthy directness, an eagerness "to hear some new thing," a freedom from dogma and formalism that is quite Athenian. And the greater Victorians (with their heirs in England and America) might say with Pericles:

We are lovers of beauty without extravagance, and we cultivate the mind without loss of manliness. Wealth we employ not for boasting and ostentation, but when there is real use for it. With us it is no disgrace for a man to acknowledge poverty; the true disgrace is for him not to do his best to avoid it. You will find united in the same persons an interest at once in private and public affairs, and even those of us who give attention chiefly to our own affairs, have a

very fair idea of politics. We alone regard a man who takes
no interest in public affairs, not as harmless, but as useless.
And we decide public questions for ourselves, or at least
endeavor to arrive at a sound understanding of them, in the
belief that it is not discussion that is an impediment to
action, but the lack of that knowledge which is gained by
discussion.